RICHARD KEITH CALL

Your Obt Servt
R. K. Call

RICHARD KEITH CALL

Southern Unionist

by

HERBERT J. DOHERTY, JR.

UNIVERSITY OF FLORIDA PRESS
GAINESVILLE
1961

A University of Florida Press Book

Preface

AMONG THE MEN who made the history of the old South, Richard Keith Call played a picturesque and dramatic part. From the War of 1812 until the Civil War he lived a life fascinating in its variety. As a soldier he fought Indians in the territories of the old Southwest, Spaniards in Florida, and British veterans of Waterloo at New Orleans. In civil life he was a lawyer, land speculator, delegate in Congress, railroad president, and planter. In politics he was successively a Democrat, Whig, Native American, and Constitutional Unionist, but was ever constant in his attachment to the federal Union and in his conservatism.

Though he was a defender of the federal form of government and of Southern institutions, Call was a nationalist at heart, dreaming great dreams of a powerful American nation. Through the antebellum South moved his figure, now prominent, now manipulating behind the scenes, now raging in frustrated political impotence. He was an outspoken, die-hard conservative and in Florida he stood almost alone against the tide of emotion which swept on toward Civil War. His is the story of a class of Southern men who had all but vanished by 1860—cultured, aristocratic and patriarchal in spirit, skeptical of democracy, but steadfast in devotion to the American Union.

In collecting materials for this study, the writer has incurred many debts. In the P. K. Yonge Library of Florida History at the University of Florida, Mr. Julien C. Yonge and Mrs. Harriet Skofield have extended courtesies far beyond the call of duty in assisting the writer and he is particularly grateful for their attentions. Mrs. Alberta Johnson and Edward Williamson of the Florida Historical Society are to be thanked for their aid, as is Dr. Dorothy Dodd, Florida State Librarian. At the National Archives countless hours were saved the writer by Dr. Clarence Carter and Dr. H. P. Beers, who generously made the facilities of the territorial records office available. A debt of gratitude is owed to Mrs. Mallie Wilson Farrell for her kind interest and her efforts in making available the researches of her husband, the late Colonel Louis Farrell, on the Kirkman family.

[V]

I gladly acknowledge my thanks to Professors Fletcher M. Green, Hugh T. Lefler, Cornelius O. Cathey, and Samuel Proctor for reading and criticizing the manuscript.

Above all, this work has been greatly facilitated by Mrs. Mary Call Collins of Tallahassee, Florida, who graciously gave the author access to the collection of Call papers deposited at the University of North Carolina. Sincerest thanks go to her and to her husband, former Governor LeRoy Collins, for the kindnesses they have shown the author.

                                    HERBERT J. DOHERTY, JR.

Gainesville, Florida

Contents

1

Soldiering on the Southern Frontier

NEAR THE BANKS OF THE Cumberland River below Clarksville, Tennessee, in the year 1813 a warm September sun shone down on a small boys' school which styled itself Mount Pleasant Academy. Ordinarily one might have expected to find there a group of restless youngsters chafing under the routine of the school, partially because of the outdoor temptations of a lazy late summer and partially because of their envy of older young men who might be leading more exciting lives full of danger and adventure in America's second war with Great Britain. The boys of Mount Pleasant were particularly distracted at that time, however, because of the recent news of an Indian massacre of hundreds of settlers, men, women, and children, late in August at Fort Mims in nearby Mississippi Territory. Creek tribesmen led by William Weatherford had surprised and annihilated the little outpost near the Alabama River in the first major action of a great Indian uprising. Inflamed by the eloquence of the great Tecumseh, and encouraged by American preoccupation in the war with Britain, most of the Creek tribes had eagerly flocked to the banner of revolt.[1*]

Throughout the state of Tennessee news of the massacre produced reactions of fear, rage, and desire for revenge. Thoroughly aroused by the contagious war spirit, the restless boys at Mount Pleasant soon allowed their imaginations to be filled with dreams of military glory and high adventure, heightened by the prospects of escaping the restraints of academic discipline. Persistently among the excited boys moved the determined figure of one who spoke to his teenaged comrades with the assurance and prestige of a twenty-year-old. Persuasively, in a voice touched with the unmistakable accents of old Virginia, this young man unfolded a plan which tantalized the students. They would form their own military company! A volunteer force would certainly be called for to resist the Indians,

*Notes begin on page 163.

and the young Virginian vowed that he would lead the students to join any body of men ready to go into action. This young man, Richard Keith Call, had come to Mount Pleasant in 1811 from Kentucky. Descended from a family proud of its participation in the American Revolution, young Call had often longed for a military career. In the spring of 1813 his taste for army life had been whetted when he took part in a brief but unsuccessful expedition to avenge the Indian murder of a family on the Tennessee River. This experience had proved heady wine to the young man, and he was determined not to pass up the new opportunity which presented itself for the realization of his dreams.[2]

When news of the Fort Mims massacre reached Nashville the call had gone out for a public meeting, which enthusiastically approved resolutions to the legislature demanding aid for the settlers to the south. On September 25 the legislature empowered the governor to call 3,500 men into the field under the command of Andrew Jackson. October 4 was named by Jackson as the date for the assembling of these forces at Fayetteville, a village near the southern border of Tennessee. Jackson directed Colonel John Coffee to go ahead to Huntsville in Mississippi Territory to evaluate the situation and to attempt to restore confidence among the frontiersmen.[3]

Meanwhile, as young Call went about organizing his company, word of his activity reached the ears of the school officials. Quite understandably those gentlemen were not enthusiastic about seeing their young charges go marching off to war. The president of the academy talked long and earnestly with Call, trying to convince him to abandon his scheme. The old gentleman pointed out that Call and his young friends were in the most important period of their lives, a period in which they should take fullest advantage of opportunities for education, and which if neglected might blight forever their future prospects for success. Under this persuasion Call relented in part and returned to his fellow students to urge them to stay on at the academy. His own course was not to be so easily altered, however, and with a few equally obstinate students he joined a neighborhood volunteer company and was elected its third lieutenant.[4]

The volunteer company which Call joined was soon coveted by a brigadier general of drafted militia who wished to attach the unit to his command. The general sought Lieutenant Call's cooperation in winning the men over to this arrangement, but the officer had not perceived the proud and arrogant character of the young lieutenant. Explosively, in a burst of temper characteristic of him when he felt his dignity had been offended, Call contemptuously replied, "I would rather be a private in a volunteer company, than a Brigadier General of drafted militia!"

"You will see," was the cool answer of the general. The angry young lieutenant now believed his sincerity was being questioned as well as his dignity offended, and—undoubtedly with visions of pistols at dawn—he haughtily asked if the senior officer doubted his word.

"Not at all, sir," came the softened reply.[5]

In later years Call looked back upon this incident with a mixture of amusement and wonder that he should have been so "very high handed" when so young. The impudence of youth, however, brought him to the attention of Andrew Jackson, who so fancied the spirit of the young man that he ordered Call's company attached to his own command. Again buoyant with hope and great expectations, Call and his comrades moved on toward Nashville to join their general.[6]

"I remember nothing in early boyhood which gave much promise of future good or usefulness," Call once remarked.[7] Undoubtedly he meant that his early life was not a privileged one which offered opportunities for leisure and education similar to those enjoyed by the sons of many wealthy Virginians. Yet the limited opportunity and occasional hardships of his early life unquestionably were important in making him the aggressive, self-reliant man that he became. Call had been born in Prince George County, Virginia, near Petersburg on October 24, 1792.[8] Shortly after his birth the family moved to Mecklenburg County where William Call, the father, died before young Richard was old enough to form a distinct impression of him.

William Call left behind him his widow, Helen Meade Walker, and six children, of whom Richard was the fourth. Richard recalled that his father had been a moderately wealthy man for the times, but had plunged heavily in speculation in Georgia real estate. This saddled his family with debts which left Helen Call with little means of supporting them. Soon after William Call's death both the youngest and oldest sons died, and Helen Call gave in to the entreaties of her brothers to move west to Kentucky and join them.[9] In their decision to move westward the Call family was not unusual.

Great masses of Virginians had moved into Kentucky, attracted by the lure of cheap virgin lands which were far more productive than the exhausted soils of eastern Virginia, worn out by generations of wasteful exploitation.[10]

Precisely when the Calls moved is unknown, but apparently it was shortly after 1800 that the four Call boys and their mother with all their worldly possessions—five young Negroes, two horses, and a wagon load of belongings—set out on the long trek across the mountains. The grandeur and the beauty of the Blue Ridge seen for the first time on a sunlit evening in October, the vast loneliness of the wildnerness between the settlements of Virginia and Kentucky, and the great white cliffs of the Kentucky River crowned with overhanging cedars and laurels made a vivid impression on the mind of young Richard. The breathtaking excitement of the journey remained with him long after the novelty of meeting his uncles had been forgotten.[11]

In due time Helen Call and her sons arrived at the home of her brother George Walker in Nicholasville, Kentucky. Remaining there but a few days, the family group soon moved on to the home of a bachelor uncle, Andrew Walker, on Barren River. After a year spent there, a third uncle of the boys, David Walker, invited them to his home near Russellville in Logan County and made them the gift of a small farm, where they lived until the death of Helen Call in 1810.[12]

All of Richard Call's uncles in Kentucky were influential and educated men respected in their communities. George Walker served in the legislature and was United States Senator from Kentucky for three months in 1814, by gubernatorial appointment. David Walker had served in the legislature about the time Call was born and sat in the United State House of Representatives from Kentucky from 1817 until his death in 1820.[13] There in Kentucky under his uncles' watchful eyes and in the companionship of his brothers, Jacob, George, and William, and his cousins, George K. and David S. Walker, Richard Call spent his formative years. While the young American union was experiencing the Jeffersonian "revolution" and doubling in size through the acquisition of Louisiana, young Call was learning to swim, ride, hunt, shoot, and fish. All was not boyish pleasure, however, for long hours of hard manual labor were put in on the little farm. There was no formal schooling for the boys for months and years at a time, but

Helen Call, a well-educated woman of determined and vigorous mind, gathered her sons about her and gave them an education rooted in biblical and classical literature.[14]

From his mother Richard Call inherited a loyal devotion to the Episcopalian Church, and an exalted sense of pride in his family and its honor. His father and grandfather had both seen Revolutionary War service, his grandfather having attained the rank of colonel in the Continental Army. The uncle for whom he was named had attained the rank of major and a second uncle, Daniel Call, was a distinguished member of the Richmond bar and a social intimate of Chief Justice John Marshall. His mother's brothers George and David were also Revolutionary veterans. His mother never let her sons forget their heritage.[15]

There is probably much in Richard Call's youth which explains the exaggerated sense of personal honor which all through his life was so easily affronted. Perhaps the young man had smarted inwardly at the more affluent conditions of life of his relatives and friends, and their greater fortune in not having undergone the hardships which he, his mother, and brothers had suffered. Perhaps his personal ambition and heightened personal sensitivity to imagined slights and slurs stemmed in part from a fear in his boyhood that somehow his branch of the family might not live up to what its heritage demanded. At any rate, the intense readiness to be affronted which we have seen in the young volunteer of twenty was still evident thirty years later in the planter-lawyer-politician.

After the death of their mother in August, 1810, the brothers separated and Richard went to live with yet another uncle, Wyeth Walker, where he studied in preparation for entry into the Mount Pleasant Academy. In 1811 he enrolled there and was content to pursue his studies until the outbreak of the Indian troubles in 1813. Under the excitment of war, Call's frontier upbringing and the family tradition of military service quickly prevailed over his inclination toward more scholarly pursuits.[16]

Call and his comrades from the Academy who had joined the local company of volunteers arrived late in September, 1813, in Nashville and moved out toward the Hermitage—as Andrew Jackson's home was called—to a point where a road branched off to the south to Murfreesboro. There they were to camp for a few days. While idling with a group of men gaping at passersby on the road one day, Call was beckoned to by the driver of a plain country coach which had stopped in the roadway. Dressed as any frontiersman might have been, in a dark hunting shirt with a bright yellow fringe, a leather belt about his waist supporting a tomahawk and hunting knife, Call stepped up to view three ladies, "one a fine looking Matron, the other two young and pretty." As they exchanged introductions the young lieutenant was astonished to learn that he was talking to Rachel Jackson and two of her young nieces. He had been in polite conversation with the ladies for a few moments when the excited shouts of the other men distracted him. He turned to see a great horse slowly approaching bearing the gaunt figure of Andrew Jackson, bent with pain and looking pale and emaciated. The general was still suffering from severe wounds which he had recently received in a tavern brawl with Jesse and Thomas Hart Benton. Jackson paused, asked a few polite questions, and then passed on with his party. But it was a day the young lieutenant never forgot. It was his first meeting with "Old Hickory."[17]

The company to which Call was attached soon moved on to Fayetteville and there on the seventh of October Jackson took command of his army. The project which was envisioned by the general was one which involved first crushing the Creeks and then moving on to seize Pensacola in Spanish Florida. Jackson was convinced that Spain and Great Britain were using the Spanish port as a supply base from which they were arming and encouraging the Indians in their uprising. For the first objective two bases were immediately established, a main supply base on the Tennessee River, Fort Deposit, and an advanced base fifty miles further south on the Coosa River, Fort Strother.[18]

Call's first taste of the horrors of war occurred in November when his unit came upon the Indian village of Tallushatchee which the troops of John Coffee had devastated a few days before. Upon this village had been inflicted the vengeance for Fort Mims. As recounted by Call: "We found as many as eight or ten dead bodies in a single cabin. Sometimes the dead mother clasped the dead child to her breast, and to add another appalling horror to the bloody catalogue—some of the cabins had taken fire, and half consumed human bodies were seen amidst the smoking ruins. In other instances dogs had torn and feasted on the mangled bodies of their masters. Heart sick I turned from the revolting scene."[19]

Jackson was seriously hampered in his operations during the weeks that followed by supply shortages and a growing spirit of rebelliousness among his militiamen. Shortly after an inconclusive battle at Talladega mutiny grew to serious proportions, but was temporarily checked by the personality of Jackson. Admiringly, Call recorded how the general with countenance like a thunder cloud vehemently hurled terrible threats at deserting units and sent them silently marching back to their posts. Call's own ambition and code of values instilled in him the greatest contempt for mutiny and mutineers. The mere suspicion that he might be connected in any way with mutiny would have been an insufferable disgrace. Consequently, when in December Jackson turned back at cannon point the regiment to which Call belonged, contemptuously rebuking it, Call was deeply troubled. He felt that the behaviour of the regiment reflected upon his own honor and he sought an interview with Jackson to request a transfer from the "infected" unit.[20]

Jackson was in his quarters slumped in his chair when Call approached him. After introducing himself the young man asked the acceptance of his resignation as third lieutenant and offered to serve in the general's body guard as a private. Annoyed by the interruption of his thoughts, Jackson rejected the request and curtly terminated the interview. As Call left, however, Jackson suddenly called him back and in an interested tone questioned him closely. Satisfied at length, he dismissed him saying, "No, Lieutenant, I cannot permit you to leave your company; as young as you are you may be of great service; . . . if I had 500 such men I would put an end to the mutiny before the sun sets."[21]

At length Jackson despaired of trying to make use of the demoralized troops and sent most of them back to Tennessee. His forces continued to dwindle away until in January, 1814, there was a brief period when only about one hundred loyal men stood with him. Among them still was Richard Call, now joined by his brother Jacob who had returned from service in the Northwest under General William Henry Harrison. By mid-January reinforcements were arriving, and with these new forces Jackson took the field and pressed toward a great Creek stronghold at Horseshoe Bend on the Tallapoosa River. As he moved toward this stronghold Jackson's forces were attacked on the night of January 21 at Emuckfaw Creek, but the blow was repulsed with few losses. The following day a report was received from Colonel Coffee indicating that the Horseshoe Bend fortification was far stronger than had been suspected. Deeming his force insufficient for a successful attack, Jackson reluctantly ordered a retreat to Fort Strother. The Indians began a constant harassing attack upon the withdrawing forces and at the crossing of Enotachopco Creek they made an attack in force. There Call distinguished himself by joining Jackson's rear guards in protecting the flank from attack after the troops assigned to that task had fled.[22]

At this low point in their fortunes, Jackson and his loyal band received unexpected support from the federal government. The Thirty-ninth Regiment of regular infantry was assigned to their assistance and was put under the command of Jackson, who was recognized as a general on federal service with full power to draw to his command men and supplies in the quantities needed to crush the Creeks. With the arrival of the regulars, Jackson rewarded the faithful handful of men who had stuck by his side throughout the campaign by dismissing them to their homes until further notice.[23]

With his brother and their friends, Richard Call turned his steps homeward and as he trudged back to Kentucky he carried in his pocket a note which he was to treasure the rest of his life. Its signature was the bold scrawl "Andrew Jackson" and it read:

> *Sir,* having been abandoned by your Company contrary to my express orders on the 4th Inst. Having yourself remained at your post, followed me and bravely faught at Emuckfau and more bravely with the guards to whom you had attached yourself at the battle of Enotachapco. there the guards and those attached to them covered themselves with glory, and by their bravery Saved my rear from havack and distruc- tion. . . . you have leave to return to your home and there await my further orders or the orders of the commander in chief Major Genl. Thomas Pinckney.
>
> On your retirement you carry with you my grateful ac- knowledgement for your Services and the bravery you dis- played with the artillery Company on the banks of the Enotachapco on the morning of the 24th Insant.[24]

The defeat of the Creeks was effected at Horseshoe Bend in March of 1814 but Call had returned home before that time. After a brief stay with relatives at Russellville, Kentucky, Call returned to Tennessee where he re-entered Mount Pleasant and applied him- self diligently to make up for lost time. Only a few months had been spent back at his books when Call received a letter from Wash- ington offering him, to his delight, a commission as first lieutenant in the United States Forty-fourth Infantry. By August 8 he was back in Russellville penning his acceptance of the appointment. As might have been expected, it had come through the efforts of Andrew Jackson, who in May had become Major General Jackson of the regular army commanding the seventh military district.[25]

After a few weeks' duty with the recruiting service Call was ordered to join Jackson in Mississippi Territory, where the latter had gathered a force of three thousand men at Pierce's Stockade on the Alabama River. The day after Call's arrival on November 1 Jackson marched on Spanish Pensacola. This unauthorized invasion of Spanish territory was not just to eliminate a source of supply for the rebellious Indians; it was a move in the larger war with Great Britain.[26] In that war the eastern portion of the United States had seen disaster come to American arms. Sir Alexander Cochrane had seized Maine, sacked the New England coast, and burned Washington before moving on to Jamaica. There a formidable force was being gathered for an invasion of the United States by way of the Mississippi Valley. In preparation for that invasion a force of British vessels rode at anchor in Pensacola Bay and British Marines were billeted in Fort Barrancas.[27] According to Call, news of the British movements had been relayed to Jackson from Vincent Gray, an American commercial man living in Havana who had many contacts in Europe and the Caribbean.[28]

Jackson had long desired to strike at Pensacola and the presence of the British there gave him all the justification that he needed. By November 6 he stood before the old Spanish town, and on the morning of the seventh he circled the city from west to east and advanced upon it in three columns from the east. The column in which Call marched entered the town and turned southward down Palafox Street against a battery of "beautiful brass four pounders." With few losses the town was soon occupied and the old Spanish governor was seen frantically dashing about with a white flag. While Jackson discussed surrender terms with him in the Government House, British vessels in the bay began to fire upon the city. Lieutenant Call, in charge of the captured four pounders, seized the initiative and moved them into position to fire upon the vessels. He opened up on some small boats near the shore with grape and canister and upon the nearest large vessel with round shot. The small ships retired and the larger one slipped her cable and put to sea as Call fired his last ammunition. He recorded, "had she not run I must have done so the next moment."[29]

During the night of November 7, as Jackson made plans for his assault on Fort Barrancas, some fourteen miles away, the British set the torch to its magazine and slipped away into the Gulf of Mexico. Fearing that they might be heading toward Mobile, Jackson abandoned his Florida conquests and rapidly moved toward Mobile Bay. When it became apparent that New Orleans rather than Mobile was the goal, Jackson sent his mounted troops on to the Louisiana metropolis overland while the infantry were transported by ship from Mobile to New Orleans by way of Lakes Borgne and Pontchartrain.[30]

The events of the battles before New Orleans from the initial one of December 23, 1814, until the last on January 8, 1815, are recounted in detail by all the biographers of Jackson and by numbers of military historians. Richard K. Call's own account of his participation was never finished and varies from the published works in some details. It is sufficient to note here that Call conducted himself creditably and won the approval of General Jackson, who cited him as "worthy of promotion." Shortly thereafter Call received the rank of brevet captain for "gallant conduct" at Pensacola on November 7 and at New Orleans on December 23.[31]

In May of 1815, the Creeks having been crushed and the war with Great Britain concluded, General Jackson and his lady returned to Nashville, where he established his headquarters as the commander of the new military Division of the South. In the same month Call was transferred to the First Infantry Regiment and settled down to several years of routine garrison duty.[32] During 1816 he was stationed at Fort Bowyer on Mobile Bay, where his major task was repair and rehabilitation of the post. In 1817 he was in command of Fort Charlotte at Mobile when trouble again flared up on the Florida border.[33]

The vast empire of Spain in America had been shaken with revolution in the second decade of the nineteenth century. As the resources of that declining European power were sapped by these upheavals the authority of Spain in the Floridas was slowly weakened until it was effective only in the confines of St. Augustine, Pensacola, and St. Marks. In East Florida slave traders, pirates, and "patriots" openly flaunted Spanish power. In West Florida runaway Negro slaves, with the connivance of Indians, actually took over an old fort on the Apalachicola River and strongly entrenched themselves. Marauding Indians freely crossed into

Georgia and Alabama for troublemaking purposes, in clear violation of the Pinckney Treaty of 1795 in which Spain had pledged to restrain such lawless bands. A United States naval expedition in 1817 wiped out the pirates' nest on Amelia Island in East Florida and a combined army and navy force destroyed the Negro fort in West Florida, but the Indians were not so easily dealt with. To check the Indians several United States military posts had been established along the northern border of Florida, some of which were virtually inaccessible during certain seasons except by water from the Gulf of Mexico. Such access, however, entailed the use of streams passing through Spanish territory and the Governor of West Florida quite legitimately objected.

In February, 1818, Captain Call was ordered to Pensacola to secure permission for the passage of United States vessels up the Escambia River to Fort Crawford. He arrived on February 21 and remained about a week, patiently trying to explain to Governor José Masot that protection of the American frontier had demanded the establishment of certain posts which were difficult of access except through Florida waters.[34] Stretching the "innocent passage" doctrines of international law, Call claimed that Spain must grant innocent passage of Florida rivers to all nations with whom she was at peace. Masot denied this contention and pointed out that he had not the least authority to grant such passage without orders from his superiors. Nevertheless Masot agreed to allow the passage of one ship on the basis of urgent need, insisting that no precedent was to be derived from his act.[35]

After the negotiations at Pensacola Call moved on to the Apalachicola River with a convoy bound for Fort Scott, another border post. The absence of Spanish posts on the Apalachicola precluded the possibility of Spanish interference there. Meanwhile, Andrew Jackson had been directed into the field by Secretary of War John C. Calhoun with orders allowing him to cross into Florida, if necessary to pursue Indians, but with definite instructions not to molest Spanish posts.[36] Jackson had advanced down the Apalachicola River to the site of the old Negro fort where, under the direction of Captain James Gadsden of the engineers, a fort was constructed which bore Gadsden's name. It was at this point that Call joined Jackson in mid-March and passed on the latest news from Pensacola. Call told Jackson of the open admission by Governor Masot that the Indians were demanding of him either arms and ammunition or possession of St. Marks, and that he presumed possession of that place would be given in the absence of the means of defense. On receiving this report Jackson informed Secretary Calhoun of his decision to seize St. Marks no matter who held it.[37]

On April 8, 1818, Jackson informed Calhoun that the seizure of St. Marks by his forces was an accomplished fact, and that the small Spanish garrison had been sent to Pensacola.[38] Call remained at Fort Gadsden until the arrival of a volunteer force from Tennessee, and then moved on to St. Marks to join Jackson's forces for the drive eastward to the Suwannee River, where the towns of Chief Billy Bowlegs were destroyed. It was on this foray that two English agents, Robert Ambrister and Alexander Arbuthnot, were seized and executed for their activities in stirring up the Indians, thus precipitating a brief international crisis. On April 25 Jackson's force returned to St. Marks to receive news that Indians were being sheltered in Pensacola and that Governor Masot had reiterated his denial of free passage through Florida rivers.[39] This news resolved any hesitation Jackson might have had about marching on Pensacola.

Jackson's permission to enter Florida had included a warning not to molest Spanish military posts. The general claimed, however, that through John Rhea, a Congressman from Tennessee, the administration had later expressed to him the desirability of seizing all of Florida. Whatever the merits of this controversy may be, by the middle of May Jackson had this project well under way. A twenty-day march from St. Marks put him before Pensacola on May 25. The town fell with virtually no resistance but Fort Barrancas appeared ready for a seige.[40] After a one day bombardment Jackson demanded its surrender, which Governor Masot refused. That night, under constant fire from the fort, Call and James Gadsden at Jackson's order supervised the erection of a battery in a commanding position near Barrancas.[41] The "daring courage" of the young officers won Jackson's admiration and he designated Gadsden his aide-de-camp and Call his second aide.[42]

On the second day of the bombardment the morale of Barrancas' defenders proved inferior to the strength of her walls and they surrendered to be shipped off to Havana by Jackson. A new government was established by fiat and its direction was put in the hands of military officers headed by Colonel William King as governor. Call was one of the provisional officials and when evacuation was ordered he was exercising the functions of Collector of Customs.[43] After the establishment of his provisional government Jackson retired again to Nashville where he began to receive intimations that his course of action would be disavowed by the administration. On August 5 he asked Call to get depositions and to try to find "every circumstance" that would prove that "the Spanish governor aided, abetted, and excited the Indians to war against us." He confided his feeling that the president was going to throw all responsibility on him but cautioned Call, "I am able to bear it—but I wish to be prepared."[44] A few days later Jackson received official word from President James Monroe that West Florida must be returned to Spain. The general ordered Call to rejoin his staff at Nashville as soon as possible.[45]

Call returned to the Hermitage and in January, 1819, went with Jackson to Washington to oppose the "combination" which Jackson thought was forming against him on the basis of his military action in Florida. By January 27 they were in the capital city witnessing a torrid debate in the House of Representatives on the Florida affair, which roared on for twenty-seven days before resulting in the general's complete triumph. In the Senate, however, an investigating committee had been formed headed by an anti-Jackson man, Abner Lacock of Pennsylvania. The committee sat from December 12, 1818, until February 24, 1819, and examined scores of witnesses and documents. Among the witnesses was Captain Call.[46]

Call's brief appearance before the committee was not sensational. He gave a brief narrative of events which had occurred in Florida within his personal knowledge, but he later pointed out that he had not been on Jackson's staff until after the attack on Pensacola and had little firsthand knowledge of the general's military views or plans.[47] From Call's remarks, however, the committee inferred that Jackson had made plans for the attack on Pensacola before learning that hostile Indians were there. Before the report was published Call left with Jackson for a grand tour of Northern cities. In Philadelphia Jackson was acclaimed and lionized in magnificent style. His twenty-seven-year-old aide apparently cut a handsome figure and produced a most favorable impression among the young ladies of Philadelphia society. The universality of his charm seems borne out by the fact that he also became a favorite of the Reverend Ezra Stiles Ely and his lady.[48]

Late in February Jackson's party passed through Baltimore on

their return to Washington and there got the first glimpse of the
report of the Senate committee. Jackson was infuriated at the unfavorable report which was given and Call made much of the
fact that the transcript of his testimony was published without his
being allowed to correct it, though he admitted that it was sub-
stantially accurate. The committee had, he insisted, erroneously
interpreted his remarks. Meanwhile, the Senate allowed the report
to die and it was forgotten as news of the signing of the Adams-
Onis Treaty swept the country. Spain had ceded Florida to the
United States.[49]

Throughout the remainder of 1819 and 1820 Jackson made his
headquarters at the Hermitage near Nashville. His staff lived with
him in the easy relationship of a large family. There Call was taken
to heart as a son by Rachel Jackson and there he mingled on
familiar terms with Sam Houston, Andrew Jackson Donelson, Robert Butler, James Gadsden, John and Samuel Overton, James C.
Bronaugh, and John H. Eaton. The young ladies of Nashville were
apparently as impressionable as those of Philadelphia and Captain
Call soon became so attentive to a young Irish beauty, Miss Mary
Kirkman, that word got back to some of his Philadelphia friends.
After a visit in the Pennsylvania metropolis James Bronaugh wrote
Call: ". . . my time was so completely occupied in visiting[,]
attending parties &c. that I really had no time to devote to anything
else. . . . I saw Miss C. You have offended her in some way . . .
& she requested me to inform you that she did not care a [illegi-
ble] for you. . . . She thinks you are not attached to her and
believes that Miss K. of Nashville has won your heart."[50]

All was not visiting and parties for Captain Call, however. In
the fall of 1819 he acted on behalf of John H. Eaton in an affair
of honor in which that gentleman had become involved with
Colonel Andrew Erwin. General Jackson also kept him busy with
routine staff duties and tasks such as the inspecting of the construction of military roads in Alabama.[51] In the summer of 1820
a rather delicate task was assigned to the young officer. The War
Department had received complaints that white squatters were
infringing upon the territory of the Cherokee Nation and it sent
orders to Jackson for their removal. Jackson named Call to head
up a detachment of Cherokee light horse and United States regular
troops to effect the removal. He assured the Secretary of War that
Call would execute the task with mildness and firmness, and ex-

pressed the hope that his troops would not be put to such use in the future.[52]

The removal of the squatters was a job which occupied Call from June until September. In the course of the operations he became quite sympathetic toward the Indians and contemptuous of the whites. At first, he reported, the Cherokee horsemen were afraid to act unless they were in the presence of the regulars, so he devised a policy of keeping the regulars hidden nearby while the Indians ejected the squatters. He believed that this plan kept up Indian morale and taught the poaching white respect for Indian authority. The scope of the work done by this force may be gathered from the destruction accomplished as reported to Jackson. Totaling the figures found in the existing letters it appears that Call's little army destroyed 610 acres of corn, 41 "farms," 18 "plantations," 1 mill, and numerous homes and fences. When he returned to Nashville in the middle of September he received a commission from the president raising him from the rank of brevet captain to full captain in the United States Army.[53]

In Nashville Call's romantic life began to strike complications and he did not long remain there. It seems that Mary Kirkman's parents were bitter enemies of Andrew Jackson, and while they had nothing against young Call personally, they would not allow their daughter to marry any protégé of Andrew Jackson. Mary governed her Irish temperament and, for the time being, stood by her parents' wishes. Call got leave from his sympathetic chief and decided to return to his relatives in Russellville and attempt to study law.[54] "Aunt" Rachel was fond of both young people and was grieved by their separation. As Call left for Kentucky she penned him a farewell note: ". . . permit me to offer you my best wishes for your prosperity[.] I had maney things to say which I cannot with this pen. Suffice it to say peac [sic] be with you going out and coming in."[55]

~ 2 ~

From Military to Political Life

RICHARD CALL had spent but a few months at Russellville at his law books when Andrew Jackson recalled him
to duty—again to go to Florida. Jackson, who was being
retired from active service on June 1, 1821, under an act of Congress
which curtailed the military establishment, had been prevailed upon
by President Monroe to accept a commission to receive the surrender of Florida from Spain and to become its provisional governor.[1]
Though Jackson expressed reluctance to accept the assignment and
reiterated a desire to return to his home, Monroe seems to have
acted on the belief that it would be both impolitic and unseemly to
turn the "Old Hero" so abruptly out of government service.

By April 12, 1821, Jackson had completed his arrangements and
informed Secretary of State Adams that he and his wife would de-
part immediately. From Nashville the general and his lady proceeded by riverboat to New Orleans, thence along the Gulf to
Blakely, Alabama, on Mobile Bay. From Blakely Jackson was to
proceed to Montpelier, an army cantonment near the junction of
the Alabama and Tombigbee rivers, where he would await notice
of the arrival at Pensacola of Colonel James G. Forbes with the
transfer orders from the Captain-General of Cuba for the Governor
of West Florida. Call was ordered to make the trip from Nashville
overland, bringing the general's horses. Expecting that the overland
journey would be completed first, Jackson authorized Call to receive
the communications from Forbes. The transfer, however, was not to
be so easily accomplished.[2]

On his leisurely journey down the Mississippi and along the Gulf
coast Jackson met Henry M. Brackenridge of Pennsylvania, a lawyer, scholar, and linguist, who was also going to Pensacola. This
gentleman had previously been the secretary of a diplomatic mission
to South America, and though Adams regarded him as a "mere
enthusiast" Monroe had been sufficiently impressed to offer him a

job in Florida. Jackson was also impressed and attached the scholarly adventurer to his official family as a legal adviser to assist in the transfer and in the erection of the new government in Florida.[3]

Jackson's party arrived at Blakely on April 29 to find that Captain Call, delayed by bad weather and high rivers, had not yet arrived. While waiting Jackson sent Brackenridge and Dr. James C. Bronaugh, his personal physician and confidante, to Governor José Callava of West Florida to announce his mission to effect the transfer. About a week was passed by the remainder of the party in Blakely before the arrival of Call. On the return of Brackenridge and Bronaugh they proceeded to Montpelier where another delay of some five weeks ensued.[4]

From Montpelier Call was ordered on May 11 to Pensacola to await the arrival of the tardy Colonel Forbes on the United States sloop of war *Hornet* from Havana. Call was authorized to enter into any preliminary negotiations which Callava might be willing to entertain. His instructions were detailed in describing the subjects which he might discuss with Callava, but had a postscript reading, "The real object is to be informed of the real feeling of the Governor and whether he is a coward full of duplicity or a candid honorable man."[5] On May 15 at ten o'clock Call was granted his first interview with the governor and found it a most agreeable experience. He observed Callava to be "a remarkably fine looking man." He was a large, fair, blonde-haired gentleman of about forty years of age, possessed of noble bearing. "I believe him to be a frank, ingenuous soldier," Call told Jackson, "and that every confidence may be placed in the professions which he has made."[6]

Besides opening preliminary negotiations for the transfer Call had been charged with obtaining permission for the deposit of American supplies in Pensacola and with arranging the concentration of Spanish troops for the evacuation. He was soon able to report to Jackson that Callava had designated a warehouse for supplies and a Spanish detachment to guard it, and had agreed to bringing the garrison at St. Marks to Pensacola for transport with the Pensacola garrison to Havana. Although the governor had denied having any power to enter into preliminary negotiations concerning the actual surrender, he had assured Call that he would grant every facility for prompt occupation by Jackson as soon as the orders arrived from the Captain-General. On May 20 Call returned to Montpelier with the news that the *Hornet* had at last left Havana with Forbes aboard.

Immediately Jackson sent James Gadsden to Pensacola to meet Colonel Forbes and empowered him to make arrangements for the receipt of the province.[7]

As Jackson cooled his heels in Montpelier, where on June 1 his military retirement became effective, President Monroe was filling the appointive offices in the government of the new territory. Jackson had submitted a list of his own recommendations for the Florida posts but Monroe ignored it, and on May 23 the Secretary of State forwarded to Jackson a list of the president's appointees. While this list was enroute, James Gadsden was ordered back to Montpelier and Call replaced him at Pensacola. Jackson had deemed Gadsden more valuable to him in Montpelier and had directed him to transfer all his powers to Call.[8] When Gadsden arrived in the Alabama village he found Jackson in a perfect rage: ". . . not one of those I recommended is appointed." Among the recommendations, Call had been named by his former general as a likely candidate for the office of Secretary of West Florida.[9] Instead Monroe had named a partisan of William H. Crawford, George Walton of Georgia, to that post. In reference to Call the president told Jackson, "It would have given me pleasure to have placed the latter near you, but, on great consideration, I thought it better . . . to pursue the course I have done. Mr. Walton was strongly supported by the two Senators from Georgia. . . . I could do nothing else for him, and Mr. Call was already provided for."[10] Call had been provided for by being retained in the army with the rank of captain, after its reduction on June 1.

Jackson's nephew, A. J. Donelson, wrote to a friend, "I am sorry to see that Call is not secretary. This disappointment is not a little vexing to the general." Rachel Jackson wrote to one of her brothers, "There never was a man more disappointed than the General has been. . . . he has not the power to appoint one of his friends; which . . . was in part the reason of his coming."[11] But the old general was not beaten yet. He told Dr. Bronaugh, ". . . say to my friend Call not to despond—that I am determined to try my influence in his behalf, next Congress, and any thing I have in my power to give him, will be."[12]

As Jackson was penning this note in Montpelier the *Hornet* arrived at Pensacola with Colonel Forbes and the transfer order from the Captain-General of Cuba. Call immediately went to Montpelier with the news and a letter from Governor Callava listing the troops and persons to be evacuated.[13] On June 12 Call returned to Pensacola with Jackson's authorization to receive St. Marks and to make all arrangements for the evacuation of Spanish personnel. Another delay ensued at this point when the Spanish governor insisted that the cannon were not part of the fortifications and were to be carried off by the troops to Havana. Jackson instructed Call to stand by Secretary Adams' orders not to surrender the cannon, but he instructed Call to inventory the cannon and give receipts for them while keeping the matter open for possible future settlement. This Call was able to do. Jackson directed Call also to require the Spanish to give receipts for the transportation and supplies given them which were not specifically required by the treaty of cession.[14]

Growing impatient with the long delay, on June 15 Jackson moved with his troops to a place only fifteen miles from Pensacola. On June 28 he sent Rachel on into the town to occupy a house which Governor Callava had allowed Dr. Bronaugh to take over for Jackson. Call, as well as Bronaugh and Brackenridge who were inventorying the archives and attending to other legal details of the transfer, was housed also at this residence, which he described as an ancient building on the plaza. After several more weeks of negotiation and delay the arrangements were finally completed for effecting the change of flags on the morning of July 17, 1821.[15]

Pensacola in 1821 was by no means a magnificent city. It had all the unpleasant airs of a boom town. Land speculators, swindlers, gamblers, soldiers of fortune—all were swarming in, swelling the population to an estimated four thousand persons—three times the ancient city's normal size. There were no brick pavements and the incessant rains conspired with the heavy traffic to turn the streets into quagmires. There were no stone houses in the town and Rachel Jackson observed that all the buildings looked "old as time." Call observed that the good woman, who wrote to her friends that she was in a "heathen land," muttered much of "Jerusalem" and "Babylon."[16]

At half-past six on the morning of July 17 Jackson entered Pensacola and was welcomed to breakfast at the governor's house by Rachel and by Call, Bronaugh, Brackenridge, and Forbes. At ten o'clock the troops of Spain and the United States were drawn up on the plaza and Call, with other officers of the United States Army and Navy, escorted Governor Jackson between the saluting ranks to the Government House. Callava greeted his American successor in the court room and the formalities were completed. There Jackson and Call for the United States, and Callava and José Cruzat for Spain, signed the *proces verbal*.[17] The entire party then passed again into the plaza where the Spanish colors were lowered and the stars and stripes hoisted, "with the tune of 'long may it wave, o'er the land of the free and the home of the brave.'" Thus Florida became a United States Territory as naval guns in the harbor boomed a salute.[18]

Immediately Jackson, who had been vested by his government with all the indefinable power of the Spanish governors of Florida and the Captain-General of Cuba, except the powers of taxation and land granting, began to organize the new government. Henry Brackenridge was named to the post of Alcalde of Pensacola, and Call became a member of the town council. Since none of Monroe's appointees had yet arrived, Jackson temporarily organized the government with his old staff, making Call the acting Secretary of West Florida. Bronaugh was put at the head of a Board of Health.[19]

The outward signs of the "Americanization" of Pensacola were evident. On the evening of the day of exchange Andrew Jackson Allen opened the Jacksonian Commonwealth Theatre and played to capacity crowds. Across the square from the theater, E. Hathway opened the Eagle Tavern, which boasted hot and cold baths and "an elegant ten pin alley." In August a printing press arrived and the *Floridian* began weekly publication just in time to notify the public of the arrival of Victor Pepin's equestrian circus. Though cultural developments were not so rapid as some others, within a year W. Hassell Hunt's circulating library was open and L. Patrick's reading room boasted files of forty to fifty newspapers "and other periodical literary publications."[20]

Some of the changes of the new regime were highly commendable from Rachel Jackson's viewpoint. Observing that "really a change was necessary," she approved of the Sunday "blue laws" imposed by her husband and noted that shops were now closed, fiddling and dancing had ceased, and cursing was not heard on the Sabbath. Though she thought "the Lord had a controversy" with the inhabitants, she obviously enjoyed the role of first lady. The local Catholic priest "seems a divine looking man," the stern puritan lady wrote. He and the former Spanish officials, and French, Spanish, and American ladies were feted at her table, and she boasted, "I have as pleasant a house as any in town."[21]

Shortly after the transfer Captain Call formed a partnership in law with Henry M. Brackenridge. Their notice in the *Floridian* stated that they were ready to practice in the various courts of West Florida and the Mobile region of Alabama.[22] The arrival in mid-August of George Walton, the secretary appointed by Monroe for West Florida, freed Call for his law practice. In this profession he soon became involved in the most controversial dispute of Jackson's governorship.

The heirs of Don Nicholas Maria Vidal retained Brackenridge and Call to institute suit against John Innerarity, the debtor of the Vidal estate, and instituted proceedings to get the papers relating to the administration of the estate. An order was delivered to Domingo Sousa, a Spanish officer holding the papers, to surrender them. In his capacity as alcalde Brackenridge was allowed to examine the papers, but Sousa refused to turn them over to him. The mild-mannered Brackenridge then withdrew and informed Jackson. Sousa meanwhile sent the documents to former Governor Callava whom Jackson believed to be conspiring with Innerarity to defraud the Vidal heirs. Jackson promptly jailed the former governor when he, too, refused to surrender the papers, thus precipitating a mild international incident.[23]

At the time of these proceedings Call was sick and not able to take part in the interview with Sousa. Call was more prone to direct action *à la* Jackson than to Brackenridge's regard for legal niceties, and had he been present it seems improbable that Sousa would have been permitted to retain the documents in question. In later years Call was bitterly critical of his former partner for not seizing the papers when he inspected them. In Call's opinion it was the "weakness and folly" of Brackenridge that got Jackson involved in the Vidal affair.[24] He regretted the incident as much for Callava's sake as for Jackson's. In the memory of his daughter, Call never criticized any act of Jackson in Florida except his jailing of Callava whom he described as "a gallant, high-toned gentleman, as much so as Gen. Jackson himself."[25]

The trials and disappointments of the Florida post weighed heavily on Jackson's health. Call thought that the governorship took as great a toll of his strength as had the Indian campaigns. By October Jackson decided that his task had been completed and he could return to the Hermitage. Florida had been received and a provisional government had been established; more than this he had not promised to do. On October 4 the officers and citizens tendered their governor a farewell dinner, and he took his leave of Florida on October 8.[26] Richard Call sent a letter after his departing patron thanking him in effusive terms for the generous friendship and favors bestowed upon him. "To have followed your fortune," he assured Jackson, "to have been tutored by your councils and honoured with your confidence is the proudest and happyest recollection of my life, and . . . be assured my gratitude will only terminate with my existence."[27]

"Your gratitude . . . shews the godlike virtue of a heart susceptable of friendship," Jackson replied. He recalled Call's loyalty in 1814 and commented that from that time "my opinion was formed of you." The old general expressed his regret that the president still had found no civilian appointment for the young captain, but urged him to turn this neglect to profit by applying himself to the improvement and development of his mind.[28]

Jackson had more interesting matter of which to write than appointments or compliments, however. On the trip back to Nashville he and Rachel had met Mary Kirkman and her uncles on their way to New Orleans. From this meeting Jackson learned that Mary was to tarry in Natchez a few days while her uncles inspected nearby lands. He advised Call, ". . . there is but one course you can pursue—that is to see her either at Natchez or New Orleans. . . . Take her to yourself, your industry and the aid of your friends will enable you to support her."

In this fatherly vein Jackson continued, "I need not say to you that as far as I have the means it will be afforded you—and industry and ecconomy will do anything. . . . I would not hesitate to see her . . . and put an end to the pain full situation of you both."[29]

Another letter followed within two weeks: "You and Miss Mary ought to forget each other, for ever, or at once marry." A month later came another message: ". . . receive her to your bosom—and protect her from all the fury of an exasperated & infuriated mother." Jackson assured Call that Mary still cared for him and would "no doubt" marry him if he were to see her. "Despond not," he wrote, "as long as I have property it will be cheerfully divided with you."[30] "Aunt" Rachel wrote an awkward, emotional account of the meeting with Mary: "We met in the roade betwene Florenc and Nashville. I cold not Help Exclaimeing O I am so sorry. She caut my hand as tho she Expected something from mine. Her Uncle came so

close to us & she apeard a stricken Dear. . . . May you be happy
is the sincere wish warm from my Heart who thinks on you as a
son or younger Brother."[31]

Call was appreciative of the information which his old chief
sent even though he did not act upon it. He assured Jackson that
". . . on my success in this affair my happiness in life depends. The
old People may annoy me for some time but if I live the period shall
yet arrive when I can look on them and their opposition with the
contempt they merit. They have indeed given me much unhappi-
ness but they shall learn that I have a spirit not easily subdued."[32]

Jackson was correct in his estimates of Mary Kirkman's feelings
toward Richard Call though he may have misjudged her willingness to break with her family at that time. On her journey to New
Orleans Mary wrote back to her mother, "As to happiness, I don't
expect much as long as I remain in my present situation. I will not
pretend to deny that my feelings are not changed. I am and must
continue attached to Capt C." Mary Kirkman was not yet of age,
however, and in closing she added, "Still it is a satisfaction to me
and a duty I owe my parents to obey them as far as I can."[33] Wed-
ding bells were not yet to ring for Mary and her Captain Call.

After Jackson quit the territory of Florida in October the government devolved upon the secretaries in Pensacola and St. Augustine.
George Walton was the acting governor in the former place and
his actions won Call's general approval. Call wrote Jackson that
the government was running quite smoothly and that Walton had
performed his duties "beyond my expectations."[34] Judge Brackenridge, Call's law partner, had a different reaction, however. The
judge declared that since Jackson had left he had been obliged to
do everything for Walton. "His companions are persons of no character, or the subalterns of the army with whom he passes almost
every night over the gaming table. . . . He is in truth an object of
universal contempt."[35]

Jackson had hoped to have a friend, Colonel William King, succeed him in the governorship and some of his followers in Pensacola got up a petition to that effect. President Monroe again turned
a deaf ear to Jackson's desires, however, and named William P.
DuVal to the post. DuVal, a former resident of Kentucky, was at
the time of his appointment United States Judge for East Florida.[36]
He was the first civil governor of Florida under the act of Congress
of March 30, 1822, which also provided for a Legislative Council

to be appointed by the president. Call was named to membership in both the first and second councils.[37] His career as an army officer was brought to a close about the same time that he launched upon this new phase of political activity. He submitted his resignation from the service in January, 1822, and was immediately given leave until its acceptance.[38] After a brief trip to New Orleans for his health he settled down in his office to go at law with new life. He wrote Rachel Jackson that Pensacola was a fine place to study for he found no distractions there; but, with an eye to the future, he told her to let all the girls know that he was becoming a very clever fellow and had developed a strong partiality for western ladies. In a year or two, he warned, they had best watch out for a dashing young Floridian in search of a wife.[39]

The new career which Call had chosen for himself was not one in which he was expertly versed. There is no indication that he had ever studied law except spasmodically and without direction. No records have come to light to indicate that he attended any law school or read in any lawyer's office before coming to Florida. Under the circumstances it seems highly probable that his partnership with Brackenridge was partially in the nature of an apprenticeship. Fortunately for him little knowledge of law was necessary in the primitive courts of frontier territories where the judges were not infrequently less well versed in the law than the attorneys arguing before them. Call probably felt that his self-directed study and his association with Brackenridge made him the equal of any other member of the Florida bar.

The change of governments in Florida brought in its wake a great flood of litigation which kept throngs of lawyers busy for a number of years. Cases connected with land titles and with claims against the United States were the most numerous and Call was engaged in many cases of both types. Less than two months after Jackson had left the territory Call boasted, "I believe there is scarcely a suit on the docket in which I am not engaged, and my practice even at this time promises me a competent support."[40]

There are few descriptions of Call's physical appearance, but those which do remain stress his temperament as much as his visual features. Friend and foe agree that he had a terrible temper and was an imperious and commanding man. A friendly observer has pictured him as tall and erect, with fair personal appearance and a bright and intelligent eye. He was noted for the melody and power of his voice and for his dynamic and ostentatious manner. We have already noted that he cut a dashing figure in female society. Even a "cracker" who had served under him in the military observed, ". . . he is the powerfullest man among the women that I ever seen." His critics saw him as a man of intense ambition, exclusive selfishness, lofty and arrogant pride, and "vanity beyond conception." His daughter observed that "inferiors" rebelled against his imperious manner.[41]

As Call rose in prominence as a lawyer and politician his ardent temperament not infrequently led to his making enemies among important men. There can be little doubt that he was an ambitious and acquisitive man strongly desirous of advancing his material wealth and personal prestige. His opponents, however, seized upon all the weak points in his character and painted them large. They belittled in particular his competence as a lawyer. According to one of his detractors Call had entered law practice after reading the first volume of Blackstone the first time. This critic claimed that after winning his first case Call was ready to cast aside his friend Brackenridge, "who kindly took him as a student and partner."[42] Whatever his personal defects may have been, Call was becoming a successful frontier lawyer and politician. His friends found him to be as able and enthusiastic a partisan as his enemies a tenacious and bitter opponent. Among the rough spirits of the new territory his outspoken manner and directness of action won many followers.

As his law practice flourished and he took part in the Legislative Councils of 1822 and 1823, Call more and more felt the attraction of political life reaching out to him. Both he and his partner Brackenridge had been appointed to the first Council and before it convened they dissolved their partnership on July 15, 1822.[43] Brackenridge, however, never sat in the Council, for in the same month he was appointed United States Judge for West Florida to preside over the Superior Court at Pensacola. In the Council, which met in Pensacola in August, Call came into conflict with Dr. Bronaugh, its presiding officer, and Joseph M. White. The latter was an able lawyer, but was viewed as something of an interloper owing to the fact that he had not been a resident of Florida until after his appointment by Monroe. Throughout the territorial period White and Call were to be on opposite sides of virtually every important political issue, and Brackenridge eventually became a staunch friend of White.

At the first session of the Council White introduced a measure which would have given the vote to military personnel in Florida. This was seen as a thinly veiled means of promoting Bronaugh's ambition to go to Congress, the theory being that the troops, who outnumbered the rest of the voting population, would support Bronaugh who was a favorite among them. Call took a stand as a defender of the rights of the civilian population, insisting that the measure would virtually disfranchise them. Despite his opposition the measure passed the Council by the vote of its presiding officer, Bronaugh, who acted to break a tie.[44]

Bronaugh appeared to be Call's major stumbling block to political advancement, and because of long intimate army association the doctor was closer to Andrew Jackson than was Call. When Call made exploratory inquiries as to the advisability of seeking the post of Delegate to Congress, Jackson sought to discourage him. He warned that Call should wait a few years to secure his own fortunes before entering public life. By waiting, he advised, he would assure his financial position "and a standing in public opinion, that cannot be shaken by every breeze. . . . On the other hand . . . the services of every man belongs to his country when that country requires it. . . ."[45]

From Richmond came a letter in a similar vein from old Daniel Call, Richard's uncle. He heartily applauded his leaving military life but warned that politics could be as profitless as soldiering if it were to become an obsession with him. "You will readily perceive from all this," he told his nephew, "that I am of opinion you had better pursue your own business, and let that of the public alone. If you go to Congress you will infallibly lose your practice and . . . spend the best part of your life in ennui and your old age in poverty."[46] Call's passion for political advancement was discouraged, but only temporarily. James Bronaugh died suddenly of yellow fever in September and Joseph M. Hernandez, a Spanish resident of St. Augustine, was sent to Washington for the closing session of the Seventeenth Congress.

Meanwhile Call was busy trying to assure "a standing in public opinion." After dissolving his law connection with Brackenridge he had formed a new partnership with Richard J. Easter, an old army crony. Call maintained the firm's Pensacola office while Easter hung out their shingle in Mobile.[47] Late in 1823 another young man, Benjamin D. Wright of Pennsylvania, joined the partnership. In

the same year honors were added to Call's name when he became
a general. On January 28 President Monroe commissioned him
brigadier general of the militia of West Florida.[48]

The election for Delegate to Congress was scheduled for June
of 1823 and speculation was rife for months in advance about who
the candidates would be. In April a public meeting of citizens in
Pensacola placed Call's name in nomination. The group discussed
no great issues of national or local importance and adopted no platform or party name. The only issue was a sectional one. The Pensacola citizens were backing Call because he was from West Florida
and they opposed the re-election of the incumbent, who was from
East Florida. In the East candidates were nominated on much the
same basis. Hernandez was most popular in St. Augustine and
Alexander Hamilton was a close second. In Fernandina the favorite
son was Farquhar Bethune. All four men made the race.[49]

The factionalism of the Florida political scene reflected the national political picture. This was the twilight of the so-called "era
of good feelings" in the United States and there had been no clearly
defined national parties since the death of the Federalist party after
the election of 1816. Factions, most of them claiming nominal allegiance to the Jeffersonian Republican party, dominated the scene.
Behind such names as Jackson, Adams, Calhoun, Clay, Webster,
and Crawford gathered the politically conscious men of the day,
seeking to build personal political organizations dedicated to the
elevation of their respective heroes. Personalism and sectionalism
were the dominant cohesive forces in these political factions, and
the picture was even more sharply focused in this direction in Florida. It is important that the formative years of Call's political life
were the years of this American one-party era in which factions
struggled for power and place, and party loyalty and great issues
of principle played secondary roles. This may help one to understand Call's frequent hostility to party regularity and his recurring
distrust of party organization.

The second session of the territorial Legislative Council began
in May at St. Augustine and was still in session when the congressional election was held. Call played a dominant role in that session,
holding the floor more often than did any other single member. He
took the lead in legislation to organize the territorial judiciary and
was instrumental in securing the passage of the act for the establishment of a permanent seat of government. His hard-working role

won him the admiration of the *East Florida Herald*, which ventured the opinion that should Call be elected to Congress East Florida might rest assured that its interests would be well represented.[50]

In East Florida, as was expected, the vote in the congressional election was about evenly split between Hernandez and Hamilton, with Call receiving only six votes of the 543 cast. In the West, however, it was a different story. Call was the only candidate from that section and received every vote cast, giving him a total of 490. Had the East been united he might have been beaten. Coincidentally, in October came the news that the Tennessee legislature had elected Andrew Jackson to the United States Senate.[51]

The Eighteenth Congress to which Call and Jackson had been elected was to convene in December, 1823. Late in October Call set out from Pensacola and met Jackson at Rogersville, Tennessee, from which place they proceeded to Washington in the company of John Henry Eaton, the senior senator from Tennessee.[52] In the capital Eaton directed his friends to the establishment which he had patronized for the past ten years operated by his good friends the O'Neales. Jackson was quite pleased with the arrangements and wrote to Rachel that he, Call, and Eaton were "private and comfortably accomodated in a worthy family."[53] Jackson appreciated the comradeship and attentions of both young men, but Eaton made the greater impression on him and he confided to Rachel that the latter had been "more than a son."[54]

The Call-Jackson-Eaton trio had been a few days late in arriving in Washington, and though Call presented his credentials in the House of Representatives on December 3 he was not sworn in and seated until December 5. Four days later he moved that the Committee on Public Lands be instructed to look into the expediency of granting a tract of land to the Territory of Florida for a seat of government. This ultimately resulted in the passage of an act granting a quarter section of land for a territorial capital.[55] Before the end of 1823 Call had also initiated inquiries which resulted in bills excluding foreign wreckers and fishermen from Florida waters, and authorizing the laying out of certain public roads in Florida.[56] Andrew Jackson spoke in the Senate only five times during this session, and on two of these occasions he was supporting the Florida road-building program. He saw no constitutional objections to the Congress building roads in federal territories, and he justified the

Florida roads as defense measures and aids to settlement.[57] Call went further than Jackson in his support of internal improvement projects and became an enthusiastic adherent of the internal improvement bloc in Congress. In the House debate on his road bill the Florida delegate was supported by Westerners and representatives from New York and Pennsylvania.[58] Though he had no vote Call, in turn, gave his oratorical support to other measures of internal improvement in the states.

Call was interested in canals as well as roads. In the debate on the passage of a bill to open a Wabash-Erie canal through public lands, Call came out strongly for the measure. He proposed to amend the bill, which originally gave a ninety-foot right of way to the canal company, to grant "the square of a mile" from the public lands on each side the entire length of the route. He defended his amendment as being in principle the same as assistance to a public road, and noted that a similar grant had been made for a road in Ohio. John Test of Indiana, Andrew Stewart of Pennsylvania, and William McLean of Ohio all backed Call's amendment. As had Call, they stressed the point that such a grant would generally enhance land values in Indiana. The amendment received lengthy attention on May 8 and 11 but failed to be incorporated into the final bill.[59]

Call's work in behalf of the land grant for the Wabash-Erie canal was directly related to his efforts to advance the interests of Florida, for at the time of the debate his bill for a canal from the St. Johns River to St. Augustine, Florida, was pending in the House. The amendment to the Wabash-Erie bill would have set a precedent for granting to the Florida canal similar tracts. This Florida canal bill was passed through the House without land-grant features but failed in the Senate.[60]

Two other bills of some importance which Call sponsored were approved during the first session of the Eighteenth Congress. One concerned a reform of the judiciary of the Territory of Florida. The act of 1822 had vested the judicial power in two Superior Courts at Pensacola and St. Augustine and such inferior courts as the Legislative Council might create. These courts were to have jurisdiction in criminal cases, exclusive jurisdiction in capital cases, and original jurisdiction in civil cases of $100 or more arising under the territorial laws. Each court was also to have such jurisdiction under federal law as was possessed by federal district courts, appeals to be taken in federal cases direct to the United States Supreme Court

under the same rules as governed appeals from United States Cir-
cuit Courts.[61] One objection immediately voiced to the 1822 law
was that it spelled out no right of appeal from the Superior Courts
in territorial cases.[62] The bill sponsored by Call divided the territory
into three Superior Court districts, one centered in Pensacola, one
in St. Augustine, and one in the new seat of government, which was
to be Tallahassee. The judges of these three Superior Courts were
also now empowered to sit annually at Tallahassee as a Court of
Appeals having appellate jurisdiction over the Superior Courts and
the territorial courts. Appeals could be made from the Court of
Appeals to the United States Supreme Court in all cases.[63] Marshals
and district attorneys were to be named for each Superior Court.
The day after the act received the president's signature Call's young
law partner Benjamin D. Wright was named United States District Attorney for the Tallahassee district.[64]

The second bill of importance was one which granted land to
actual settlers in Florida who could prove habitation and cultivation as of February 22, 1819. The amount of such grants was not
to exceed 640 acres to each settler who was over twenty-one years
old and the head of a family. The grants were for the benefit of
squatters and were not to include any claims based on Spanish or
English grants.[65] This measure was approved May 26 and was the
last successful bill introduced by Call at the first session. Though
Call is due much credit for his able advocacy of the interests of
Florida, he should not be given full credit for originating the legislation which he introduced and saw passed. Virtually every measure with which he was connected had been requested by the two
Legislative Councils of which he had been a member or by the
Council of 1824.[66]

Despite the activity in Congress the weeks in Washington were
not all work. Call took his meals at O'Neale's with Eaton and Jackson and there came to know the effervescent and attractive Mrs.
Margaret Timberlake, the married daughter of the O'Neales, who
quite often attended the table of the congressional trio. He also met
Prince Achille Murat and spoke persuasively to him of Florida as
a region in which he ought to settle.[67] Call was an optimistic, enthusiastic promoter, and impressed many, including John Branch,
William Wirt, and the Marquis de Lafayette, with the boundless
opportunities opening in the Florida territory.

Call enjoyed the sessions of Congress almost as much as the social life of the capital. He was entranced by the oratory of the seasoned politicians with whom he brushed shoulders daily. In the House Henry Clay, Daniel Webster, and John Randolph of Roanoke impressed the young delegate. One gathers from his admiration of senatorial eloquence that many hours were also spent in the Senate galleries. Thomas Hart Benton drew his praise as a senator who possessed a superior mind.[68]

Though the Congress held Call's fascinated interest as a school of oratory and debate, the Floridian found time to pass interesting hours with his colleagues in the barroom beneath the legislative chambers. There he heard bold tales about the beautiful Mrs. Timberlake.[69] Popularly known as Peggy, she was a vivacious young lady who had grown up in her father's inn, where Call resided, and had married a young naval officer who was frequently absent on long cruises. She was a coquettish, impudent girl who was known as a spoiled favorite of all the gentlemen of her father's tavern. Having grown up in such surroundings in a lusty era in the raw young capital, it is not surprising that her conduct was unpuritanical. Indeed, positively scandalous tales were circulated about her and she had never been accepted in "good society." Despite her beauty and a certain charming wit she was regarded as a conniver with persistent and unscrupulous ambition. When angered her fearful temper was said to lead her into "the conversational methods of a fishwife, and a habit of unbridled profanity."[70]

Ben Perley Poore, a contemporary observer, compared Washington society in the first half of the nineteenth century with that of England in the seventeenth century and judged extravagance and recklessness to be characteristic of both. Moral laxity was seen to be widely prevalent in the city on the Potomac where Peggy Timberlake moved at her enchanting and unscrupulous best.[71] In this context "good society" chattered eagerly about the activities of the tavern-keeper's daughter and the senator from Tennessee, John H. Eaton. Such stories came to Call so frequently that he soon formed the opinion that the lady was a loose woman on intimate terms with more notables than the senator from Tennessee. That Call always held to this conviction thereafter is quite clear. Beyond public gossip, what was involved in the shaping of this opinion, if anything, is not clear. All the documentary evidence bearing on this phase of Call's life was produced five years later, after the death of John Timberlake, Peggy's husband, and her marriage to

Eaton. At that time Peggy was the center of a controversy raging around the unbending refusal of Washington society to accept her even though her husband, Eaton, was then the Secretary of War. Consequently, we must take into account possible errors on the part of all who reduced their memories of 1824 to writing in 1829. We are, however, certain of Call's attitude toward Peggy's morals and of the fact that relations between them were far from cordial. Call himself declared, "Mrs. T. and myself quarreled so frequently, I cannot remember the time or the cause of our first disagreement."[72]

No matter what the state of affairs between them may have been, it seems unlikely that two persons possessed of the mercurial temperaments of Call and Mrs. Timberlake could have long coexisted peaceably. On one occasion which Call has noted he refused bluntly to be seen with her in public and she flew into a rage; on another she charged him with looking at her too hard at the dinner table, saying she feared that Eaton might notice. All in all, it must have been a tense household in which Call, Jackson, and Eaton lived. It may be that even at this time, while her husband still lived, Peggy had set her cap for Eaton and feared that her free and easy ways might weaken her hold on him or that Call's opinions about her unworthiness might influence him. Call, on his part, belived that even at this early date Eaton and Peggy had decided to marry.[73] He believed, too, that this woman would be the ruin of the man whose friendship Jackson prized so highly. Accordingly, Call had several conversations with Eaton about his association with Peggy, on one occasion rebuking him for having taken Jackson and himself to "a house which he had brought into disrepute." In this exchange Eaton denied any impropriety in his friendship with Peggy and angrily challenged Call, since he thought so badly of her, "Why do you not try her yourself?"

"You do not give me an opportunity, Sir," Call replied, "but if you will go to Baltimore for three days, on your return I will make a faithful report to you."[74] Call gives no indication that this arrangement was agreed upon, but Jackson, who was convinced of Peggy's virtue, declared positively that one day in the spring of 1824 Peggy came to him in tears. She bitterly complained that "Call had grossly insulted her, by making to *her and urging upon her*, very indelicate propositions, and attempting to inforce them by *great rudeness*, which she was compelled to extricate herself from, by seizing a pair of tongs, or shovel. . . ." Jackson was incensed and, after quieting her, promised to speak to Call and put an end to such conduct. As Jackson remembered the incident, he severely lectured Call, who admitted the incident but insisted that Mrs. Timberlake had resisted from a sense of mock modesty.[75] Call declared that he had "no such recollection" of an event such as Jackson remembered but admitted that he quarreled with Peggy often.[76]

We shall possibly never know precisely what the truth is. Was the story to Jackson a figment of Peggy's imagination to discredit Call as a source of stories about her? Did Peggy lead Call into an incident to exhibit her faithfulness to Eaton? Was the incident arranged by Eaton and Peggy to gain Jackson as a defender of their friendship? Or, despite all the contrary evidence, was Peggy truly innocent of any wrongdoing and was she actually telling the truth about an encounter with Call? No matter how we may speculate on Peggy and her activities, the overwhelming volume of evidence seems to indicate that she was not innocent. Even her defender in the cabinet crisis of 1829, Martin Van Buren, thought little of her character.[77] Though we may not go so far as John Floyd of Virginia who asserted, "I know, myself, that all is true which has been said of her," about the most charitable judgment of Peggy Timberlake which can be made is that of historian J. Franklin Jameson: "It is possible that she was chaste; it is certain that she was vulgar."[78]

When the session of Congress was about to end in May, 1824, Call again had a serious talk with Eaton about Peggy's bad influence upon his reputation, and he thought he had convinced Eaton to leave her and return to Tennessee with Jackson and himself. Peggy, however, prevailed upon Eaton to stay, and when the session ended Jackson and Call made their way back to Nashville without him. In Tennessee Call talked with Eaton's brother-in-law, William B. Lewis, urging him to write to Eaton and use every effort to get him back home. Lewis agreed at the time and said that he even prepared a letter, but he did not mail it when he heard Eaton was planning to return anyway.[79] For the time being Call considered his duty done and put the Eaton-Timberlake affair in the back of his mind.

In Nashville Call resumed his courtship of Mary Kirkman. This young lady, now almost two years past her twenty-first birthday, had decided to break with her parents and marry the thirty-two-year-old militia general from Florida. Andrew Jackson offered the Hermitage to the young couple and plans were made for the marriage there on July 15. Call informed Mrs. Kirkman that he would call for her daughter at eleven o'clock in the morning. Her dwelling was on the public square in Nashville and when Call drew up before the door in a carriage the interested neighbors quickly gathered around, for the courtship had been as talked of as the Jackson-Kirkman feud with which it was connected. When the embarrassed couple appeared they were hailed by the crowd and drove off to the Hermitage as handkerchiefs waved and good wishes were shouted.[80]

After the marriage the Kirkmans voiced threats of disinheritance and Jackson tried to intervene to patch up the quarrel. In Mrs. Kirkman, however, the old general found an unyielding enemy. When he called upon her she refused to discuss the matter with him and ordered him from her home at pistol point. For one of the few times in his life Andrew Jackson retreated.[81]

During July and August the Calls remained in Tennessee. Despite his insistence that Florida was a fine place in which to live, Call managed to avoid it in the summer months whenever possible. This was the period generally referred to as the "sickly season" because of the occurrence of malarial and yellow fevers. In September, however, he returned for a brief visit with his constituents, leaving Mary in Tennessee. In Pensacola Call busied himself with preparations for the next session of Congress. He wrote the Secretary of the Navy Samuel L. Southard to hurry the survey of Pensacola harbor so that the plans might be used in a bid for a navy yard to be located there. He also urged Calhoun, the Secretary of War, to strengthen the army garrison at Pensacola which was to be used in building the newly authorized road to St. Augustine.[82]

On Saturday, September 18, a committee of citizens held a public dinner for Call in celebration of his return to the territory. A respectable number of gentlemen gathered "to participate in the general joy" and to toast their guest, a man whose popularity "is the popularity which follows; not that which is sought after." After a number of toasts Call honored his hosts with a "handsome" and "concise" address. After the young politician's schooling in the halls of Congress, however, it seems a safe bet that his address was more handsome than concise.[83]

Call remained in Florida less than a month. He took leave of Pensacola on Sunday, October 3, and travelled directly to the Hermitage. There he and Mary, with Andrew and Rachel Jackson, set out on their trip to Washington. The two couples boarded together but not at the O'Neale tavern.[84] This was a presidential election year and Jackson was figuring prominently in the race. Jackson was, in fact, the leading candidate and Washington was agog with speculation over the outcome of the election when the Calls and Jacksons arrived for the second session of the Eighteenth Congress. By December 16 it was known that Henry Clay was out of the running and that none of the three other candidates had gotten a majority of the electoral vote.[85] The effect of this development was to throw the election of a president into the House of Representatives where the influence of Clay, its speaker, was seen as a vital factor in determining the choice. Jackson, John Quincy Adams, and William H. Crawford were the contestants and Jackson, with the largest popular vote, was thought by many to be a sure winner.

Call professed to believe that Jackson's election was sure until he was approached by an unnamed friend of Henry Clay. This friend told Call that "from his knowledge of the value which Mr. Clay set upon the office of Secretary of State, and its patronage, that he was convinced that Mr. Clay had determined to dispose of his interest in a manner that would secure him that station." Call replied that he did not know Jackson's views on that subject and that it was one which his best friends could not discuss with him. The gentleman then remarked, "Without pretending to have more sagacity than others, I venture to say, that Gen. Jackson will not be elected."[86]

From December until the election in the House of Representatives on February 9, intrigue, rumor, speculation, claim, and counterclaim kept the adherents of Jackson, Crawford, and Adams at fever pitch. As the delegate from a territory Call had no vote in the House but throughout the controversy he was an unflagging Jackson man. On the appointed day, however, Adams was elected and when he made Clay his Secretary of State the Jacksonian adherents felt that a "corrupt bargain" had been made between the two men. From 1825 until 1828 they spread the charge and labored unremittingly for Jackson's election in 1828.

Despite the exciting business of the election of a president the House had to conduct its usual business. The Florida road building program was again an item on Call's list of projects. The measure which he had secured in the first session for a Pensacola-St. Augustine road was pushed along by an additional appropriation of $8,000 which Call secured on the advice of General Thomas Jesup who was directing the construction. An additional $12,000 was voted for a new road from the St. Marys River to Tampa Bay.[87]

Call's other major accomplishment at this session was the passage of an act to establish a navy yard on the Gulf coast of Florida. His original bill had located the installation at Pensacola but on motion of Daniel Webster it had been altered to allow the Secretary of the Navy to locate it at any point on the Gulf coast of Florida. Edward F. Tattnall of Georgia was a strong supporter of the measure and the amended bill was backed by Henry Clay.[88]

Meanwhile, political opposition against Call was rising in Florida. The leaders of this opposition were Joseph M. White, now a federal Commissioner on Land Claims, and Joseph L. Smith, the United States Judge for East Florida. With the help of Edgar Macon, the district attorney in East Florida, Call sought to have Judge Smith removed. Macon informed Call that Smith was receiving fees for transacting business during vacation which had previously been done in term.[89] With such information Call attempted to build a case against Smith for taking fees for his services. On February 3, 1825, Call rose in the House and moved the adoption of a resolution to investigate the receipt of fees for services by "the Judges of the District Courts of Florida." He arraigned Smith by name for impairing the purity and integrity of the courts:

> Sir, the paltry pence which the learned judge has wrung from the hands of honest industry, or from the unfortunate victim of oppression, who has sought protection in your courts of justice, is not the only evil we deprecate; it is the pernicious effect of his example in showing a disregard to law, reason, and decorum, which we most deplore. . . . ignorance or corruption in your judiciary, is an evil not less to be lamented than apostacy in your religion. . . . But, sir, it is your officer of whom we complain; you sent him to us, and we ask you to take him away.[90]

Samuel A. Foote of Connecticut immediately rose and took Call to task for going into a statement of the facts of the case "in this stage of the business," and stated his wish that Call had waited until the investigating committee had made its report. The Committee on the Judiciary took up Call's charges but reported that it was wholly impracticable to make an investigation into the particulars of the case because of the distances involved.[91] Smith bitterly charged that Call had deliberately asked for an investigation so late in the session that one could not be undertaken, while his character would be blackened by the unproved charges.

Smith branded Call "a flighty man actuated by personal pique." His attack, Smith asserted, was "distinguished by one of those blunders, which of him, may be said to be characteristic." He declared that had Call read the law "with ordinary intelligence" he would have noted that he was not a district judge, but a judge of a Superior Court who was authorized to receive fees for performing non-judicial duties imposed upon him by the territorial government. Call, he concluded, "has made a false and flagitous charge against me."[92]

Though the point at issue is an arguable one, Smith seems to have had the better side of the argument. He was not a district judge, as Call charged, though he was vested with many of the duties of a district judge. He also was a territorial judge having jurisdiction over cases under territorial law. Certain duties imposed upon him by the territorial government, he argued, caused great expense and inconvenience. Because of this he took advantage of a law of the 1823 Legislative Council which justified the collection of fees by any officer not compensated by law when such officer "shall perform any service under, and by virtue of any law of this territory. . . ."[93]

Call did not back down on his charges though he was content to let the dispute rest with a parting reply in the *Pensacola Gazette* in which he referred to Smith as one "familiar with vice and dissimulation."[94] Judge Smith's friend, Joseph M. White, was meanwhile being talked of prominently in Florida as a candidate for Congress in the 1825 election. The *Pensacola Gazette,* which took a stand opposed to Call, asserted that it was well known that Call had no intention of running again and had privately so informed his friends. In the new seat of government located at Tallahassee, however, a circular was published under the letterhead of the *Florida Intelligencer* putting Call's name in the race. The first edition of the *Intelligencer* had not yet been published, but after it began publishing in February, 1825, it was generally regarded as expressing Call's views. This circular, dated December 20, 1824, praised Call's principles as "honorable even to chivalry" and assured the public that he was "incapable of descending to the low acts of electioneering."[95]

There was no clear public statement from Call on his intentions

in regard to running again, apparently because of indecision in his
own mind. It seems likely that his Tallahassee friends tried to push
him into the race with their premature announcement of his candidacy. An anonymous letter to the editor of the *Pensacola Gazette*
expressed the view that Call had not concurred in this announcement and commented, "We hope it [the announcement] was not
done to gratify that private rancor which it is well known has been
engendered in the breasts of disappointed land speculators."[96]

White, who appeared to be Call's opponent, had gained fame in
Florida for uncovering land frauds at Pensacola and much of the
violent abuse of him came from disappointed land speculators. Call
and many of his political associates in Florida were big landholders
and that fact, taken with the fierce rivalry between him and White,
caused Call to become identified in the popular mind with these
speculative interests. Call's cause was not materially assisted at this
time by the antics of some of his political associates, many of whom
were quite as imperious as the young delegate and acted often in a
highhanded manner. One of these men, Peter Alba the former
mayor of Pensacola, made a vicious physical attack upon White
and it was widely rumored that White did not dare to offer for
Congress, for if he did it would not be settled by the people "but
by the pistol."[97] A meeting to console White for his assault by
Alba was broken up by a band of men armed with dirks, who afterward went *"hooting, halloaing, and hurraing through the streets!"*[98]
In this atmosphere White announced his candidacy for Congress
with the comment, ". . . proscription and violence are no part of
my character."[99]

Call's delicate ego was quickly offended by the many attacks directed toward him by White's partisans and he was provoked to
sharp replies. He apparently did not view himself as a public
servant and when it was suggested that he maintain better relations with his constituents he angrily wrote:

> I am free to admit that I am not calculated for a success-
> ful politician so far as success must depend upon a time-serv-
> ing humiliating policy which would degrade the reputation of
> a gentleman.—I treat every man with politeness—I am mind-
> ful of the rights and interests of all. . . . In serving the Terri-
> tory, I have made great personal sacrifices. Under these cir-
> cumstances if the people of the Territory are disposed to aban-
> don me because I will not lie, fawn, flatter, and deceive—be
> it so; I care not; I am able to take care of myself.[100]

In another letter to John Pope of Jackson County Call bitterly criticized White and his followers, and implied that all men who questioned his conduct were questioning his honor.[101]

The rash remarks which the opposition drew from Call were turned upon him with vehemence. His legal ability was questioned, his militia rank was belittled, and the idea that he had made sacrifices to represent the territory was found to be perfectly laughable: "A young man resigns a Captaincy in the army, embraces a new profession . . . in a poor decayed village, and is then suddenly transferred to Congress, seated among the *patres conscripti* and yet talks of *personal sacrifices*." His attitude was seen as betraying a young man "too suddenly elevated beyond his proper sphere." This critic observed that army officers in civil life had a tendency to assume more importance than their talents merit and warned, ". . . voters will not be *drilled* in favor of anyone."[102]

Another critic thought that Call was forgetful of the duty he owed his constituents and reminded him that office holders were answerable to the people, who also possessed the right to criticize their representatives without being called to the field of honor for so doing. This man expressed the opinion that many voters who had previously had nothing against Call were being alienated by his belligerent attitude.[103]

Call's internal improvement friends in Congress noted the opposition forming against him and tried to come to his aid. Andrew Stewart of Pennsylvania hoped that Call felt "no uneasiness about the opposition which has recently shown itself," and testified, "If ever there was a portion of this Union indebted . . . to the zeal, talents & industry of its representative . . . that portion is Florida, and she will be unfaithful to herself, and forgetful of her own interest should she make a change."[104] The *National Journal* praised Call as "an ardent and industrious representative" who was unusually successful in getting bills passed which he brought forward.[105]

Undoubtedly Call was troubled by the attacks upon him, which were a new experience to him. He probably also was finding that the early advice of Jackson and of his uncle about the meager rewards of public service were true. Perhaps his apparent indecision about running again actually reflected an unwillingness to commit himself until some other means of livelihood were certain. At any rate, on February 14 Call directed a letter to the *Pensacola Gazette* informing the editor that he no longer aspired to the honor of representing Florida in Congress, and on February 28 the Commissioner of the General Land Office transmitted to him his credentials as Receiver of Public Monies at the land office in Tallahassee. With a wife to support and a family on the way, Call now had the security of a regular income in Florida where he could also rebuild his law practice and establish himself financially.[106]

⟿ 3 ⟿

Reaping the Unearned Increment

AFTER THE CLOSE of the second session of the Eighteenth Congress Richard and Mary Call returned to the Hermitage and after a brief stay made a leisurely water journey to Florida by way of New Orleans. They were well received in New Orleans and spent several pleasant days in the company of the Marquis de Lafayette, whose friendship they had made in Washington. When they arrived in Pensacola on April 19, 1825, Call's political supporters gave him an "elegant dinner" and ball at Mr. Collins' Hotel. The several toasts at the dinner ranged from tributes to the Union and the Constitution to praise of Call, Bolívar, and "the Fair." After a few weeks in Pensacola the Calls pushed on to the new capital which was still being hacked out of the wilderness. Call's duties as Receiver of Public Monies required his residence in Tallahassee where the land office was to be located.[1]

Tallahassee had been selected as the new seat of government in 1823 by John Lee Williams and William H. Simmons, commissioners named under an act of the Legislative Council of that year. It was a high location eighteen miles north of St. Marks in the heart of a rich farming area where Spanish missions had flourished in the seventeenth century. Call looked with favor upon the location and believed that it might allay the extreme east-west sectionalism in Florida. The first meeting of the Legislative Council in the new capital was held in a log house in 1824. By 1825 lots had been sold, and soon a church, shops, houses, and a hotel rose around the capitol square, but for a number of years unbroken wilderness extended in every direction from this center of activity.[2]

Early in 1825 the *Florida Intelligencer* began publication at Tallahassee under Ambrose Crane and Adam Gordon. When a post-office was established at the capital in 1825 one of its publishers, Crane, became the postmaster. The paper maintained a friendly attitude toward Call, and his opponents looked upon it as reflecting his views and those of the "land office faction." In addition to Call this land office group included George W. Ward, the Register of Public Lands, and Robert Butler. Butler was a Jacksonian crony who had been named Surveyor General of Florida in 1824. He brought with him from Tennessee Robert W. Williams and Isham G. Searcy as his clerks. These men, with other Jacksonian cronies such as James Gadsden, Benjamin D. Wright, and Samuel Overton, were the early leaders of the political faction variously known as the land office gang, the Tennessee surveyors, the Call party, or the "Nucleus."[3]

After Call's refusal to stand for re-election to Congress and his return to the territory his feud with Joseph M. White continued. The main point at issue was Call's letter to John Pope in which he had denounced White's friends as being as "base and unprincipled" as their leader. Letters from White men appeared regularly in the *Pensacola Gazette*. Finally White himself gave notice that if he had ever injured Call he stood ready to give him "satisfaction." Call did not overlook the fact that this was the language of the duelling ground. Had he been disposed to overlook it the next few words would have obliterated that disposition. General Call, White wrote, "had made not only a rude but groundless charge, that had an existence only in his imagination. . . . Should Gen. Call ever favor the public with his proofs, I shall endeavor to shew whether the epithets are more applicable to myself or the General."[4]

Before this missive was made public White left Pensacola and remained away until the following year. In a public reply Call apologized to the people that private wrongs had been brought before them and contemptuously derided White for not publishing his letter until after taking "flight" from the territory. Call assured all who were interested that *he* did not seek distinction "in paper warfare."[5] From the Hermitage Andrew Jackson commended him upon his reply, saying that it was the only proper notice of White that could be made in his absence. The old general ventured a guess that White would never return to Florida.[6]

Call complained that in the controversy the press in Pensacola had been hostile to him and had denied him a fair chance to defend himself. The *Gazette* denied his charge and rashly asserted that Call's name had been "too fully identified with that of slanderer" to give him serious notice. The editor asserted that Call had been denied access to his columns only once, when he wrote an article of "scurrility and abuse." He asserted that he would defend himself against Call's abuse at all times, "even under a threat of having our THROAT CUT."[7] The editor's friend, Joseph M. White, had meanwhile been elected to Congress at the 1825 territorial election, defeating James Gadsden and Joseph M. Hernandez. Gadsden was known as one of the land office crowd and was generally conceded to have been Call's candidate. The *Intelligencer* supported him while the *Gazette* backed White.

Scurrility and abuse were characteristic of both sides in the verbal battles of 1825. Though White had temporarily moved beyond the range of Call's temper, some of his satellites had not. Robert Mitchell of Pensacola, who had been named to Call as the author of an anonymous newspaper attack upon him, was unfortunate enough to meet him face to face. The encounter occurred on a cool day in December, 1825, just before Christmas, in the Pensacola public market. Call accosted Mitchell and inflicted a beating upon him, but the *Gazette* reported that the latter suffered no serious injury.[8] Public thrashings were not uncommon in these days when high-spirited men were insulted by persons who were not "gentlemen" or by gentlemen who ignored the challenge to a duel. If Call followed the example of his old mentor Andrew Jackson, he deliberately had sought out Mitchell to deliver to him a public horse-whipping.

Though preoccupied by personal and political controversies Call was establishing himself in Tallahassee and laying the foundations for his material prosperity. He resumed his law practice with Benjamin Wright as his partner, organized the land office, and began building his home. Precisely when the Call mansion was completed has not been ascertained, though his daughter wrote that it was built in 1825. In that year Call wrote, "We are now settled on our own place within half mile of Town, and in a short time we shall be very snugly fixed."[9] It seems highly improbable, in view of the isolation of Tallahassee and the insecurity he felt still about his finances, that Call's imposing brick residence was completed so early. It seems more reasonable to believe that the house was completed early in the prosperous thirties. Certainly it had been finished by the time Mary Call died in 1836. It was located at the north end of Adams Street where it still stands, a magnificent structure overshadowing the neighboring official residence of Florida's present-day governors.

In his early years in Tallahassee Call did not engage in farming on a scale impressive enough to term him a "planter." In 1825 he possessed only ten slaves, five of whom were house servants. He asserted that this was quite as many as he wished to employ but conceded that he might add more later if he found that farming would not interrupt his professional pursuits.[10] For the next ten years, however, Call occupied himself predominantly with his professional work. Litigation arising from the transfer of Florida and title disputes provided legal employment and the frequent public land sales kept him busy in his capacity as Receiver. In addition, Call himself became a land speculator and made frequent purchases and sales of quite large tracts. His inside knowledge of the land office could not have been disadvantageous, and such an advantage was not considered a "conflict of interests" by the government or many citizens in his day. His purchases of public lands were selected from the richest in Middle Florida and he seldom paid more than the minimum $1.25 per acre.

Florida lands had been the object of speculation since before the cession of the territory by Spain. As early as 1817 John H. Eaton and James Jackson of Nashville had formed a company to buy lands in West Florida. This was done in the expectation that Florida would soon be acquired by the United States. John Donelson, as the agent of this group, had gone to Pensacola with a note of introduction signed by Andrew Jackson and had purchased town lots as well as some 2,600 acres of outlying lands. After the signing of the treaty of cession in 1819 a genuine boom in Florida lands set in, *Niles' Register* reporting a price rise of from 500 to 1,000 per cent, with city lots selling from $500 to $7,000. About the time of the transfer in 1821 Call managed to secure several tracts near Pensacola. In partnership with James Innerarity he purchased 800 arpents of land on Santa Rosa sound and a like amount on Escambia Bay in partnership with Henry M. Brackenridge. An arpent in Spanish Florida was slightly more than an acre. In the city of Pensacola Call secured one town lot.[11]

Call's interest had early shifted to the richer lands of Middle Florida where most of his subsequent purchases were concentrated. He received early reports of the fertility of these lands from John Lee Williams in 1823. When reporting on his trip to select a site for the seat of government, Williams wrote in glowing terms telling Call that the Ochlockonee River and Tallahassee lands were first rate. "The cotton fields," he declared, "exceed by one half, any I have before seen & the sugar cane better than the Mississippi affords."[12] Call waxed enthusiastic about such fertile lands while in Washington and became noted as an ardent Florida promoter. His enthusiasm may have been a factor in the government's decision to locate the Lafayette land grant in Florida.

The Marquis de Lafayette had been granted a township of land by the Eighteenth Congress in appreciation of the services which the French nobleman had rendered to the United States in the Revolution. Since the French Revolution and Napoleonic Wars the wealthy Frenchman had fallen on hard times and this land grant, with an accompanying cash grant of $200,000, was the third attempt of the United States Congress to lighten Lafayette's financial burdens.[13] President Monroe selected Florida as the territory in which the tract was to be located and Lafayette named Colonel John McKee to select the lands for him. Land officials in Florida were instructed to give McKee all the information they possessed in order that he might make the best possible selection.[14] McKee selected a township adjoining Tallahassee on the northeast, designated as township one, north, in range one, east. Over the years Lafayette named a number of persons as agents to dispose of his tract. McKee was initially authorized to receive and transmit purchase proposals and to carry out Lafayette's instructions on them. Call says that in 1825 at New Orleans the Marquis also commissioned him to dispose of the lands. In 1829 the *Florida Advocate* reported that George Graham, the head of the General Land Office in Washington, was authorized to dispose of a part of the lands. Lafayette, in 1831, told Call that he had given John Skinner of Baltimore power of attorney to sell the land, but added that "I continue to depend upon your kind local advice and exertions for the disposal of one half of my Florida lands."[15]

After his return to France in 1825 Lafayette had written to Call suggesting the formation of a company of local capitalists to purchase part of the township. Call could make no arrangements, however, and a few years later expressed doubt that any such company could be formed in Tallahassee. In 1833 he offered Lafayette $50,-000 for half of the township but his offer was rejected.[16] Though Lafayette had hoped to retain a part of the land as a family holding, the entire township was eventually disposed of in piecemeal fashion. At Call's suggestion the portion adjoining Tallahassee was

divided into lots and sold; the remainder was disposed of in tracts
of varying sizes.[17]

In the fall of 1825 the first child of Mary and Richard Call was
born—a daughter whom they named Ellen. Call apologized to Jackson saying, "We are . . . greatly disappointed in not having a son
as we had flattered ourselves with the hope of giving our first borne
the name of our best and dearest friend Andrew Jackson."[18] Shortly
after this event Call was forced to absent himself from his official
duties for two months because of a severe illness. Described as
"bilious fever," it was to become a chronic disease with him, frequently recurring throughout the remainder of his life. Rachel and
Andrew Jackson anxiously awaited news of his recovery and added
to their expression of relief and pleasure their felicitations upon
the birth of a daughter. The old general added that Mrs. Kirkman
had "ceased to make you the object of her abuse; and I fondly hope
. . . she may in some measure attone for past improprieties."[19]

In April, 1826, Jackson conveyed to Call the news of the death of
Mary's father, and discussed steps which he had taken to protect the
Call interests at the probation of Thomas Kirkman's will at the
next session of the county court. Jackson had engaged three lawyers,
headed by the noted John Bell, and suggested that Call should
bring action to have Kirkman's sanity at the time the will was made
determined by a jury.[20] A codicil to the will had given Mrs. Kirkman the power to withhold the share of the estate due to the daughters in case of their marriage. In the event that said shares were
not withheld, they were to be settled upon the daughters and their
heirs exclusive of any control by the husbands.[21] Call approved
Jackson's selection of lawyers but hoped that everything could be
amicably "adjusted with the old Lady." After correspondence on
the matter for a year Call ultimately instructed Jackson not to contest the will in court. Eventually Mary Call received a portion of her
father's estate, and at her death the remainder was bestowed upon
her surviving daughters, Ellen and Mary.[22]

Meanwhile, in the winter of 1825-1826, Joseph M. White had
been aiding Judge Smith's attempts to clear himself of the charges
which Call had brought against him in the previous session. White
presented two petitions asking for an investigation of the judge, one
memorial from the inhabitants of East Florida praying for Smith's
acquittal, and one from Edgar Macon, the district attorney, charg-
ing Smith with malfeasance and corruption. However, the Judiciary

Committee, to which the subject was referred, made no report and was discharged from consideration of the subject.[23]

Smith and his friends were more successful in presenting their case to President John Quincy Adams. Elias B. Gould, editor of the *East Florida Herald,* assured the president that Call's charges "arose from personal hostility" and expressed the belief that Smith's conduct had been worthy of approval. After convincing Adams that Smith had been unjustly accused, White persuaded the president in April, 1826, to remove the troublesome district attorney Edgar Macon, who was an adherent of the Call faction in politics.[24]

The month of April also saw the beginning of an attempt to reconcile Call and White. Daniel E. Burch, one of Call's army acquaintances, asked him if a friendly settlement could be made. Burch revealed that Edward Tattnall, a Georgia Congressman, and Colonel Duncan L. Clinch had discussed the desirability of a settlement and stated his opinion that "nothing but the necessity of the case has ever made Colo. White your enemy." He assured Call that he would advise nothing that was not entirely honorable.[25]

Call exhibited no haste in seeking a settlement. It was rumored that if White were to return to the territory it would be in the fall, and no progress was made in bringing the men together until that season approached. Call named as his intermediary J. W. Ramage, a naval officer who was also a devotee of the pistol; Ramage excitedly threw himself into the intrigue. In August he told Call that Pensacola was buzzing with talk about the affair, with the general opinion being that White would never return. General opinion to the contrary notwithstanding, White arrived in Pensacola on September 21.[26]

Within a week after his arrival White was waited upon by Ramage who brought this note:[27]

> Sir:
> Your return to this Country affords me the opportunity I have long anxiously awaited, to demand from you, reparation for the injury and insult, received by me, in consequence of your publication in the Pensacola Gazette of the 4th June 1825 which appeared long after your departure from this Territory.
> My friend Capt. R. of the Navy, will deliver you this letter and he is fully authorized by me to make any arrangements which may be agreed upon.
> > R. K. Call

White referred Ramage to his friend John McCarty of Tallahassee for further negotiations. When McCarty was found to be out of town, Ramage melodramatically met with White "in the woods" near Quincy on October 16 and insisted that he name another representative immediately. White told Ramage that he could not immediately find a friend to act for him, but after some argument Daniel Burch was agreed upon. On October 18 Ramage sent an urgent express to Call asking to have Robert Butler associated with him to balance off Henry Yonge, who had appeared with Burch on behalf of White. Ramage also advised Call that his sympathizers were becoming too warm in their advocacy of his cause. The naval officer told Call that it had become difficult for him to "parry the many attacks of Religion, masonry, friends, etc which has been levelled against me."[28] On October 19, however, the four intermediaries held a full discussion of all the issues in dispute and concluded "an honorable and amicable termination of them."[29] Afterwards Call's friends were again overly exuberant and circulated handbills interpreting the settlement as a Call victory. This was dispelled by Henry Yonge's statement in the *Gazette* that each side had retracted all offensive statements concerning the other and that the settlement was an honorable one for both men.[30]

Jackson, who had become the very embodiment of discretion since entering the presidential lists, approved of the settlement. He told Call, "My friend, we ought as we pass through life not to break our shins, against stools, not in our way, when we can honorably remove them."[31] Adams, who had become White's confidante, noted in his diary that the delegate had barely escaped a duel and was seeking to be made *chargé d'affaires* to Denmark. He crisply observed, "Mrs. White very unwilling to go back to Florida."[32]

Despite the unwillingness of Mrs. White to return to Florida, White remained in Congress as the delegate from Florida until 1837. Though he and Call never became friends, their relations were never again as close to the point of actual armed combat as they had been in 1826. In 1827, 1829, and 1831 Gadsden ran unsuccessfully against White, each time backed by Call and the "Nucleus" at Tallahassee. During Adams' presidency White, enjoying the confidence of the administration, usually had the decisive word on patronage in Florida. The main critics of both Adams and White in Florida were the old Jackson followers who clustered around the "Nucleus." Call warned Jackson that White might be

his friend in his presence but that in Washington he was a slave
to Adams.[33]

The concentration of Jackson men in the land office furnished
their opponents with an excuse to attack the administration of the
public land policy in Florida. The "Nucleus" at the territorial capital was never a sharply defined political faction, but the opposition
gave it a more clear-cut membership and program than it in fact
possessed. It never seems to have been more than a group of men
having similar property and political interests who cooperated in-
formally on matters in which they thought alike. It was not a party
so much as it was a "community of interests." To the followers of
White, however, the term "Nucleus" became an epithet connoting
a group of grasping, self-seeking land speculators and men of wealth
intent upon their own enrichment whatever the cost. One opponent
of the "Nucleus" defined its purpose as "to guard with vigilance
the surveys and sales of the public lands, and to see that no one was
appointed to any office in relation to them, that was suspected of
complaining of an injury." Persons from Tennessee were always
favored, this critic observed, and he noted the great importance
attached by the "Nucleus" to control of the office of Delegate to
Congress. He described "Nucleus" men as solidly united in opposition to anyone presuming to peep into their arrangements.[34]

Eventually charges were made that Call and George Ward were
running the Tallahassee land office in a corrupt manner. One citizen complained that Call had tried to obstruct his pre-emption
claim because he had supported White for Congress. He charged:
"speculators buying to sell have had much less trouble in procuring
titles than the actual settlers who voted for Colonel White."[35] An
anonymous individual wrote to the Secretary of the Treasury that
the public money at Tallahassee was being misappropriated, and
that Call was using it to purchase lands for himself. This charge
was refuted by Call's accounts which arrived in Washington about
the same time. George Graham, head of the General Land Office
wrote Call about the letter "to guard you against the machinations
of your enemies." Call thanked him with the observation, "I have
no doubt it was written by some minion of Col. Whites. . . . You
are aware that we are personal enemies, and I know him to be
capable of such an act."[36]

"The abuses and temptations to fraud," wrote another of Call's de-
tracters, "must occur to every reflecting mind. The combination of

receiver with speculators is an infamous thing." This man stated
that Call had often put aside titles to choice lands, and had later
sold them at advanced prices, pocketing the increase himself in a
manner "little short of criminal."[37] Though these charges hurled at
Call doubtless were exaggerated and were calculated for political
effect, there can be little doubt that Call the land speculator was
in a very favorable position.

Charges of shady profiting were not all on one side, however.
White also dabbled in the buying and selling of land, and while in
Congress sold to the government a large tract to be used as a live
oak plantation for producing a supply of oak timbers to the navy.
Call and Ward charged that White had acted improperly and to
his own profit in the transaction, foisting off upon the government
a worthless patch of sand. Call tried to uncover any improper influence which might have been brought to bear by White to get
his own property selected but Duff Green replied to his inquiry,
"Your delegate is a *smart* man, and manages his matters with the
Dep'tments here in such a way that it is difficult to ensnare him."[38]
White was indignant at Call's suspicions and declared that he had
made only $28 on the deal. A portion of the tract had been bought
from Call and White asserted, "If I sold *worthless* property to the
Government, Gen. Call sold a part of this *same worthless* property
to me. . . . A man who has had his sickle in so rich a field, might
find better employment than by looking after my gleanings."[39]

Although Call did have his sickle in the rich field of land speculation, his wealth and the extent of his land transactions did tend to
become exaggerated in the heat of dispute. He was not the largest
purchaser of public lands nor did he make tremendous profits on
each tract he sold. Most of his public land purchases were in Leon
County. Between 1825 and 1831 he purchased over 8,000 acres of
land at public sales at a total cost of about $12,000. The Leon
County Court records indicate that his land sales in the same time
period totalled about 3,000 acres which brought in to him about
$19,000. His purchases from the public lands came largely from
the Lake Jackson and Ochlockonee River areas and the region on
the northern limits of Tallahassee. Both were wisely chosen regions.
The lands near Tallahassee cost him from $2 to $5 an acre; the remainder he purchased at $1.25 per acre.[40]

The land office duties of Call and Ward were increased by legislation in 1825 and 1826. While Call was in Congress in 1825 the

Board of Commissioners to settle land claims based on Spanish or English grants had been abolished and this duty had been vested in the Receiver and Register of the land offices. This meant that they were to decide upon all claims of less than 1,000 acres which had not already been decided by the Commissioners. For this extra duty each received $1,000. In 1826 more duties were put upon them connected with the adjudication of pre-emption claims but no extra compensation was granted. Call's regular salary as Receiver was $500 per year plus 1 per cent of the public monies received. From 1826 through 1829 he received a total of $8,889.69 in salary and commission from the land office. He petitioned Congress for an additional $5,630 for extra duties under the pre-emption act, but the claim was denied.[41]

From a financial point of view it can be seen that by the end of the Adams administration Call was doing fairly well. Though he could not be described as a man of great wealth, his legal practice, his land speculation, and his land office job brought in a comfortable income. Call retained the land office position until he became governor in 1836, and the thirties were even more rewarding than the twenties. In the early years of Jackson's first administration the "Nucleus" wielded much influence and enjoyed the life giving substance which patronage provided. To its ranks were added influential men who were not actually personal cronies of Jackson. In Tallahassee such men as Romeo Lewis, Sheriff of Leon County; Richard C. Allen, a land speculator; William B. Nuttall, a planter; and George K. Walker, Call's cousin, were associated with the "Nucleus." In East Florida Joseph Sanchez, an old inhabitant; Charles Downing, a lawyer; and Samuel Bellamy, a lawyer-planter, were leading men associated with the group. By 1829 Governor DuVal was also acting with the Call faction and became one of its most loyal adherents.[42]

As Call was growing financially independent and more influential locally, his mind did not close out events occurring beyond the limits of Florida. He watched with great interest the progress of the "bargain and corruption" campaign against Adams and he told Jackson in 1827, "I feel daily more sanguine that we shall have a happy triumph on the 4th of March 1829."[43] Mary and the young daughter Ellen visited the Hermitage in the same year, but the old general was so busy refuting the attempts of Clay "and his hired panders" to "harrow up the feelings of Mrs. J. and myself" that he was prevented from giving Mary "a final blow out" before she left. He promised Call that he would atone for it the next year "should it take the last shot in the *locker*."[44]

Richard Call and his brother George both turned their efforts to Jackson's cause. George W. Call was a doctor in Russellville, Kentucky, and could actively sway votes as Richard could not do in voteless Florida. George Call was in favor of the tariff and internal improvement features of Henry Clay's "American System" and he urged Jackson to endorse them. He assured the old general, "I have embarked my political all in your cause."[45] In Florida Richard Call took up his pen in Jackson's behalf to assure various questioners and newspapers that Jackson had not stolen another man's wife, that he had not brawled with Commodore Stephen Decatur in the Senate lobby in 1819, and that he had never threatened to cut off the ears of Congressman Abner Lacock.[46] When Henry Clay quoted Call to prove that the Jackson men, before the 1824 election, had not expected Clay to aid them in electing Jackson, Call again took up his pen.[47] "I have no recollection whatever of having made the remark attributed to me by Mr. Clay," he told Charles A. Wickliff; to John P. Van Ness he wrote, "I am confident that the assertion is without the least foundation."[48]

Jackson was appreciative of the efforts of his former aide, but was grieved that "every virtuous and patriotic act of my life is charged upon me as a crime." He comforted himself with the thought that "if the whole weight of Executive patronage . . . wielded in the most corrupt manner . . . does not prostrate me, then I have right to exclaim 'truth is mighty and has prevailed.' "[49]

By the summer of 1828 Jackson's lieutenants saw his victory as virtually certain. Call told him that he felt "a strong inclination to be with you in January next," but that imperative circumstances would prevent it. In December Rachel Jackson died only a few weeks after the confirmation of her husband's election, and for a time the president-elect was prostrate with grief. In January, however, Jackson buried his personal feelings and moved on to Washington to serve the people.[50] Call did not accompany him but was in Washington by inauguration day. There Call found that the proposed cabinet appointments were being received with mixed emotions. Many of Jackson's appointees were relatively unknown men, which prompted the use of the derisive term "the millenium of minnows." In "good society" shock was being expressed at the naming of John H. Eaton to the cabinet, because in January he had married the former barmaid Peggy Timberlake. Among the scandalized was the Reverend John N. Campbell, a Presbyterian minister of Washington. Campbell was understandably reluctant to speak to Jackson about the matter, but he talked freely about Mrs. Eaton to the Reverend Ezra Stiles Ely, a Jacksonian admirer from Philadelphia who was in Washington for the inauguration.[51]

Two days after his arrival in Washington Call visited with Ely and his lady, and in the course of the conversation the subject of Mrs. Eaton was broached. It developed that Ely had heard all that Call had heard and more. Call made it plain that his opinions coincided with those held by both Ely and Campbell. The opportunity did not arise, however, for Ely to speak to Jackson on the subject and he returned to Philadelphia without doing so. Call later visited the minister in Philadelphia and again they discussed Peggy Eaton. The Floridian, believing that a clergyman's words would win a more respectful hearing from Jackson on this explosive topic than his had, suggested that Ely address a letter to Jackson on the subject. On March 18, 1829, the minister wrote the fateful letter.[52]

On its arrival Ely's letter aroused a storm within the walls of the White House. Jackson collected all manner of "proofs" that the stories about Peggy were false and demanded to know of the clergyman his sources of information. At this counterattack Ely retreated, and Jackson set William B. Lewis to collecting testimonials on the spotless nature of Mrs. Eaton's character.[53] In a second letter Jackson tried to discredit any information which Call might have given to the minister.

"In all General Call's conversations with me," wrote Jackson, "and they have been frequent and *confidential*, he never did intimate any knowledge of Mrs. Eaton which was calculated, in my opinion, to cast even a shade of suspicion on her virtue. The very act which gave rise to his suspicions was one which, in my judgement, should have given him a more exalted opinion of her chastity."[54]

Jackson's vehemence and tenacity in defending Peggy Eaton stemmed in part from his friendship for her husband. In larger measure, however, it stemmed from Jackson's firsthand knowledge of the damage which wanton gossip could cause. His late wife Rachel, whom he had idolized, had been the victim of such gossip when through a mixup she had married Jackson before her divorce from her previous husband had become final. The pain which

Rachel had suffered was ever in Jackson's mind, and in fighting Peggy Eaton's fight he became so emotionally involved that it almost seemed he was defending Rachel's honor again as he had so many years earlier.

After Jackson's slashing replies to Ely, the minister's sources came forward. Campbell revealed that he had been one and Jackson had already guessed that Call had been one. In a long letter he took Call to task for his part in spreading tales about Peggy. Call replied with the hope that he might be wrong and Jackson right, saying: "Yours is certainly the most charitable belief, and one which I would embrase if I could. . . . I tell you in confidence . . . she will not be recd. in the families of the other members of your cabinet." Though Call's prediction was an accurate one Jackson scrawled on the back of the letter, "evidence of the falibility of man and how far he will be carried by his prejudices. . . ."[55]

Impatiently Jackson prepared another long letter to Call setting forth his "proofs" of Mrs. Eaton's sterling character with the taunt, "my Dear Call *you* have a right to believe that Mrs. T. was not a woman of easy virtue." He advised that the proof he enclosed was enough to warrant Call's telling Ely that he had been wrong in his information about Mrs. Eaton: "Justice to truth and to my friend, and your friend, Major Eaton requires this statement."[56]

Jackson reminded Call that his advances toward Mrs. Eaton had been rebuffed and asserted that Call had told William B. Lewis about the incident; should there be an investigation a denial would place him in an unpleasant predicament. The president professed not to be surprised that the "hired slanderers" of Henry Clay had spread stories about Peggy Eaton but expressed astonishment that confidential friends should have aided "in such unhallowed work." He wished to be rid of the unpleasant subject, however, and gently told Call, "You and I will not quarrel about it. . . . we always differed about these slanders . . . but as you have given me no evidence, entitled to any weight . . . I must be excused for still adhering to my own opinion."[57]

A man with the sensitive pride of Call could not let so incriminating a subject drop so easily. He admitted that the topic was one which he would like to let "slumber in oblivion," but decided that duty to himself required a reply to the president's letter. "I am much mortified," Call wrote, "that you have thought proper to class me among your enemies for doing that which could only have been dictated by the most devoted friendship." He pointed out that he realized he would incur Eaton's displeasure, but that he thought it a small price to pay to save Jackson from embarrassment. He believed that Eaton and Lewis were conspiring to keep Jackson deceived, and to discredit him was part of their plot. He denied that he was the only source or the major source of gossip, saying that the affair between Eaton and the former Mrs. Timberlake had been "talked of at Washington as publickly as the meetings of Congress."[58]

Call insisted that he had not told Lewis a story of any encounter with Mrs. Eaton and that he would call any man a liar who said that he had told such a story. He observed to Jackson, "I am satisfied that you are mistaken in the belief you entertain on the subject." Call declared that he had not carried tales to any of the president's enemies and wished that he had never carried any to him. "I have created enemies among men in power, whose enmity I expect to feel."[59]

Call was not successful in having Eaton removed from the cabinet, but Eaton was not the only appointee who he felt would embarrass the administration. John M. Berrien of Georgia, the Attorney General, was a most improper appointee in Call's opinion. The basis for his objection to Berrien was his connection with important cases against the government involving the validity of large land grants made by the Spanish in Florida. These grants were believed by many to be fraudulent, and Berrien was one of the attorneys representing the claimants. Call asserted that these engagements were "incompatible with his duties as attorney-general of the United States." He tried to defend Jackson from criticism by publishing a statement that Jackson had appointed the Georgian without knowledge of his pre-existing engagements.[60] Berrien immediately authorized Duff Green to deny this allegation in the *United States Telegraph* and he reminded Jackson that he had mentioned his connection with the Florida land cases and that, "You thought, as I did, that this circumstance presented no difficulty, and I acquiesced in the call with which you had honored me."[61]

Three years later Duff Green informed Call that the denial which he had published on behalf of Berrien had not been authorized by Jackson. In response to Call's inquiry Jackson declared that while he had known that Berrien was involved in cases against the government, it had never entered his mind that the large Florida land cases were included among them. He told Call that "you were the only individual who gave me the idea, that he was concerned in those large land claims." However, since the appointment had been made Jackson felt that no action ought to be taken against Berrien. Again with futility Call had tried to play the role of presidential adviser, but he had had Jackson's good name at heart. He told the president, "If I have erred it was in defending you with too much zeal from charges which I thought were calculated to do you a serious injury when ever the history of the Florida land claims is known."[62]

Call's efforts to save Jackson's administration from embarrassing appointments won sympathy from some of the men around Jackson, particularly from those who agreed with Call about Peggy Eaton. John Branch, the Secretary of the Navy, and Andrew Jackson Donelson, the president's private secretary, were among them. Branch told Call in a confidential letter, "You may have been indiscreet, you may . . . have committed a trivial sin in the indulgence of those fine and chivalrous feelings for which you have ever been characterized, but. . . . I wish that your efforts to rescue an old valued and venerable friend from misery and mortification in disguise, could have succeeded." Branch said that he did not entirely agree with Call about Berrien and was not disposed to condemn him. He wrote that Donelson "wished to write and unbosom himself to you, but that he could not under existing circumstances."[63]

During the early years of the Jackson administrations the good feelings between the president and Call were somewhat strained by the disputes over Eaton and Berrien. Their relations were not to receive a serious, severe test, however, until after Call became governor of Florida.

4

Defending the Public Domain

THE CONTROVERSIES BETWEEN Jackson and Call
over Berrien and Eaton for the most part had taken place
through the mails, since Call had returned to Tallahassee
after the inauguration to continue his law practice and pursue
his official duties at the land office. In the first year of the Jackson administration Tallahassee was little changed from the rough
village it had been at the beginning of the Adams administration
except that it had grown to larger proportions. The population
numbered about 1,000 and there were now three hotels, two
private schools, nine stores, two groceries, and a grog shop. One
wing of a more permanent capitol had been completed and the
Legislative Council no longer met in a log house. In the fall of the
year 1829 the Council incorporated St. John's Parish of the Episcopal Church, and Call was named one of three wardens empowered
to govern the church. The parish did not have its own church
building until 1837, however, toward the building of which Warden
Call had subscribed $500. Call's economic status was on the up-
swing even in 1829. The county tax rolls show that he owned 8,754
acres of land, thirteen slaves, and town lots valued at $500. He was
also assessed for one four-wheel pleasure carriage. In little Tallahassee Call was a big man and only one other paid more taxes
than he did.[1]

Call and his friends looked hopefully to the new administration
as heralding a new era for them in terms of political influence. Call
himself was not disappointed for he soon received a new federal
appointment and kept his old job as Receiver of Public Monies as
well. Three weeks after taking office President Jackson proposed
to Call that he take an appointment as assistant counsel for the
United States in two large land cases, those concerning the Arredondo grant and the Forbes grant. The Congress in 1828 had
:nacted a law providing for judicial settlement of all remaining

land claims which were larger than one league square, and authorizing the president to appoint a law agent to superintend the interests of the United States and an assistant counsel to assist in the prosecution of the cases.[2]

In the last days of the Adams administration William Wirt, the Attorney General, pointed out that the outcome of the Florida land cases would be finally determined by the Supreme Court and that the success of the United States would depend upon a proper presentation in the lower courts. Therefore, he told Adams, it was important that in the lower courts counsel should be employed "who are masters of the whole law upon the subject." Wirt suggested that the counsel also be required to make a compilation of the Spanish land laws. He named Joseph M. White as the best qualified man for the job and Adams ultimately appointed him.[3] White, however, had been engaged with Berrien and Daniel Webster to defend the claimants in the Arredondo and Forbes cases and was unwilling to act for the United States in those two cases.[4]

Adams finally consented to White's being employed on his own terms, it being understood that his chief duty would be the compilation of the Spanish land laws. White also stipulated that he should receive $3,000 as a retainer fee not to appear against the United States in any but the Forbes and Arredondo cases. The only cases in which he specifically agreed to defend the United States were those founded on British grants and those founded on claims which the old Board of Land Commissioners, of which White had been a member, had declared to be fraudulent. So it was that under President Adams the assistant counsel for the United States was appearing against the United States in the two cases involving the largest Florida land grants.[5]

When Jackson took office the Commissioner of the General Land Office suggested the appointment of an additional assistant counsel to represent the United States in the Forbes and Arredondo cases. He also recommended that the appointee be authorized to go to Havana to try to acquire originals of all papers relating to lands granted by Spain in Florida. It was as a consequence of this suggestion that Jackson proposed to engage Call as assistant counsel. The ebullient Floridian was to receive $500 for each case which he argued before the Superior Courts of the territory and $1,000 for each case which it was necessary for him to defend before the Supreme Court.[6]

Though Jackson hired Call to assist in the cases which White could not handle, he was still faced with the problem of having an Attorney General, Berrien, who was defending the claimants in the same cases. The initial responsibility for the defense of the United States rested with the local district attorneys who normally could have consulted with the Attorney General and, in these cases, the assistant counsel. When the district attorneys called for aid, Berrien advised Jackson to appoint "some professional gentleman" to act in his capacity for the Forbes and Arredondo cases. Berrien wrote that "the magnitude of the cases, as well as the novelty of some of the questions involved, will make it important to secure to the Government professional talents of the highest order."[7] Acting upon this advice, Jackson turned to former Attorney General Wirt and named him to supervise the United States side of the cases in which Attorney General Berrien was defending the claimants.[8]

Call's role in this complex arrangement was to assist the district attorneys in Florida before the Superior Court and to assist William Wirt in cases which might be carried on appeal to the Supreme Court. Like White he also had a major task aside from the actual preparation of cases. Call was commissioned to go to Cuba to procure original documents, or authentic copies of documents, relating to the large claims. At the end of March, 1829, James A. Hamilton, who was acting Secretary of State pending the arrival of Martin Van Buren, instructed Call on his mission, pointing out that his special agency was to find out whether suspicions that the Forbes and Arredondo grants were fraudulent were well founded.[9]

Under Spanish rule just before the cession, Florida had been a part of the Captaincy-General of Cuba and since the cession in 1821 the United States had been unsuccessfully trying to get from the Captain-General of Cuba certain of the Florida archives which included the records of land grants and title transfers. Four agents —James G. Forbes, James Biddle, Thomas Randall, and Daniel P. Cook—had already made fruitless journeys to Havana in quest of the missing archives. Yet despite the refusal of the authorities in Cuba to deliver the records, the claimants of Florida lands continued to produce originals or authenticated copies of documents purporting to establish their claims. This caused many persons, Call among them, to believe that Spanish officials were in collusion with the holders of questionable land claims in Florida.[10]

The appointment of plain spoken, energetic Richard Call was looked upon by many as a move which would at last get some action one way or the other. It should be made clear, however, that Call's mission differed somewhat from that of the previous agents sent to Cuba in that his major task was not to secure the Florida archives but was to get information about certain land claims. The instructions which he received from the State Department specified that if he could not get original documents he was to content himself with "authentic copies of them." He was to make plain to the Spanish authorities that his mission was in no way to be construed as relinquishing the "undoubted right" of the United States to absolute possession of all original archives.[11]

Call did not immediately leave for Cuba. His wife was expecting another child and he informed Jackson that he would not leave until its birth. The president consented, but expressed his anxiety to hear of Call's return from Havana with documents relating to the land cases. In a few months Call was seeking another reprieve on the grounds that it would be dangerous to go to Cuba during the "sickly season."[12] Jackson was dubious and wrote that White wanted to bring the land suits to trial in October, but he conceded that Call might wait if the trial could be delayed. The delay was secured and Call so informed Van Buren. In this interim the controversy about Peggy Eaton, as well as the one about Berrien's appointment, was dragging on. Call also was occupied in seeking the opinions of the three federal district attorneys in Florida as to which documents would be most useful in the government arguments.[13]

Finally, on December 22, 1829, Call left Tallahassee for Key West and proceeded thence to Havana. Arriving in the Cuban capital on January 5, 1830, he immediately notified the Captain-General in writing of his presence and requested an interview. On January 7 William Shaler, the American consul, verbally informed Call that the Captain-General would see him on the ninth. Call felt that this was no way to treat a Special Agent of the United States and, deeming this mode of communication unusual and disrespectful, he declined the interview. This treatment quickly brought an explanation and apology from the Captain-General, who sent his interpreter to Call with an invitation to meet with him.[14]

Call accepted this invitation and demanded of the Captain-General "such original documents relating to the land claims in Florida as might exist in the archives of Havanna." That functionary informed Call, as previous agents had been informed, that all papers in the archives of Florida had already been surrendered and that none remained in his hands. Call denied this contention and insisted that in the hands of the Spanish government there still were papers which rightfully belonged to the United States. In the face of Call's insistence, the Captain-General gave way and agreed to make a search of the archives and to make copies of any papers that might be found. "After the procrastination and delay common to these people," Call reported, original title papers to the big grants were produced. While they were being copied Call observed that certain documents varied so materially from the copies which the claimants had used to prove their ownership that he believed it would be necessary to produce the originals in court.[15]

The Captain-General was very reluctant to deliver over the original documents; however, after much difficulty and delay Call succeeded in obtaining them. He also obtained copies of papers concerning the power of local officers to make grants of land. The latter were secured by surreptitiously employing archives workers. Afterward the Captain-General genially authenticated the illicit copies. With the acquisition of the original grants and the papers bearing on the powers of the officials Call believed that he had secured everything necessary for the defense of the United States in the Forbes and Arredondo cases. He informed the State Department, however, that many documents relating to Florida which might be of great importance still remained in Havana. Call suggested that an order be secured from the King of Spain for their delivery, and asserted that with the knowledge he had gained of their existence and situation, "I feel well convinced that I could with the proper authority procure them."[16]

Call spent about two months in Havana and there enjoyed the pleasures of Cuban society. The American merchant Vincent Gray seems to have been his chief host, and the two men spent long hours recounting events of the War of 1812. Gray claimed that it was his intelligence which informed Jackson on British plans to attack New Orleans. In March, 1830, Call returned to the United States arriving in Tallahassee about the twentieth. He was "mortified" at the delay which had attended his mission but expressed satisfaction that he had done everything possible to protect the public interests in the Florida land cases. He reported that most of the grants "bear on their face conclusive evidence of their fraudulent character," and that the "prejudices in behalf of the claimants" were clearly apparent among the Spanish officials.[17]

The papers which Call produced relating to the grant to Don Fernando de la Maza Arredondo indicated that although the grant was a genuine one, it had been made on condition that two hundred families be settled on the tract within three years. The documents relating to the Forbes grant indicated a more complex situation. In the first place, the so-called "Forbes grant" was really a series of claims based upon several alleged grants to the commercial house of Panton, Leslie and Company and its successor John Forbes and Company, as well as to John Forbes individually. One large grant, estimated at about 1,500,000 acres, and located between the Apalachicola River and Choctawhatchee River, was granted by the Captain-General of Cuba to John Forbes and Company for services rendered to the Spanish government and losses sustained by the company. This was the only obviously fraudulent grant, bearing on its face a clumsy alteration of the date of execution. Under the treaty by which Florida was ceded to the United States all grants made after January 24, 1818, were "declared and agreed to be null and void." The alteration of dates was attempted in an effort to validate this grant.[18]

The other grants to Panton, Leslie and Company, John Forbes and Company, and to John Forbes individually, took in most of the land between the Apalachicola and St. Marks Rivers and were estimated to have a total acreage of about 1,200,000. These grants were made by Florida Indian tribes in payment of debts owed to the commercial houses, and were confirmed by the Spanish governor of West Florida. These grants were presented for adjudication by Colin Mitchel, a Havana merchant who claimed American, English, and Spanish citizenship, who had purchased the rights of the original grantees.[19] One historian of the Supreme Court says that the real promoters of the Mitchel claim were George Griswold, a New York shipper, "combined with other capitalists and with some of the most noted politicians in the country."[20] A conservative historian of the Court observes that "a large number of these Spanish claims had been assigned to and were being prosecuted by bankers, financiers, and speculators in New York and London" thus giving Andrew Jackson, in his fight upon the money power, a vivid interest in the outcome of the cases.[21]

The first of the grants to come to trial was the Arredondo case.

It was first tried in the Superior Court at St. Augustine and the decision went in favor of the claimants. An appeal made to the Supreme Court by counsel for the United States came before that tribunal in March, 1832. Call, Wirt, and Roger B. Taney, who had succeeded Berrien as Attorney General the previous year, represented the United States, while White, Berrien, and Webster represented the claimants. The arguments began on March 2 and ended on March 7. The eminent historian of the Supreme Court, Charles Warren, ranks this case as one of the few in this period which had a permanent effect upon the history of the country. He says that "in this case the Court established the public land policy of the Government on the basis of the most scrupulous respect for treaties, preferring to preserve the honor, rather than the property of the government, and to run the risk of confirming possibly fraudulent claims rather than to impair the reputation of the Government with foreign nations."[22]

In the Arredondo case Call contended that the condition imposed by the grant—the settlement of two hundred families—had not been met. He also claimed that the Intendant of Cuba, who made the grant, had not possessed such power.[23] The Court rejected the arguments of government counsel and upheld the decision of the lower court for the claimants. The major arguments of the government attorneys were waved aside in favor of a liberal construction of the clauses in the treaty of cession protecting property rights. The Court excused the non-performance of the conditions of the grant on the grounds of change of circumstances and jurisdiction.[24] Despite the fact that the Court was satisfied that the Intendant of Cuba had the land-granting power, it asserted that it was unnecessary to inquire into that fact because the act of a duly appointed official was to be presumed to be a valid official act with the burden of disproof lying with the United States.[25]

The Arredondo grant had embraced 289,645 acres and was one in which Northern capitalists had been involved. Call was convinced that it was a fraudulent claim and that all the large grants were patent efforts to cheat the government of land which was rightfully its property. After the decision in the Arredondo case he became quite pessimistic about the prospects of defeating any of the other "evidently fraudulent" claims.[26] He was, nonetheless, to be successful in two cases before the Superior Courts of Florida, one of which was not appealed.

John Innerarity, a member of the house of Forbes and Company, instituted suit for the immense tract between the Apalachicola and Choctawhatchee Rivers on behalf of the firm. The case came to trial in the Superior Court of West Florida and the claim was invalidated for being based on an obviously forged document. No appeal was made and the decree of the lower court became final.[27] The tract east of the Apalachicola, which Colin Mitchel claimed, came before the Superior Court of Middle Florida and was also invalidated. Call figured prominently for the government in both cases.

The government arguments against Mitchel included three points of major importance: (1) As the title to all lands in Florida was vested in the Crown, the Indians ceding the land had no title to it, nor did they have prescriptive rights to it since most of them lived in the United States at the time of the grant. (2) The Governor of West Florida had possessed no power to ratify Indian grants. (3) Even had the governor possessed such power the lands granted were in East Florida. The Superior Court, in upholding the government, made much of a discovery by the judge that watermarks on the confirmation papers were said to indicate that the paper had been made subsequent to the dates upon them.[28]

The claimants appealed this case to the Supreme Court and it was docketed on February 2, 1831. It was not tried for four years, however, because of continuations granted at government request in the hope that more evidence could be turned up in the Havana archives. In line with Call's suggestion of 1830, the American minister to Spain had applied for a royal order for the delivery of all Florida archives remaining in Cuba and had been successful in getting it. Secretary of State Edward Livingston named Jeremy Robinson, an experienced hand at Latin American affairs, to carry out the order. He said that he had not asked Call to go because Call had already left Washington when the royal order arrived.[29]

Robinson was directed to get from Call before going to Cuba all information which the latter might have about the disposition of the archives. He arrived in Tallahassee on May 28, 1832, and waited impatiently for Call to return from the sessions of nearby county courts. After several weeks in Tallahassee, during which time Call related to him his experiences with Cuban officialdom, Robinson proceeded to Pensacola and took passage for the Cuban capital. There he soon adopted the same views toward the land

grants as were held by Call. He became convinced that Colin
Mitchel had bribed Spanish functionaries to forge or alter records
to assist him in his suit before the United States courts.[30]

Robinson's progress in getting into the archives was slow, owing
in large measure to the apparent determination of the officials not
to execute the royal order. He copied Call's example, however, and
bribed the Spanish clerks and employees for the loan of indices and
inventories of the archives. For two years he remained in Havana
examining and copying documents. His work, however, was delayed
not only by official indifference but by ill health, and in November
of 1834 he died. Though he was not successful in returning a single
original document to the United States, he did send inventories of
the Florida papers and copies of official reports bearing on land
grants. Upon Robinson's death Nicholas Trist was sent to Havana
to return ten specific categories of documents which were thought
to be necessary in the Mitchel case. Trist returned forty-five documents, but none was admitted as evidence by the Supreme Court.[31]

While Robinson worked in Cuba the Supreme Court continued
the Mitchel case and Call was occupied in other land cases. In 1831
White's services were terminated and Call was engaged to act as
assistant counsel in all suits instituted in Florida on land claims.
In this capacity Call spent most of 1831 and 1832 assisting in these
cases before the territorial courts. Several hundred cases were
brought, most of which concerned East Florida claims. The Attorney General, Roger B. Taney, reported to Jackson that the government could not afford to recompense Call for each case argued
on the basis of their earlier agreement and recommended an annual
salary of $2,500 for him. Taney observed that this was far less than
the claimants would have paid him to represent them.[32]

During 1833 Call's legal work took a back seat to his electioneering. In that year he ran against White for Congress but was defeated. He still also held the post of Receiver at the land office and
it required some of his time; however, much of the work was dele-
gated to clerks, to the apparent detriment of the records of the
office. The files of the General Land Office are filled with letters
from the Commissioner reproving Call for not sending in his reports
on time, and correcting errors in his accounts. Call continued to
hold the posts of Receiver and assistant counsel until his appointment to the governorship in 1836. Actually he held all three posts
for a brief period in that year.

At the January, 1834, term of the Supreme Court the government got another continuance of the Mitchel case. On February 19 William Wirt's death left the prosecution of the remaining cases in the hands of Call and another new Attorney General, Benjamin F. Butler. Call travelled to Washington for the January term and represented the United States in eleven East Florida claims which were heard by the Court at that session. The most important was the case of George J. F. Clarke in which the Court reaffirmed the doctrines laid down in the Arredondo case. To Call's argument that the governor had exceeded his powers in granting Clarke a tract larger than he was authorized to do, Chief Justice John Marshall asserted, "A grant made by a governor, if authorized to grant lands in his province, is *prima facie* evidence that his power is not exceeded. . . . His orders are known to himself and to those from whom they proceed, but they may not be known to the world."[33]

The Court upheld the lower court in validating the claim though it ordered the lower court to restrict its size to the acreage in the grant, which that court apparently had expanded.[34] The ten remaining cases were also terminated in favor of the claimants but three of those, too, were diminished in size. In the Clarke case Call alone had appeared for the United States while Berrien and Wilde appeared for the claimants. In the remaining cases Call represented the government and White appeared for the claimants.[35]

After this term of the Court ended Call returned to Florida and remained until the January, 1835, term began. In December, 1834, as he was preparing to return for the Mitchel case, news arrived of the death of Jeremy Robinson in Havana. Assuming that this would delay the documents which Robinson might have turned up and that the Court might grant another continuance, Call delayed his departure. "The recent afflictions, and present delicate situation of my family," he wrote to Butler, "would render my absence from home exceedingly painful, and unless required by necessity, should be avoided on my part."[36]

The afflictions to which Call had reference were the deaths of his daughter Mary Jane and his only son Richard Jackson Call. Since the birth of Ellen in 1825, Mary and Richard Call had had five more daughters and one son. In 1826 twin daughters, and in the fall of 1832 two other infant daughters, had died. In September of 1834 the infants Mary Jane and Richard joined them, both being buried on the eighteenth in a single coffin. The "delicate situation" to which Call referred was the pending birth of the last child, Mary Call.[37]

Despite the affliction of these personal difficulties Butler felt that Call was badly needed in Washington. "I regret exceedingly," he wrote, "that you should have determined . . . to remain at home . . . inasmuch as it is altogether doubtful, whether the case of Mitchel will be continued . . . and the Court have already decided that the Missouri cases in which I also desired your assistance are no longer to be connected with that of Mitchel, but to be brought on at an early date."[38] To the Secretary of the Treasury, Butler wrote, "The aid of the surviving assistant counsel General Call will be essential in the argument of this case." Some of Butler's anxiety was no doubt due to the fact that Wirt had not written a full argument before his death and had left only notes on the defense which he had prepared.[39]

On March 14, 1835, the Supreme Court refused to grant another continuation in the Mitchel case. White and Berrien for the claimants and Call and Butler for the United States heard Chief Justice Marshall denounce the delay as already excessive and declare that "no rational foundation is laid for the opinion that new and important additions will or can be made to the information the record at present contains."[40] The Court then reversed the decision of the lower court and declared the Mitchel claim to be a valid one.[41] The Indian grants were upheld as, in the opinion of the court, having been made according to Spanish law and practice, and the copies of the confirmation documents were accepted despite Call's protestations that they were not even notorial acts, but were private copies entitled to no credit. The Court brushed aside these objections with the observation that the questioned confirmations were only a part of numerous undisputed documents tending to establish the grant.[42]

Call was much disheartened by the loss of this case and two other land cases in 1835. With disgust he left Washington, writing to his friend Donelson, "I am now fairly launched on the bosom of the great Potomac, but the power steam, tide, and wind, combined does not carry me over the troubled waters so fast as I am borne by my feelings and wishes toward the South."[43] Call was bitter in his criticism of the Supreme Court for its decisions on the Florida land claims and declared that its precedent in the Mitchel case would remove all objections to the confirmation of any of the remaining claims. He ridiculed the Court policy of regarding the grant itself as evidence of the power to make a grant, and asserted that the Supreme Court had vested Spanish officials with powers which even their own king had not given them. Much expense and inconvenience could have been saved, he wryly suggested, had Congress merely enacted a bill confirming every grant of any kind.[44]

Many have been critical of the course of the Court in the Florida land cases and the decision in the Mitchel case did raise questions worth pondering. The Court apparently closed its eyes to the hindrances which Spanish officials put in the path of those who sought to uncover original documents. It would be interesting to know why, in the face of contrary evidence, the aged Chief Justice stated that no difficulty had been put in the way of American agents and that every facility had been accorded them.[45] Another point which seems questionable was the inclusion in the decree of a 7,000-acre tract, Forbes Island, which was not even in the claim being adjudicated before the Court.[46] The island was at that time the subject of a case being heard in the Superior Court in Florida. Attorney General Butler expressed his amazement at this enlargement of the claim by the Court, and Call declared, "I was indeed surprised to find that the island . . . is included in the decree. I listened with great attention to the decree when read in Court, and feel most confident that the island was not mentioned at that time."[47]

One historian of the Supreme Court, Gustavus Myers, saw the decisions in the Florida cases as part of a pattern of decisions by which "judicial dictator" John Marshall designed to strengthen the governing and capitalist classes.[48] The more conservative Charles Warren viewed the decisions as designed to protect private property rights and preserve the national honor of the United States by strict adherence to the article of the treaty of cession which recognized property rights existing before 1818.[49] A third historian, Ernest Sutherland Bates, points out that the rights of Spain were not at issue in any of the claims because the actual claimants were American capitalists not Spanish citizens. It is his contention that the Court was governed less by respect for treaties than by the formalistic procedure established in the Yazoo land fraud cases whereby it refused to consider the evidence of fraud behind a formal grant.[50]

What was Call's attitude toward the Court and its decisions? Why did he consent to defend the public interests when he could more

profitably have given his services to the speculators who were press-
ing the claims? Call was critical of the reasoning of the Court, as
we have shown, and was convinced that the Court was disposed
"to avail itself of every circumstance however remote, or trivial to
sustain the claims against the government."[51] Yet there is no evidence which indicates that Call believed the courts to be in league
with capitalists or speculators. He did firmly believe that the speculators were in league with the Spanish officials to cheat the United
States. He never gave up the idea that the grants were made by
local officials who thought proper to transcend their powers because of the pending cession of the province.[52]

Call had been approached to defend the Mitchel claim in 1828
but had requested a fee which Mitchel had declined to pay. Later
when his personal hero, Andrew Jackson, requested him to defend
the United States, at an admittedly lower fee, he gladly consented
to do so. There is no indication that Call had any idea of being a
part of any Jacksonian crusade against the money power or against
vested privilege. The evidence seems to point, however, to a strong
personal conviction on Call's part as the motivating factor in his
defense of the government. He was certain that the grants were
frauds perpetrated by the wily Spaniards and, as he possessed some
of Jackson's tendency to attribute evil motives to political enemies,
this belief was probably strengthened when White undertook to
defend the claimants. It cannot be ignored, too, that confirmation
of the grants would eliminate any federal revenues from them and
would remove large choice tracts from Call's own speculations.
He thus stood to incur personal economic loss, in that as Receiver
he would lose the commission from the sale of the lands by the
government and as a speculator he would lose the opportunity of
buying them at the government price of $1.25 per acre.

Despite the fact that great vested interests were involved in push-
ing the Florida land cases, Call's opposition to them apparently
stemmed from these more personal sources: his friendship for
Jackson, his hostility toward the Spaniards, and his own economic
interests. Probably the fact should not be overlooked that the appointment as assistant counsel for the United States, with the opportunity of appearing before the Supreme Court, was a great
feather in the cap of a frontier lawyer with little formal training.
He could not have foreseen that from fifteen cases argued before
the highest court he would record fifteen defeats.

5

To the "Nucleus" Go the Spoils

THE EXPECTATIONS of the members of the "Nucleus" that the election of Andrew Jackson would redound to their benefit were soon fulfilled. In April, 1829, Governor William P. DuVal wrote to Jackson that his friends in Florida were "solicitous that the benifits resulting from the salutary reforms which you have commenced should also be extended to Florida." He reminded Jackson that when he had been governor the administration had not allowed him to utilize his friends in filling the appointive offices and asked, "I beg of you to remember them now and aid us in giving a character to our Territory it richely deserves."[1]

DuVal named a long list of officeholders who should be removed to effect the "salutary reforms" which he had in mind. Call also suggested removals from time to time and his suggestions usually were acted upon in the first years of the administration. Joseph M. White, who had been more influential with the Adams administration, assumed an air of naive surprise and indignation that his recommendations no longer carried much weight at the White House. He visited his old patron, the former president, and together the two men consoled each other about the dreadful changes being wrought by the new administration. In a tone of shocked righteousness White related to Adams that twelve removals had been made in Florida with no justification. The former president nodded sympathetically as the Florida delegate related how Jackson had "bristled into a passion" when he had questioned the Florida removals and had shouted that every last man had been removed for "oppression or defalcation." Shaken, White had retreated to the office of Secretary of State Van Buren where he complained that his recommendations had been ignored, and asked what instances of oppression or defalcation had occasioned Jackson's removals in Florida. The urbane Secretary of State soothed the ruffled Floridian and assured him that either he had misunderstood the president or the president's memory was at fault for, he quietly observed, no reasons were ever given for their removals.[2]

We have already noted the elevation of some of Call's friends to federal jobs. In 1825 Benjamin D. Wright, his law partner, had become federal district attorney at Tallahassee, and Ambrose Crane had become postmaster of that city. Wright was later transferred to Pensacola. Crane edited the *Florida Intelligencer* in 1825 and 1826, a paper known as the organ of the "Nucleus," and he was followed in the editorship by Algernon S. Thruston. Thruston's reward came early in 1830 when he was named Collector of Customs at Key West in place of William Pinckney, removed. In 1827 Call's friend Edgar Macon, whom Adams had removed as district attorney in St. Augustine, succeeded to the editorship of the *Intelligencer*, which then became the *Florida Advocate*. Leslie A. Thompson, another member of the "Nucleus," was the last editor of the *Advocate* before its failure in 1829. From August, 1829, until December, 1830, the "Nucleus" was without a newspaper voice.[3]

The impending Congressional election of 1831, however, demanded that newspaper support for the "Nucleus" and its candidate be secured. William B. Nuttall approached the editor of the *Floridian*, William Wilson, with the proposal that he not favor White in the forthcoming election. Nuttall further suggested that if Wilson would take Edward R. Gibson on his staff and be favorable toward the "Nucleus," then he need fear no competing press in Tallahassee. Wilson declined to enter into any such arrangement, and on the following day he was approached by Call. In the course of their discussion of the political leanings of the *Floridian* Call asked Wilson, "Is there no possibility of making an arrangement?"

"None whatever," was the editor's reply. That afternoon the prospectus of a new paper, the *Florida Courier*, was published.[4] This new publication was favored in 1831 by a resolution of the Legislative Council awarding to it the contract for the public printing despite charges of its competitor that it was a vehicle of abuse and filth and the organ of "land speculators and political mercenaries."[5] Gibson edited the paper until 1832 when he joined Duff Green in the management of the Washington *United States Telegraph*. The *Courier* press is notable not only for its support of the "Nucleus," but for having published the first novel in Florida, Don Pedro Casender's *The Lost Virgin of the South*.[6]

The patronage of the federal government was also bestowed upon a number of other persons associated with the "Nucleus." Richard C. Allen, a Tallahassee land dealer and crony of Call, replaced Samuel Brents as Law Agent in Florida, thus becoming associated with Call in the land claims cases. Thomas E. Randolph became United States Marshal at Tallahassee and George K. Walker, Call's cousin and business partner, became United States Attorney for West Florida when Benjamin D. Wright gave up that post in 1830. In 1834 Wright became editor of the *Pensacola Gazette.* Call's old duelling crony, James W. Ramage of the navy, was appointed to the post of master commandant in that branch of the service.[7]

The peak of the power and influence of the "Nucleus" was reached during 1830 and 1831 when its ties with the Jackson administration were strongest. The Congressional election of 1831 and the attempt by the followers of Joseph M. White to unseat Governor DuVal are events of those years testifying to the support which was given to the Florida group from Washington. The campaign for delegate began in 1830 and, as usual, featured White, the incumbent, against James Gadsden, representative of the "Nucleus." In this campaign Call was a vigorous supporter of Gadsden, as he had been in the past. He particularly assailed White for his connection with the claimants of the large land grants, and his sale of land for the controversial live oak plantation.[8] Call and his friends tried to make political capital among the squatters on the huge Mitchel claim by showing that White was doing them a disservice in upholding the claimants. Should the claimants win, Call pointed out, actual settlers would not be able to pre-empt the land at $1.25 per acre but would have to pay the prices demanded by companies of speculators. In this campaign the tables were turned on White, former foe of speculators, by Call—now fighting as champion of the people against White, champion of the vested interests. Call's participation in the campaign became so vigorous that a stranger was reported to have asked which of the two, Gadsden or Call, was running against White.[9]

White's friends, with their control of the influential papers in Pensacola and Tallahassee, set up a very damaging outcry against the machinations of the "Nucleus." They represented it as a powerful, invisible, evil force ruling the territory through tributaries and auxiliaries in every quarter. Some saw great speculative combines injurious to the public welfare growing from the influence of the "Nucleus." The clamor against this phantom power grew so great that Gadsden at length felt it necessary to state that he was not then and never before had been a member of it.[10]

To combat the power of the "Nucleus" an attack designed to drive a wedge between the Call-Gadsden faction and the Jackson administration was launched. The opposition press played up the disagreements between Call and Jackson over Eaton and Berrien, and tried to show that Call's opposition to them was opposition to the Jackson administration. Dark insinuations were also made that there was a Clay supporter in the land office, and assertions were made that the main support for Gadsden came from the friends of Henry Clay. Gadsden, it was rumored, had pointedly condemned the appointment of Martin Van Buren to the cabinet; Gadsden, it was implied, was opposed to the administration. Later events were to show some truth in the latter implication. With the election a month away, "Cato" wrote the editor of the *Floridian* that the "Nucleus" was opposed to the measures and the principles of Andrew Jackson, but that it would invoke his name to benefit by his popularity. General Jackson, he wrote, "carries more dead weight than ever man run with."[11]

Despite the great pressure brought to bear for his defeat White was re-elected to Congress, though his majority was a narrow 85 out of 3,891 votes cast. In Middle Florida the "Nucleus" had triumphed in giving Gadsden a majority of almost two hundred, but White's majorities in East and West Florida carried him to victory. The delegate was bitter and charged that Washington had directly interfered in the election and had used every influence "over contractors, deputies, dependants and expectants."[12]

Besides the public attempts to split the "Nucleus" from the Jackson administration, White had been moving against that faction behind the scenes. Working with William Wyatt and the Indian Agent Gad Humphries, he was attempting to discredit Governor DuVal and prevent his reappointment by Jackson. White first forwarded to Jackson a list of charges by Wyatt against DuVal. Wyatt was a little known, maverick politician who was very active in White's behalf. The charges which he made accused DuVal of favoritism, misappropriation of funds, fraud in the handling of Indian gifts, carelessness in the preservation of public records, negligence of official duties, and general maladministration. Jackson retorted that Wyatt was a man of very bad character and that White should either prefer charges himself or forget the matter. On White's insistence, however, Jackson examined the proofs presented and came to the conclusion that no impropriety existed in DuVal's conduct.[13]

DuVal and the "Nucleus" counterattacked. Richard C. Allen wrote to Jackson that White was leagued with an "inconsiderable" party in Florida opposed to the administration. Romeo Lewis, Allen's partner and sheriff of Leon County, wrote in DuVal's behalf as did Call and, of course, DuVal himself. As a result Jackson showed his confidence in DuVal by giving him an interim reappointment until Congress should convene. In the meantime, DuVal prepared a body blow at Delegate White.[14] In July rumors were current that DuVal was planning to order another election for Delegate to Congress, and on the tenth of August the *Floridian* carried the news that he had indeed ordered a new election.[15] He had seized upon a technicality of the law which required the submission of lists of voters along with the returns and had thrown out enough votes to cause a tie between White and Gadsden. On the pretext that no one had been elected the governor had ordered the new canvass. What Call's precise role was in this farce is not clear. DuVal, however, had removed the returns to Call's office "for safety," and presumably the rejection of certain returns was done there. Incredulous, White exploded that DuVal "admits he removed the returns to the office of my greatest personal, and political enemies, for safety!!"[16]

This bold move by DuVal was nonetheless a colossal failure. White chose to ignore the second election and was seated by the House on the basis of the first one; even so the new election resulted in his victory with a more decisive majority. But the war was not over. In the Senate DuVal's name was presented for appointment for another regular three-year term on December 7, 1831. On the ninth Ezekiel F. Chambers of Maryland rose to present White's charges of "malversation and corruption" against DuVal. They were referred to the Committee on the Judiciary which conducted an investigation. Among the witnesses who testified before the committee was Call, who spoke in favor of DuVal and reportedly declared that thirteen of the sixteen members of the Legislative Council also favored the reappointment. In April, 1832, the committee reported that the charges were not substantiated and that "his nomination ought to be confirmed," which the Senate did on the thirtieth.[17]

By this time the campaign for the election of 1833 was underway and alterations were taking place within the "Nucleus." To some extent the changes in the "Nucleus" reflected shifts in the national alliance which had carried Jackson to the presidency. Two hostile factions had taken shape within the Democratic party during the first year of his administration. One had pressed Calhoun's claims to the succession and the other supported Van Buren. Some of Call's associates in Florida were admirers or adherents of Calhoun and resented the decline of his influence after the cabinet was dissolved in 1831 and Jackson personally broke with him. This probably produced some discord within the "Nucleus," despite the personal admiration which many of its members also felt for Jackson, for some of these men did not like Van Buren, whose interests were now in the ascendancy, or the old Crawford faction with which Van Buren had been allied. The Peggy Eaton affair had been one incident symptomatic of the party division, with the Calhoun forces leading the ostracism of the Secretary of War's wife and the Van Buren forces posing, with Jackson, as her defenders. Call seems not to have suffered much diminution of prestige at the White House by his enmity toward Eaton, possibly because his opposition to Berrien, a Calhoun man, served to cancel out any hard feelings which Jackson may have entertained toward him for his attitude toward Eaton.

Further strains in the national Jacksonian alliance were apparent in 1832. The major events of that year were the nullification controversy and Jackson's veto of the recharter of the Bank of the United States. The reaction to both events caused changes in Florida politics, generally serving to increase the factionalism as men took opposing sides on the national issues of bank, nullification, the nature of the Union, and presidential prerogatives. For all practical purposes, 1833 was the last year in which the "Nucleus" was able to act as a political force with any semblance of unity.

Local issues also entered into the increase of factionalism. In part the decline of the "Nucleus" reflected the growing diversification of interests among propertied men in Florida. By the 1830's the land office was ceasing to be a center of attraction for ambitious men seeking their fortunes. Banking and railway corporations were rising in importance and were seeking their attention and resources. Pensacola, Tallahassee, and St. Augustine each had rather important banks, and railroad schemes were projected in virtually every populated place in the territory. Competition for the favors of the territorial government divided propertied groups among themselves and promoted sectionalism. Late in the thirties the statehood movement also promoted factionalism and sectionalism. In prosperous, populous Middle Florida where statehood sentiment was strong the politically articulate groups were anxious to be free of federal control. In East Florida, less populous and ravaged by Indian warfare, statehood was opposed by many influential men on the grounds that Florida could not yet financially sustain a state government and needed continued material benefits from the federal government. Much the same sentiment prevailed in West Florida, where there was also some feeling for annexation to Alabama.

Though no sharp change is evident in the influence which leaders of the old "Nucleus" exerted with the administration, the appointments to Florida posts after 1833 show the presence of other influences. Call himself continued to be on good personal terms with the president despite the gradual entry into Florida posts of men personally repugnant to him. More and more after 1833 men sympathetic to Van Buren and hostile to local banking institutions began to appear in federal posts. It was from these men that the Democratic party in Florida was to take its direction—not from Call and the old Jacksonian followers who had clustered around the "Nucleus."

In 1832, however, the old Florida political alignments still maintained a degree of surface unity. Jeremy Robinson, visiting Call in Tallahassee while en route to Havana, noted that party politics were "distinguishable by the Gadsden and White interests, or the administration and anti-administrationists." He noted it was common knowledge that the former group was led by Governor DuVal, Call, and James D. Westcott, Jr., the territorial secretary.[18] The surface unity was more apparent than real, for rival ambitions and conflicting national and local interests threatened to tear the "Nucleus" asunder. Benjamin D. Wright sought to preserve the alliance by convincing Call that he should run for Congress as the only candidate upon whom all could unite. Call gave his consent, but became so discouraged by the dissension within the group that he asked Wright to withhold his announcement as a candidate. Wright, however, was not to give up his plan so easily and replied that Call's request had not been received early enough to withhold the announcement. He urged that there be no further delay in getting on with the campaign. "What you mistake for a want of heartiness & zeal in your friends," he wrote, "is in fact but the want of concert." He assured Call that

> the opponents of honest Joe are almost unanimous in the opinion that you are the only man who can beat him. In this part of the Territory they would not go to the polls unless you were a candidate. . . . I must do those of our little caucus who were themselves aspirants the justice to state that they yielded their pretensions with as much grace as could have been expected. I think they will support you. . . .[19]

Call accepted the decision and made the race, but Gadsden and many of his followers did not receive the new nominee with pleasure. Call believed that his defeat in the race was in part the fault of Gadsden.

Important national issues came up in the campaign in relation to the nullification controversy. In November, 1832, the new tariff bill of that year was nullified by South Carolina. Jackson countered this action with a ringing proclamation maintaining the supremacy of the Union but committing himself to a theory of the nature of the Union which frightened the state rights men among his followers. Call supported the proclamation of the president and thereby undoubtedly lost some support. Gadsden did not publicly favor nullification at this time, but he ultimately broke with the Jacksonians on that issue. Actually White was opposed to nullification as was Call, but he tempered his views and claimed to be more in favor of state rights than was Call. White also announced that he favored Calhoun for the presidency but would accept Henry Clay before he would support Martin Van Buren.[20]

The press, for the most part favorable to White, denounced Call for his support of the president's views. "He goes the whole for the proclamation and the enforcement bill," wrote the *Floridian*. "There is no reservation in favor of State Rights. . . . We fear the General has become infected with doctrines which, . . . however current they may be at Washington, are rather unsuited to this latitude."[21] Call later modified and defined his views on the great controversy by assuming a position favorable to secession, but in opposition to nullification. He conceded that secession was a technical right which the states possessed but which he believed would be disastrous if used.[22]

Call was subjected to an unmerciful campaign of criticism and sheer personal abuse. He was accused of having used Gadsden to head up the opposition to White, and was charged with having made certain Gadsden could never be elected so that he could be pushed aside when Call himself wished to run again. "It was not convenient for him to offer," wrote a critic, "until the land office 'tit' was sucked dry: but now it seems, it no longer gives milk, and he must take to rooting."[23] Others brought up the Eaton and Berrien affairs and taunted him for keeping silent when Jackson kept them in the cabinet: "Verily this devotion 'surpasses the love of women' —it not only is ready to sacrifice life, but *honour*."[24] Call's critic "Junius," who is believed to have been James D. Westcott, Jr., sought to establish that he had neither "the abilities, temper, character, or principles" to represent Florida in Congress.[25]

As might be expected, Call's connection with the land office came under fire. In March, 1833, Jackson reappointed him to the post of Receiver, indicating his disbelief in the criticisms of those who claimed that Call had used the office "to oppress the citizens of Florida" and to enrich himself.[26] On the very eve of the election a group of Jackson County men had published over a dozen charges alleging serious maladministration by Call and Ward.[27] Despite all the unfavorable press there is indication that, at least in Tallahassee, sentiment for Call was strong. The violently partisan *Floridian* felt constrained to print one letter in its columns favorable to Call. That letter praised Jackson's course towards South Carolina, defended Call, and stated that the writer was voting for him because "he *is* the personal and political friend of Jackson."[28]

The most dramatic episode of the campaign was a duel between Leigh Read and Oscar White. Read was the protégé and law student of Call and White was the nephew of Joseph M. White. Oscar White's slighting remarks in public about Call brought a challenge from Read. It was accepted and at the appointed time a great crowd gathered to watch the encounter. Shots were exchanged and then the two young men closed with knives. Rolling and tossing in the dust, they fought until exhausted. Neither was killed.[29]

Call showed remarkable public restraint throughout the campaign. He did suspect that White penned some scurrilous letters but White hastened to assure him, "I . . . do not intend to write one line derogatory to your character. . . . Shall I be under the necessity of writing anything in relation to you it will be over the signature of your observant Jos. M. White."[30] With the frustration common to politicians who feel themselves persecuted by the press, Call declared that freedom of the press in Florida had degenerated into licentiousness. He defended the "Nucleus," saying: ". . . the motives and conduct of no men have been so much and so incessantly the subject of misrepresentation and calumny, as those of the high minded and honorable men, with whom it has been equally my pride and my pleasure to act."[31]

White proved to be an unbeatable candidate in Florida and Call went down before him in 1833 as Gadsden had done three times before. Call felt that Gadsden's friends and the "nullifiers" had beaten him. Jackson read of the defeat of his former protégé and demanded, ". . . how this has happened I wish you to explain to me. There are so many rumors of treachery in your ranks, and nullifiers in your Territory, that I am anxious to be correctly informed, for whatever good opinion I may entertain of individuals, I can never invest one with office under the General Government . . . who would nullify its laws and oppose their execution. Is it possible that our friend Gadsden is a nullifier? and his political friends voted against you, or did not vote at all."[32] Gadsden asserted that he had not opposed Call and blandly denied that he controlled any votes. He coyly professed to believe that in his own campaigns Call's friends had been perfectly free to support whom they chose. That he was a nullifier was soon proved by his break with Jackson on that issue.[33]

Another great issue in national politics, the Bank of the United States, apparently had little immediate effect in Florida. President Jackson had vetoed the recharter of that institution in July, 1832, but its effects upon Florida politics were not felt for several years. Little indignation was evidenced and Call privately approved of the act, probably largely from personal loyalty to Jackson. Perhaps there were other considerations, however, for Florida was feeling the need of its own banks as its planters grew in wealth and its speculators dreamed grander dreams. The Bank of Florida had been chartered by the Legislative Council in 1828 and was followed in 1832 by the Central Bank of Florida. In this latter institution Call was one of the superintendents of the subscription of stock.[34]

Numbers of smaller banks followed these, many of which never opened. In 1831 the Bank of Pensacola was established followed by the Union Bank of Tallahassee in 1833 and the Southern Life Insurance and Trust Company at St. Augustine in 1835. These were

the "big three" of Florida banking. The board of directors of the
Union Bank read almost like a roster of the old "Nucleus." William
B. Nuttall, J. K. Campbell, Isham G. Searcy, and Leslie A. Thompson were included on the list, and among the large stockholders
were Romeo Lewis, Richard C. Allen, George W. Ward, and James
Gadsden, but not Call. He owned no stock in any of the three big
banks, nor has evidence been found to indicate his ownership of
stock in any of the smaller banks.[35] Yet the identification of a large
number of influential men with the local banks might tend to increase the indifference which they and their associates felt about
the fate of the Bank of the United States, for local banking interests
all over the country resented the deflationary policies followed by
the Bank of the United States and joined with the "hard money"
men in opposition to the Bank. The demise of the Bank would turn
the business of the government to the state banks and would remove
the check which the national bank exerted on their inflationary
policies. It is not unreasonable to suggest that this climate of opinion
prevailed in Florida and that Call was affected by it. He was not a
hard money man, and had no doctrinaire antipathy to banks as such.

The new influences in the Jackson administration began to make
their presence known in Florida through the appointments which
were made in 1833 and after. In 1832 Jackson failed to reappoint
two United States Judges in Florida who had become obnoxious to
the "Nucleus." These were Joseph L. Smith in East Florida and
Henry M. Brackenridge in West Florida.[36] Brackenridge was Call's
old law partner but had drifted away from the "Nucleus" and become a close friend of White. Both judges were indignant and
Brackenridge charged, "The secret malice of an ignorant, con-
ceited, and avaricious pettifogger, who happens to bask in the sun-
shine of General Jackson's favor, has succeeded in removing honest
and independent Judges, who possessed the confidence of the people."[37] Smith declared that a secret petition had been circulated
against him by Charles Downing, "a person of bad character, but
a member of the bar of East Florida."[38] Downing and Joseph Sanchez were two of Call's leading adherents in East Florida. Sanchez
had been prominent in earlier attempts to remove Judge Smith.

Though Call and old "Nucleus" leaders may have been instrumental in impressing Jackson unfavorably with Smith and Brackenridge, it seems doubtful that they influenced the selection of the
new judges. Robert Raymond Reid of Augusta, Georgia, was named

to the East Florida post and John A. Cameron of North Carolina went to the West Florida post. The appointment of Reid was the more important one. He was a member of the old Crawford faction and was warmly sympathetic to Van Buren. More important, he was very critical of the inflationary state banking people.[39] It does not appear likely that White had anything to do with the appointments, but he did exult that "The Nucleus is no longer the hive from whence swarms of officers go forth to suck honey from Treasury blossoms."[40]

Reid was a remarkable man: an urbane scholar, a gentleman, an intellectual who shrewdly evaluated his fellow men; he analyzed his own mind, dissected his vices with philosophic resignation, and wrestled with religious dogma, always wanting to believe but never quite able to do so. In his calm introspection, his tact, his discretion, his humanitarian impulses, his shrinking from physical exertion, he presents a picture of a man quite opposite in temperament from Call. It is worth noting that Reid was ever on friendly terms with Call, though he differed with him politically, and from Reid's diary come some of the most favorable evaluations of Call.

In January, 1833, Reid arrived in Tallahassee for the session of the Court of Appeals. It was his first trip to the territorial capital and his diary reflects his initial impressions. The banking fever was in the air and the judge observed, "There is a passion for bank making existing at present in the Territory, which must prove injurious to the general interests. Banks must be founded upon capital to be useful, and the idea of making the capital the superstructure and the bank the basis, is erroneous. Such schemes are fit only for the brains of speculators."[41]

Reid agreed with Call on the nullification controversy and was contemptuous of the extreme state-rights viewpoint. "I think we shall have a *row*," he wrote, "but the *Union* will weather it—no thanks to the South Carolina aspirants."[42] Reid did not care for the associates of Call in the old "Nucleus" group and particularly despised Governor DuVal. On first meeting he judged the governor to be a weak man, lacking in dignity. His chief virtue was found to be that "his friends say he is a fine story teller!"[43] After a two-year acquaintance Reid confided to his diary, "Duval . . . is a ninny."[44] The Georgian wholeheartedly shared Call's veneration for Andrew Jackson. Looking back on Jackson's first administration, Reid approved of his attack upon the Bank, which he thought to be "a dangerous machine," and he wrote of the president, "D—n him, he frocks and unfrocks at pleasure, but he is a magnificent fellow and the best Constitutional president since the days of Jefferson, who was himself not sinless."[45]

Reid reserved his most devastating criticism for the society of frontier Tallahassee. After the ending of the term of the Court of Appeals in 1833, he summed up his impressions:

> I have seen a noisy senseless crowd; a legislative council with little wisdom, a fashionable circle with little taste. . . . a Governor's daughter, pretty, rouged, and sour; a Governor, shallow, blasphemous, and coarse; a Secretary, (sometimes Governor) rough, factious, and egotistical; . . . Col Murat's wife—Queen of Naples—queenly indeed—lovely, but conscious of her beauty and rank; General Call and Lady, highminded, unsophisticated, and good-hearted; . . . Judge Randall, chivalrous, intelligent, and opinionated; Judge Cameron, Scotch! Scotch! Scotch![46]

Throughout the diary run favorable impressions of Call. Reid thought Call to be a good lawyer, and after hearing him in court would note in his diary that he had heard a good argument from the general. He was always happy to receive a visit from Call, who was often in St. Augustine during 1833, 1834, and 1835 in connection with the land cases. The judge noted that Call was always a sensible man while his friend Downing was witty and smart, "but neither studies nor thinks enough."[47]

The second important Florida appointment which shows the declining influence of the "Nucleus" was the appointment in 1834 of Call's old enemy, John Henry Eaton, as governor. Call's opponents were gleeful at this turn of events and Joseph M. White was not reluctant to take credit for the selection. Achille Murat told James Gadsden, "The appointment and particularly the confirmation of Eaton were all his [White's] doings with a view to the prostration of Call and he made no mistery with me in the delight of his successes."[48] The "success" was hardly a smashing White victory; and it may be that White actually had very little to do with it, for at the same time that Eaton was appointed Call's cousin and business partner, George K. Walker, was made secretary of the territory. James D. Westcott, Jr., the former secretary, had been getting increasingly troublesome to DuVal and Call. Westcott was an anti-bank, Van Buren man, however, and was merely shifted to the post of district attorney for Middle Florida.[49]

Eaton did not sit out the entire term for which he was appointed. He arrived on December 11, 1834, to assume his duties and remained the nominal Governor of Florida until March 16, 1836. He was absent from Florida much of the time and the gubernatorial duties devolved upon Secretary Walker. The glamorous Peggy could not bear Tallahassee and spent most of her time in Pensacola. She left Florida for good, however, only three months after their arrival.[50] Soon after the new governor and his wife first appeared Reid was in the capital and noted, "The latter place is full of filth— *of all genders. . . .* Gov. E. is a rowdy—his wife drunk or crazy, and several other ladies but so-so." Again there were kind words for Call, "Call and his wife . . . are clever and indeed excellent people."[51]

During Eaton's administration the atomization of the "Nucleus" became complete. Probably the loss of the governorship speeded the breakup. Indeed, it seems that if the death blow to the "Nucleus" had been plotted it could not have been more effectively accomplished than by the failure to reappoint DuVal. In the election of 1835 the split was obvious with Gadsden and Nuttall as well as White and Wyatt all in the race for the single seat in Congress. Reid observed, "There is an Eastern and Western, and Middle Party, a Call party, a White, a Nuttall, a Gadsden—the whole community from the point of the Peninsula to the St. Mary's and Pensacola split up into bits. This should not be so—the party should divide upon principle."[52] Reid was to be one of a triumvirate around which the next powerful coalition was to form.

∽ 6 ∾

A Frontier Entrepreneur

THE DECADE BEFORE THE Panic of 1837 was one of expanding economic activity in Florida as well as the nation as a whole. Opportunities for profit seemed limitless as new banks were launched, the amount of money in circulation increased, and lands were bought up with great rapidity. From older sections of the country came immigrants to the West and South buying land and slaves and reaping quick profits from the high prices of cotton. Call reported in 1830 that lands in Florida had not yet attained their highest prices, but he foresaw a rapid rise in the next few years. Even so, he declared, planters could make from $200 to $300 per hand in one season.[1]

During these years Call's major interests were directed toward business, professional, and political pursuits rather than planting. He had become practically a one-man chamber of commerce in extolling the virtues of Florida, however, and in persuading others who were planters to make their homes in the new territory. He had inspired the Marquis de Lafayette with enthusiasm for the Middle Florida region where his gift township had been located. He induced Prince Achille Murat to become a Florida planter and resident, and he had done much work in spreading the fame of Florida among Virginians who were leaving their exhausted lands for virgin fields.

Lafayette toyed with visions of planting a colony of German immigrants upon his Florida lands and tried to impress upon Call the desirability of white labor as opposed to Negro slave labor. The French nobleman suggested employing the Germans in vineyards, in silk culture, and in the growth of mulberry and olive trees. These, he thought, would be valuable additions to the industry of Florida.[2] In 1831 he wrote to Call that a M. Delaporte had determined to purchase 370 acres in the township and settle about thirty immigrants there.[3] A few Europeans, probably French, actually did settle on the tract, but the utopian dreams of duplicating the agrarian patterns of the Mediterranean were not successful.[4]

Call's friend and legal associate, William Wirt, was sold on Florida at an early date and bought large tracts near Tallahassee about 1827. Wirt divided his land between his sons-in-law, Thomas Randall and Louis Goldsborough. The latter encouraged him to undertake a settlement scheme similar to that contemplated by Lafayette, and the aged Virginian soon became quite enthusiastic over his Florida ventures.[5] He told his daughter, "I count sanguinely myself on settling a plantation and coming out to live. . . . Florida bids fair to become a perfect Arcadia."[6] A few months later Governor DuVal visited Wirt and painted glowing pictures of the potentialities of Florida for growing sugar cane and sea island cotton.[7]

Like Lafayette, Wirt wanted no Negroes in his model settlement. As the idea matured in his mind it took on patriarchal, almost medieval aspects, and his plans sound more fitted for a manor of the middle ages than for a colonization project in the New World. The colonists were to be Germans governed by Louis Goldsborough with their spiritual needs cared for by their own Calvinist minister. Wirt meticulously specified the layout of their village, to be called Wirtland, even detailing the games the children should play and the avocations which should be fostered among the adults. Though he detested the idea of Negro slaves being used, nonetheless his attitude toward the Germans smacked of the outlook of a slaveholder. He told his son-in-law, "You will have to exercise your authority, occasionally, to settle their little disputes and keep them in goodhumour with each other. This, done gently, kindly and firmly, will make them all revere and love you the more."[8] To his wife he confided, ". . . it will be, if Providence blesses the design, a most princely establishment for you and our children."[9]

Despite his cheerful enthusiasm for his castles in the air, Wirt was not without his dubious moments. In one of these periods of doubt he remarked to Call that no other person had succeeded in Florida with a project such as he proposed to launch. Call, in his role of promoter, dispelled all doubts and assured Wirt that "everybody had succeeded who deserved to succeed." Wirt was heartened and told Goldsborough, "Governor [sic] Call likes our plan. If the Germans continue faithful, it is, he admits, a great and splendid enterprise."[10]

Call, however, had put his finger upon a weak spot. About a hun-

dred and fifty Germans were settled at Wirtland, but they soon lost
interest and abandoned their contracts. Wirt consoled himself with
the thought that since they had proved to be such "cattle" their
desertion was "quite a happy riddance."[11] He told Thomas Randall
that "those rascals having gone so far to play so ridiculous a caper
. . . seems to me rather more laughable than cryable."[12]

Among other prominent Virginians coming to Florida in this
period were Robert and John Gamble, and Thomas Brown. In the
thirties also came Dr. George W. Call and his family.[13] The Gamble
brothers were brothers of Mrs. Wirt.[14] Thomas Brown was later to
win fame as the only elected Whig Governor of Florida, and held
office during the crisis of 1850. Brown came from the Rappahan-
nock River region of Virginia in 1827 and settled near Lake Jackson north of Tallahassee. After the failure of his sugar plantation
there he moved to Tallahassee and devoted himself to business and
inn-keeping.[15] The Gambles did not actively enter politics as did
Brown, but John Gamble became president of the Union Bank of
Tallahassee and later a leading member of the Whig party. Both
men were considered leaders in many walks of life.

In 1832 Call's old friend and Jackson's former Secretary of the
Navy, John Branch, arrived in Tallahassee.[16] He, too, had been sold
on the charms of Florida and established a plantation on Lake
Jackson. He purchased a portion of his lands from Call and part
from Lafayette. Like Wirt, Branch was followed by his sons and
daughters. Two of his daughters married prominent men: one,
Daniel S. Donelson, a "Tennessee surveyor"; the other, Robert
W. Williams, the land speculator and member of the "Nucleus."
Two of Branch's sons, Joseph and L. O'B. Branch, were purchasers
of Tallahassee lots from Call.[17]

Call's business interests were more extensive, however, than selling land or promoting Florida's potentialities. He often acted as
agent in the sale of real estate; in 1832 he participated in the organization of the Central Bank of Florida; and in 1834 he was a
trustee of "Mrs. Brown's female school."[18] He became one of fourteen trustees of a proposed University of Florida in 1836, in which
capacity one of his functions was to convince Congress to put up
for immediate sale the lands which Florida would normally get
after statehood for the support of education.[19] Call was evidently a
shrewd and competent businessman for he became known to some
people as a sharp bargainer. The Parkhill family transacted deals

with him and George W. Parkhill testified to Call's hard bargaining. Commenting on the sale of an estate in which both Call and John Gamble of the Union Bank were interested, Parkhill wrote, "They are great scoundrels—they will cheat each other."[20]

Call's most important venture in the business world was in the field of transportation. As Middle Florida grew in population and the produce of its plantations grew to sizable proportions, banking and credit facilities were needed and access to world markets became important. The planters who had access to the Apalachicola River used that great artery to gain entry to the Gulf of Mexico. There at the port of Apalachicola their cargoes were transferred to waiting vessels for transshipment to the markets of Europe and America. The planters of Leon County and the Tallahassee region, however, had no great navigable stream opening a highway into their midst and no great port from which to ship their produce.

The old Spanish fort of St. Marks, twenty miles south of Tallahassee, was the closest point from which these planters could embark their goods. As yet there was no town there, and there were no facilities except a few ramshackle buildings haphazardly put up around the fort. The fort itself, presumed to be public property, was in the area claimed by Colin Mitchel and his associates, so the residents there were unable to purchase land.[21] In March, 1829, Call wrote to the head of the General Land Office favoring steps toward laying out a town at or near St. Marks. He stated that the makeshift town was already becoming a commercial depot and that "the imports and exports to and from this point are already considerable and are increasing with great rapidity."[22]

The head of the General Land Office, Graham, told Call that a town could not be laid off without the express authority of Congress, but that as a result of his representations he was ordering Robert Butler, Surveyor General of Florida, to survey a town with Call's cooperation. The plans would be presented to Congress for action. This was done but Congress did not act until March, 1833. At that time Congress authorized the laying off of a town but prohibited the sale of lands until it should be definitely ascertained that the site was not in the limits of any unsettled grant. This further delayed the sale of lands but did not prevent the territorial legislature from chartering the town of St. Marks in the same year.[23]

Meanwhile, a group of local men conceived the idea of constructing a railroad from Tallahassee to the Gulf as a substitute for a river which nature had neglected to provide them. Early in 1831 a group of men met at the Planter's Hotel in Tallahassee and discussed the feasibility of a railway to St. Marks. As a result of this meeting a charter was drawn up and presented to the Legislative Council for enactment.[24] Six men were behind this move among whom were Robert W. Williams, Isham G. Searcy, and Thomas Brown. Call was not associated with this first railroad scheme. The Council modified this charter to eliminate certain monopoly features and the next year issued a completely new charter, but nothing resulted from either of these beginnings.[25]

A third railway project got underway on February 10, 1834, when the Legislative Council chartered the Tallahassee Rail Road Company.[26] The road was capitalized at $100,000, with the privilege of increasing that to $200,000 if construction costs should make it necessary. The corporation was headed by a board of seven directors who were empowered to choose from their number a president. The directors were to be named annually by the stockholders. The first election of directors was held on June 27 and Call was elected to the board. The directors then named him president.[27] There were a hundred and ten stockholders, but Call appears to have had the controlling interest. He directed the affairs of the railroad until he disposed of his stock in 1855 to the Pensacola and Georgia Railroad.[28]

At the same time that the Tallahassee railroad was being organized, the Union Bank was being formed. The concurrent organization of these two corporations probably explains why Call invested no money in bank stock. The founding of the bank was looked upon as a necessary aid to the building of the railroad, however, for in 1834 the *Floridian* reported the sale of one million dollars' worth of Union Bank stock and observed, ". . . we may now calculate with certainty on the construction of a railway to St. Marks; for the early completion of which, proper measures will be immediately adopted."[29]

In December the company petitioned Congress for aid in the form of land grants. It asked the grant of a right-of-way two hundred yards wide through the public lands from Tallahassee to St. Marks and a hundred acre grant at St. Marks.[30] In 1835 the Congress granted a sixty foot right-of-way and ten acres at the junction of the St. Marks and Wakulla Rivers.[31] Actual construction work began in January, 1835, under the direction of John D. and William Gray,

contractors of Columbia, South Carolina, who had participated in
the building of the Charleston and Hamburg Railroad. The brothers
contracted to build the road, the terminals, and to furnish two pas-
senger and twenty freight cars for $107,000.[32]

The contract was almost entirely lacking in precise specifications,
reflecting, perhaps, the general ignorance of railway building which
prevailed. Where ordinary conditions were encountered, five by nine
inch wooden rails were laid on eight by ten inch cross ties. On top of
the rails were laid strips of iron two and one-half inches wide and
one-half inch thick. The contract specified the use of the best
heart pine in construction, "on the most approved principal." No
provision was made for the acquisition of a locomotive.[33]

In November, 1837, the road was completed to St. Marks and
was in operation for its full length. It was the second railway to
open in Florida, the first being the St. Joseph Railroad which began
operation in 1836. In the month in which it commenced operation
the Tallahassee corporation filed suit against the Gray brothers for
$50,000 damages. Eighteen breaches of contract were charged, sur-
mounted by the declaration that the Grays had built "the very
worse road known in the United States, in the worse possible manner." The case, however, was dismissed several months later.[34]

The motive power of the road throughout Call's presidency was
mule or horse power. In December, 1837, the company bought a
locomotive as a result of an increase in business, but after several
trips the cap of the boiler exploded. The *Floridian* assured the public that repairs would have the engine moving again before long.[35]
Apparently the locomotive was doomed, however, for a few days
later Call wrote to his mother-in-law, "We have taken the Locomo-
tives off of our Road, and intend never to use them again. We find
Horse power superior."[36]

The St. Marks site proved to be an unsatisfactory terminal to
the railway company because of shallow water and the prolonged
disputes about the ownership of the surrounding area. Consequently, in 1837 the directors determined to push on to a site near deeper
water where they could locate their ten-acre grant and lay out a
city. The new town was called Port Leon and lots were first offered
for sale there in 1838. The location was highly recommended by
the *Floridian* as one of the highest points on the St. Marks River
and as being particularly suited to business or summer residence.[37]
Call told his mother-in-law that it was just the place for her to

come to live with him and his daughters. "It is improving more rapidly than any little place I have ever seen," he wrote, "and will become the largest business place in Florida . . . [and] will become the fashionable part of the country."[38]

Call directed much personal attention to the new town and to the operation of the railway and its subsidiary enterprises, a saw mill and a grist mill. His promoter's zeal functioned full time proclaiming the virtues of these ventures. To foreign visitors who travelled in Florida, however, Call's enthusiasm may have seemed somewhat exaggerated. The Comte Francis de Castelnau found little to admire in the railroad or in either Port Leon or St. Marks. He depicted St. Marks as a town "wretchedly built" with streets often covered by salt water from the river. He described Port Leon as a low, submerged locality two leagues from St. Marks. Castelnau agreed with the railway company's charges against the Gray brothers and described the railroad as "the very worst that has yet been built in the entire world."[39]

A New England visitor has left similar accounts. "Port Leon," he wrote, "is a new town but the houses (about 20 in number) are about the meanest kind. . . . The people Oh my! . . . Law and Justice are not in their vocabularies." He recorded that on the trip from Port Leon to Tallahassee the train was derailed three times.[40] Conditions had not improved by 1855, according to Earnest Malvern writing in the *Florida Sentinel*. He was astonished that the railway had no locomotive and questioned the Negro driver about the absence of that seemingly vital piece of equipment.

"They once had such a thing," the Negro replied, "but it ran away one day; nobody could stop it. It went straight to St. Marks, and roaring and hissing, it dashed plumb into the bay; and since that they have never dared to try one." Malvern soon found that he had little reason to regret the absence of a locomotive. He observed the railway ahead of him gently undulating like the sea. The rails in many instances were no longer attached to the cross ties, and separated so that one wheel of the car was off in the sand. Occasionally, he noted, there was no rail at all. The iron bands atop the rails often were fastened only in the middle and the ends had a tendency to curl upwards to such an extent that, as Malvern was solemnly assured, Negroes sometimes had to run ahead of the trains to hold down the ends of the bands until the car came upon them. In the course of this epic journey the car came upon a section of the road which had been ignited by a forest fire. Malvern was startled to see that they merely hurried on "like salamanders," the driver protesting that he was not a fireman. When they came upon a derailed freight train, the incredulous visitor abandoned the party and walked on ahead to St. Marks.[41]

Despite comic opera aspects of the Tallahassee Rail Road Company, it served as a means of transporting the cotton from Leon County plantations to the Gulf for shipment abroad. With all its defects the railroad was a more efficient mode of transportation than the wagon trains that toiled along the sandy roads to the Gulf of Mexico. The road carried the mail and an estimated 30,000 to 40,000 bales of cotton per year.[42] Its labor was almost exclusively Negro slaves, of whom the company owned twenty-five in 1840.[43] The Port Leon extension of the railroad was opened in 1839 and from that date began an attempt on the part of the company to throttle the town of St. Marks. The company closed the terminal at St. Marks and eliminated that town as a freight stop on the road. Passengers could continue to get off and on at that town but freight had to be handled through Port Leon. Had this policy been effective it would virtually have forced the entire town of St. Marks to move to the Port Leon location. The railroad company might then sell them land there and be assured of the successful operation of its terminal facilities.[44]

The mill operations of the road were money-making propositions adding to its success. A steam engine, perhaps the one removed from road operation, powered the mills which Call valued at $30,-000. The saw and grist mills were both operated from the single steam engine. The saw mill delivered six to eight thousand feet of lumber daily which, in 1840, sold for $25 per thousand feet.[45] The mills were, however, destroyed by a fire in May, 1840. It was set by one of the slaves belonging to the firm.[46]

In the fall of 1843 a major disaster struck the company when Port Leon and the railway extension to it were totally destroyed by a hurricane. The drawbridge across the St. Marks river, viewed locally as something of a wonder, was completely washed away as was the railroad itself for a good distance above St. Marks. The *Sentinel* reported, "The rail-road bridge was found some distance up the river, *an entire bridge yet,* but injudiciously placed."[47] In the midst of the hard times of that year, the newspaper correctly predicted that Port Leon would be abandoned and the railroad would be rebuilt only as far as St. Marks.[48] Some of the merchants of both towns withdrew to a new location even farther inland, which they named Newport. Call's company refused to cooperate with them in rebuilding the road and built it back to its old terminus at St. Marks.[49]

Aside from his land sales and legal practice, the railroad was the most important business venture in which Call was engaged. When he rid himself of his interest in the corporation in 1855, most of his law practice had been abandoned and he long since had ceased to hold public office. After 1845 he increasingly turned his attention to the development of his plantation on Lake Jackson which he turned into one of the finest establishments in Middle Florida. There were, however, minor business ventures through these years. In 1848 he was a member of a partnership which established a ferry across the Apalachicola River at Chattahoochee, and in 1851 he served as a Commissioner to receive stock subscriptions for the Florida, Atlantic, and Gulf Central Railroad Company and for the Leon and Gadsden plank road company. Such things were, however, side activities of little importance. From 1836 on, Call's major interests increasingly were planting and politics. They were unquestionably his major interests in the decade of the fifties.[50]

⌒ 7 ⌒

War and Politics

IN THE FALL OF 1835 Richard and Mary Call were in Washington where Call was clearing up some details of his land office work at the General Land Office. Mary did not spend all her time in Washington despite the fact that they were house guests of President Jackson. Nine-year-old Ellen was at school in Franklin, Maryland, and relatives in Baltimore were anxious for Mary's company. So while her husband conducted his business she visited in the neighboring towns, often accompanied by Emily Donelson.[1]

Whether Jackson and Call talked about a replacement for John Eaton, who was becoming restive as governor of Florida, is not known. Rumors soon spread, however, that the governorship had been discussed and Robert Reid heard that it would be offered to Call. Apparently Call had offered to recommend Reid for that post for the latter told him, ". . . you may probably be embarrassed, in consequence of what has been understood *between us* respecting that appointment," but he insisted that Call not allow any consideration to deter him from taking the post if offered to him. Reid magnanimously wrote, "The success of my friend *is* and has *ever been* as gratifying to me as my own."[2]

Speculation about the governorship was soon overshadowed, however, by the growing unrest among the Florida Indian tribes. When the United States came into the possession of Florida the Indians had been free to roam virtually unmolested throughout most of the peninsula, and many of their towns were located in the most desirable portions of the territory. Under the English and Spanish governments they had enjoyed many important privileges and had been subjected to few restrictions. In the face of the loud demands of American citizens who were seeking homes and land in the new territory, however, it was inconceivable that the old system should be continued by the federal government. It became imperative for the government to formulate policies to dispossess the Indians of the richest portions of the territory and confine them to limits within which friction with the whites would be reduced if not eliminated. Accordingly, James Gadsden, William P. DuVal, and Bernardo Segui had been named as early as 1823 to negotiate a treaty for the removal of the Indians to the lower part of the territory.[3]

Three treaties were concluded with the Florida Indians. The first, the treaty of Moultrie Creek in 1823, segregated them on a large reservation in the interior of the peninsula. In these bounds the Indians were to be protected against white depredations and were to receive certain stipulated payments; however, the boundaries of the reservation were poorly defined and the federal government was unable or unwilling either to protect the Indians or restrain them within their own boundaries. Gradually it reached the decision that the only solution was the removal of all the Indians from Florida to the trans-Mississippi West.[4]

The second treaty, that of Payne's Landing in 1832, provided for the emigration of the Indians to the Creek country west of the great river and was conditioned upon Indian approval of the territory in the West. A delegation of chiefs was taken to inspect lands in Arkansas, and while there was induced to sign an "Additional Treaty" agreeing to the move. But on their return to Florida the chiefs repudiated their action when their tribes accused them of having exceeded their powers by making such an agreement. The principal chief, old and vacillating Micanopy, was forced by the fervid young Indian patriot Osceola to oppose the move. Four other chiefs of high rank declared their total dissatisfaction with the lands in Arkansas and with the idea of uniting with the Creeks.[5]

Two years after the signing of the treaty of Payne's Landing the Senate, on April 9, 1834, ratified it and the "Additional Treaty" and vigorous measures were instituted to enforce them. Wiley Thompson of Georgia was appointed Indian agent to superintend the emigration and General Duncan L. Clinch was ordered to use the army to enforce compliance with the treaty if necessary.[6] Governor Eaton, seeing the impasse grow more serious, questioned the validity of the treaties because of the time lapse between signing and ratification. He urged caution in the use of force and recommended that militia not be used owing to the prejudices of the local citizens against the Indians.[7] Call, who still retained the militia post of brigadier general, later explained Eaton's attitude toward the militia as nothing more than opposition to his having a command.[8]

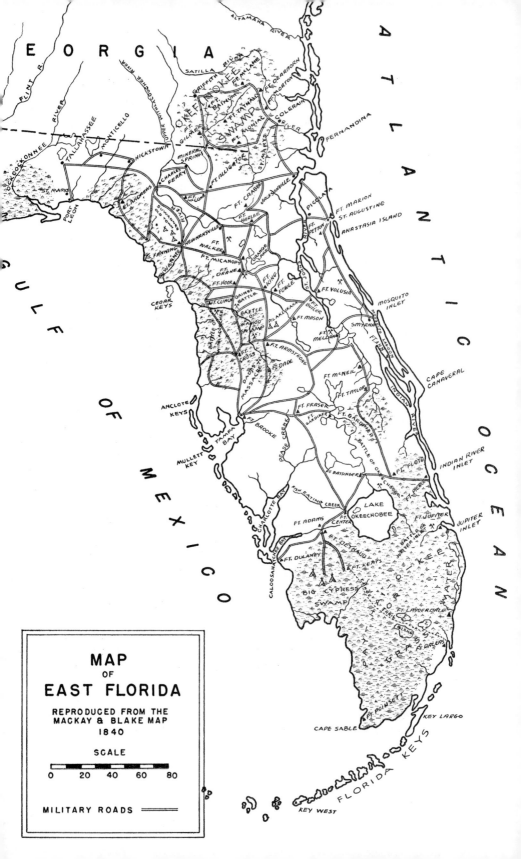

MAP
OF
EAST FLORIDA

REPRODUCED FROM THE
MACKAY & BLAKE MAP
1840

SCALE

0   20   40   60   80

MILITARY ROADS

By December of 1835 several chiefs had agreed to emigration but the remainder grew more determined in their opposition. Led by Osceola, the uncooperative Indians met in private council in the fall of 1835 and decreed death for those cooperating in the removal. On November 26 they executed this decree on Charley-E-Mathla, a prominent chief friendly to the emigration plan. The death of the federal Indian agent was also plotted by Osceola and his allies. Meanwhile, these recalcitrant Indians began to concentrate their women and children in a dense region of lakes and swamps adjacent to and south of the Withlacoochee River.[9] When news of the Indian resistance reached Jackson he ordered General Clinch to move with his regulars to the Indian settlements and inflict "meritted chastisement" after taking the women and children into custody. In addition, Jackson instructed that militia were to be summoned if necessary.[10]

Clinch meanwhile had called for aid from acting Governor Walker, who authorized General Call to raise volunteers to bolster Clinch's small force.[11] Call raised about two hundred and fifty mounted but poorly armed men in Middle and West Florida and joined them to a like number from East Florida at Micanopy. There they joined with Clinch and preparations were made to move against the Indian towns in the Withlacoochee River valley.[12] On December 28 Wiley Thompson, the Indian agent, was murdered near Fort King, about thirty miles south of Micanopy, and a detachment of two companies of regulars under Major Francis L. Dade was massacred while marching north from Tampa Bay to reinforce Fort King.[13] By this time Call's volunteers, called up for only four weeks of service, had only four days left to serve. Having had much trouble with deserters, Call realized he could not hold his men beyond their term of enlistment and he urged upon General Clinch an immediate movement. Clinch agreed to the action, and on December 31 they arrived at the Withlacoochee River with a combined force of about seven hundred men.[14]

Their guides had misled them, however, and the point at which they reached the river was not fordable but deep and swift. The only means of crossing was one canoe which held six to eight men. Using this conveyance Clinch had transferred all of his command and about thirty militiamen when the Indians attacked. In the ensuing battle the regulars were hard pressed and the militia would not risk their lives in the swift river to come to their assistance.

Call and several of his staff crossed over and gave valiant service, but the bulk of the militia were spectators of the engagement.[15]

The volunteers did render some service in covering the retreat of the regulars back across the river, and Call claimed that it was due to the volunteers that the regulars were not entirely cut off. The regulars, however, were bitterly critical of the militia and Call himself was unmercifully abused by some of the newspapers of the country. Although Clinch made no charges of negligence or non-cooperation at the time, a bitter controversy later developed between him and Call over the battle. After the repulse of the regular troops the entire force withdrew, the militia returning to their homes. Call returned to Tallahassee to raise another group of volunteers.[16]

Writing to Jackson of this, the first pitched battle of the Seminole War, Call put a good face on events saying that he and Clinch had driven the Indians back across their boundary and that he had returned to raise another body of troops to wage the war. He noted that Clinch had only 150 men on January 3, to which he had joined 150 mounted volunteers. To end the war, he told the president, 2,500 to 3,000 men would be needed. He also suggested, "I should be highly gratified to command the army, and believe I could soon bring the war to a close." He disclaimed any intent to cast reflections on Clinch. He observed that Clinch "is a brave and good man, but I fear he is too slow in his movements to conduct a war against the Indians."[17]

In January, 1836, however, General Winfield Scott was ordered to assume direction of the war against the Seminoles. Fourteen companies of regulars were ordered to the command of General Clinch, serving under Scott, and volunteers, money, and arms were offered from Charleston, Savannah, Augusta, Macon, Mobile, and New Orleans. Commodore Alexander J. Dallas was ordered to use the navy to prevent Spanish fishermen from trading with the Indians or giving them aid.[18]

About the same time, General Edmund P. Gaines, who commanded the Western military district in New Orleans, received the news of Dade's massacre and, knowing nothing of Scott's orders, he immediately made preparations to proceed to the scene of conflict. Technically the site of Dade's massacre was in Gaines's command, since Florida was divided between the Eastern and Western military districts. On February 10 Gaines arrived at Tampa Bay with

1,100 men, Louisiana volunteers as well as regulars.[19] On February 22 Gaines's force arrived at Fort King after having passed Dade's battleground, where they buried the rotting bodies of his ambushed command.[20]

By February 26 General Scott had arrived at Picolata on the St. Johns River and was furious to find Gaines "intruding" in his sphere of operations. Acting independently and with imperfect knowledge of the terrain, Scott mapped out his own campaign, which he was unsuccessful in carrying out.[21] Scott meanwhile had forbidden Clinch to cooperate with Gaines, orders which were subsequently somewhat modified. On March 13 both Gaines and Scott were present at Fort Drane, a few miles northwest of Fort King, but each refused to speak to the other. Shortly thereafter Gaines left behind the forces he had brought and departed Florida for the Texas frontier, leaving Scott in undisputed command.[22] Each man blamed the other for setbacks in their plans. Gaines claimed that he could have concluded a treaty with the Indians had not Scott moved in announcing a war of extermination which frightened the Indians into renewal of hostilities.[23]

Despite the petty squabbles between the regular officers Call had continued to collect a new militia contingent and prepared to sail with them from St. Marks to Tampa Bay. The departure date had been delayed several days owing to the illness of Mary Call and Richard Call's great reluctance to leave her. At length she seemed to recover her strength and urged her husband to go on with his men to Tampa Bay. At St. Marks on February 28 the troops were embarked and Call boarded the revenue cutter *Dallas* for the voyage. As the vessel was about to leave the bay one of the Call servants arrived and put out toward the ship in a small boat. Call recognized him and immediately put back to shore. Mary was thought to be dying.[24]

Though Call rode at breakneck speed the twenty miles to Tallahassee, driving one horse to death in the journey, he arrived too late. Mary was dead. Brokenhearted, he poured his feelings into the pages of the family Bible: "The home which she once adored and made happy is now gloomy and sad. She was the pride and joy of her husband's heart. In all the relations of life she was eminently distinguished for her many virtues and propriety. She was the most affectionate and devoted wife, the most exemplary mother, and the best and kindest mistress."[25]

On the evening of February 29 the funeral was held at the Call residence by torchlight. Mists hung heavily around the great oaks as Mary was borne out to the little family graveyard behind the house. The lurid glare of the torches on the moss draped trees and grieving figures illuminated the solemn scene. "I am the resurrection and the life," and then the hollow sound of "earth to earth" broke on the still night, and by the flickering light deep despair could be traced upon the features of the general.[26]

Call did not return to his troops but remained in Tallahassee writing letters conveying the news of the death of his wife and making arrangements for the care of the infant daughter Mary. The militia went on to their destination under Call's young protégé, Colonel Leigh Read. The long estrangement between Call and Mrs. Kirkman was ended with Mary's death, and arrangements were made for the care of the two Call daughters by their grandmother. Frequent letters began to pass between Nashville and Tallahassee, and Call and his mother-in-law were soon on the best of terms.[27]

A little more than two weeks after this great personal loss, Call achieved the highest political post of his life. On March 16 Jackson named Call Governor of Florida, succeeding John H. Eaton.[28] A few months later Call's old federal jobs, Receiver of Public Monies and Assistant Counsel for the United States, went to Matthew J. Allen and Charles Downing, respectively. His nomination to the governorship was unopposed in the Senate. The *Floridian*, however, expressed the view that Call would find himself in a very delicate situation "owing to his former relations to the local parties, and politics of the Territory." It continued, "On these questions we have been, and still are opposed to him, but we have not on that account, withholden the credit to which he is entitled for his exertions in organizing troops for the defence of the country and leading them to the frontier at a time when the Territory was left comparatively to its own resources. He has not yet accepted the office. A paper was circulated yesterday, requesting him to do so, on which we observed names belonging to all parties."[29]

Call did accept the office and asked Jackson to appoint Leigh Read to his old post as Brigadier General of Militia.[30] He took the oath of office as governor on April 4 and departed immediately for Mobile and New Orleans to procure supplies for the territorial forces. He had barely gotten past the Alabama line, however, when news reached him that General Scott was about to order the discharge of the militia and a cessation of the campaign against the Seminoles.[31] As governor, Call was the titular commander in chief of the Florida militia and he would not hear of that pitifully small force being disbanded. He had no control, however, over the militia from other states or the regulars. Scott was firmly convinced that white men could not possibly survive the ordeal of a summer campaign in Florida, and he went on with his plans to send the militia home and to concentrate the regulars in forts where they might sit out the summer.[32]

Call was furious that the field should in such manner be abandoned to the Indians and began a torrent of correspondence to the War Department requesting top-level attention to the war in Florida and offering advice as to its conduct. Meanwhile he set in motion a series of orders to officers of the territorial militia to activate their commands for battle. To fill the gap left by Scott he proposed to set up volunteer companies along the frontier, alerted as mobile units ready to move to any trouble spot on short notice.[33] While he took these steps he continued the stream of letters to Washington, lamenting the disbanding of the militia from other states and demanding arms, money for the Florida militia, and more federal troops.[34] The local people hailed his fervor and the *Floridian* reflected their feelings when it wrote, "The executive, we are glad to learn, has determined to act with vigor in this emergency."[35]

General Scott was denounced in the press as having "deceived, betrayed and abandoned" the people of Florida. Call's task of raising local militia was a seemingly hopeless one and the reaction to Scott's plans made his task even more difficult. As the *Floridian* reported, "To enlist troops here, is almost impossible now, as the immediate safety of every man's family depends on himself."[36] In a general order Scott denounced the panicky state of the public as infinitely humiliating. He denounced the "disease in the public mind" which caused the people to see "nothing but an Indian in every bush." The newspaper attacks had wounded his pride and he lamented the fate of "the general who has the misfortune to command a handful of brave troops in the midst of such a population."[37]

Call's efforts were aimed at alleviating the condition which resulted from the fact that only "a handful" of troops were present in Florida. Though he agreed with General Scott that "a panic highly dishonorable to the whole country has spread over the land," he did not agree with Scott's decision for no summer campaign.[38] Incessantly he hammered home the idea "the country is bleeding at every pore, and is threatened with desolation."[39] Indignantly he wrote to Jackson that he could evoke no response whatever from the Secretary of War. He warned, "I can hear of no measure proposed for our defence; and I assure you, sir, if something is not promptly done, that this country will be desolated during the summer."[40] Two days later the Secretary of War got the same complaint, with the comment, "I despair of producing any beneficial result by my correspondence."[41] Two more days, and a letter went to A. J. Donelson: "I have been writing to the Sect. of War . . . ever since I came into office, but can get no answer from him."[42]

Call proposed a summer campaign as a maximum effort aimed at destroying the homes and crops of the Indians. His insistence that this was not foolhardy won the ear of Jackson and on May 14, 1836, Secretary of War Lewis Cass finally informed Call that Jackson favored his recommendations. Cass wrote that information in Washington was that a summer campaign could not be endured, but that he and the president had decided to defer to Call's experience and knowledge.[43] Call apologized for the insistent tone of his letters and outlined at greater length his strategy. He suggested to Cass that if, as reported, Scott was to be diverted to Georgia to direct the battles against the Creeks who were resisting emigration, "I should be gratified by being directed to lead the expedition against the Seminoles."[44]

Call continued to criticise Scott's leadership, telling Jackson that no war had ever been "so disgracefully conducted." To Jackson he also wrote, "Nothing have I so much desired as to have the direction of the Florida War."[45] In his efforts to secure command of the forces in Florida he found an unexpected ally in Joseph M. White, still delegate in Congress. White informed Jackson that Scott had been burned in effigy in Tallahassee and that the public interest demanded his immediate removal.[46] He told the *Floridian,* "I intend to go to the President and insist that the regular forces . . . be placed under the command of Gen. Call."[47]

On May 18, Jackson wrote Call that he was going to place command of the regular army and all militia in federal service in Florida in his hands until the arrival of General Thomas S. Jesup. Though there was some delay before the Secretary of War actually invested Call with command, he immediately wrote to Jackson, "I accept with great pleasure, of the trust you have conferred on me; and I

promise you that I will soon put an end to the war in Florida, or
perish in the attempt."[48] It should be noted that the command with
which Call was invested was a temporary one to fill the interim between Scott's removal from command and Jesup's arrival. This unusual procedure is also partly explainable by the fact that the
remaining ranking federal officer, General Clinch, had decided to
retire from the service at this time.

After assuming command, Call notified Cass that he would go to
East Florida to arrange for offensive and defensive operations as
soon as his health would permit.[49] In organizing his forces Call
ran into difficulties stemming from many causes. The regulars still
nursed bitter memories of the action of Call's volunteers at the first
battle of the Withlacoochee, and resented, too, being placed under
the command of a civil officer. The naval forces cooperating in the
war resented any order smacking of anything stronger than a suggestion from this civilian who had once been an army officer. When
Call wrote to Commodore Dallas about his blockade of the Gulf
coast that officer made an explanation of the steps he had taken,
indicating that he did so "not that I feel in the least called upon to
make it, but out of courtesy to your station as Governor of Florida,
and the high consideration I entertain of you as a gentleman." He
added, "I beg that your suggestions may have less the character of
an order than those heretofore received."[50] The militia also gave
Call a goodly share of headaches. They were restless because of
uncertain pay and the slightest rumor that their homes were in
danger could cause their desertion. The regulars were badly short
of officers, Call found, one garrison reporting that in eleven artillery
companies there were only six officers. There were no ordnance,
subsistence, or quartermaster officers in the entire territory.[51] The
Adjutant General explained to Call that the absent officers were
employed in internal improvement surveys and that the Secretary
of War "will not consent that the absent officers so employed shall
be withdrawn and ordered to join their companies."[52]

The plan of operations which Call conceived won the approval of
such experienced military men as President Jackson and General
Jesup, but it would seem that difficulties were almost certain to
arise in executing the plan not only because of the deficiencies, re-
sentments, and contradictions already mentioned but also because
of the military inexperience of Call. Despite his militia rank and his
previous service in the regular army, he had never directed a far-

flung military operation involving the planning for the movement and supply of thousands of men. He had never commanded in battle a group much larger than a battalion and most of his experience had been at the field rather than the command or staff level. In view of these circumstances, and the failure of the regular general, Scott, the appointment of Call to command the Seminole War would seem to have been an unwise act on the part of the Jackson administration, unless it was meant only as a stop-gap measure during a period when no major operations were to be undertaken.

Secretary Cass informed Call in June that 1,200 to 1,500 mounted Tennessee volunteers would leave for Florida about July 1.[53] While awaiting their arrival Call pushed his preparations for a great offensive. At intervals, however, he suffered severe attacks of "bilious fever" and was often unable even to answer his correspondence.[54] Week after week passed without the arrival of the Tennessee volunteers, whom Call planned to lead overland with a small Florida militia group to the Withlacoochee River. Plans were laid for supply bases at three sides of the region in which the Indians were concentrated: at Suwannee Old Town and near the mouth of the Withlacoochee on the north, at Tampa Bay on the south, and at Volusia on the St. Johns River on the east. Original plans called for the mounted troops to be united with infantry brought into the mouth of the Withlacoochee, but this landing never actually seems to have been carried out. The army was then to penetrate the Indian territory south of the river, destroy the villages and lay waste the fields, and fall back upon the bases of supplies when necessary.[55]

September came and the Tennessee volunteers had not yet arrived in Florida, but General Jesup notified Call that he would soon be moving into Florida to take direction of the fighting as ordered by the War Department. The governor immediately tendered the command to the general, but the latter declined when he heard that Call had planned a campaign, preferring to allow him to complete his projected operation before taking over from him. Very appreciative of Jesup's consideration, Call notified Cass that Jesup had declined the command and had even offered to serve under Call until the campaign was completed.[56]

On September 17 the *Floridian* carried the news that the Tennessee volunteers had at last arrived at Tallahassee. The departure date of the troops was uncertain, however, for "Gen. Call has been confined to his room for the past week." Call was able to move very

shortly and the troops set out from Tallahassee on September 19.[57]
On October 10 Call reported from Fort Drane that the Indians had
been cleared from all the territory north of the Withlacoochee, and
he informed the War Department that about 1,350 men were being
prepared at that post for the big drive south of that river.[58]

Call marched his forces to the Withlacoochee and spent the entire day of October 13 attempting a crossing. The river was unusually high and swift and a crossing could not be effected. Having
less than two days' rations left, he decided to seek out the supply
base which General Leigh Read had been ordered to establish
from the Gulf near the mouth of the river. Owing to a series of
mishaps, however, Read had been unable to set up this base and
Call's entire force was forced to withdraw to Fort Drane. Because
of short supplies there the mounted troops were forced to retire all
the way to Black Creek, far to the northeast. On October 19 Call reported this move, which he considered an unfortunate but temporary setback, but through some circumstance his report did not
reach Washington.[59]

On November 4 Benjamin F. Butler, Secretary of War *ad interim*,
wrote to Call that the president "deems it expedient to relieve you
from the command." He explained to Call that no reports had been
received from him but that the government had received word from
other sources of a general withdrawal with serious loss of horse
from lack of forage. He also informed Call that reports had been
received of his suffering from severe sickness and fatigue. For these
reasons the administration felt that the public interest demanded
Call's removal. Butler declared that no judgment had been formed
of Call pending the receipt of his reports, but he asserted:

> I am yet instructed by the President to express to you his
> disappointment and surprise that you should have commenced
> the execution of a campaign of so much importance, and so
> long meditated, without first taking effectual measures to se-
> cure all needful supplies . . . ; and . . . after approaching with
> so large a force within so short a distance of the enemy . . .
> you should have retired without a more serious attempt . . .
> to drive him from his position. This disappointment and regret
> are greatly increased by the considerations that these retro-
> grade movements will probably expose the frontiers to new
> invasions by marauding parties.[60]

Before the letter could reach Call he had reorganized his forces and on November 13 had crossed the Withlacoochee into Indian territory. There he met the Indians in battle on November 17, 18, and 21. In this action he had been joined by a large force of regulars which had moved north from Tampa Bay and a regiment of Creek Indian volunteers. At each encounter the Indians were driven from the field, though Call admitted their losses were small. Call withdrew after the last battle to the supply base at Volusia, and it was there that he received the news of his removal.[61]

After recuperating from an illness lasting several weeks, Call replied to Secretary Butler in a bitter letter which was an index to his disappointment and chagrin at being removed from a post which he had so ardently desired. He charged that the president had visited the gravest injustice upon him by removing him "on rumor, without waiting for my official report." He went on, "The apprehensions of the President for the safety of the frontier, supposed to have been exposed by what you have been pleased to denominate my 'retrograde movements' were entirely unnecessary, and must have arisen from his want of information." He demanded a court of inquiry—which Jackson declined to grant—and declared his intent to resign the governorship. Recounting in detail his preparations, his difficulties, and the progress of the campaign, he defended his withdrawal from the Withlacoochee on October 13 with the assertion that Jackson himself could not have accomplished it.[62]

Butler, who was not sympathetic towards Call's predicament, viewed the report he submitted after his removal as excited and full of rash statements. He chided Call with indulging in "many remarks not at all necessary to the explanation of your conduct, or the defence of your character." He asserted that Call was in error in assuming that his removal had been for misconduct and reminded the governor that he had only been temporarily invested with the command and that his removal had been ordered on the basis of reports which indicated that the public interest demanded the assumption of command by Jesup, for whom it had ultimately been intended all along. He pointedly reminded Call that "no one knows better than yourself" that what had occurred was such as to excite and surprise the president.[63]

Butler conceded that Call was absolved of any blame for General Read's failure to establish the Withlacoochee supply base, but asserted that this was felt to be "the fullest measure of justice to which you are entitled." The secretary conceded that the president cheerfully allowed that Call's error lay in a patriotic desire to end the war quickly. "More than this," he wrote, "it seems to us impossible, consistently with justice, to concede." The administration would not back down on its insistence that the basic cause of the initial serious setback was Call's neglect to insure a steady and adequate flow of supplies to sustain an important offensive.[64]

After delivering up the command to General Jesup who had come with four hundred troops from Tampa Bay to Volusia, Call moved up the St. Johns River to Jacksonville. From there he returned to his home at Tallahassee, where his exploits had been followed with much pride. The *Floridian* said of his November campaign, "This brilliant affair cannot fail to have an important influence on the result of the war." It hailed Call as most fortunate in being able to close his career with a series of great achievements: "We rejoice in his success."[65]

Call arrived home from the war on the evening of Wednesday, December 28. Two miles from the city he was greeted by one hundred citizens of Middle Florida on horseback and was escorted into the town. At the city limits they were joined by the Tallahassee City Guards and the entire procession moved to the capitol. There John Branch delivered an address of welcome and thanks on behalf of the citizens. He praised Call's constancy and perseverance and declared that he had accomplished all which skill and courage could achieve.[66]

Call replied to Branch's address in an emotional speech of gratitude. He denied that he had sought the honor of command, spoke of his attempts to restore peace, and remarked on his removal from command. He asserted that his personal feelings had suffered much from the check his career had received just as success seemed in his grasp. Call maintained that he still had the kindest feelings toward the president who "might command his life, *but should not touch his honor.*" The governor began to falter near the end of his address, the *Floridian* reporting, "Gov. Call was evidently sinking under the effect of his exertions when he closed his address . . . owing to the severe indisposition under which he is still laboring." When the speeches ended Call was escorted to his home as a cannon on the capitol square boomed a salute. Yet even in this homecoming there was a touch to recall the misfortunes which had plagued Call's course. The cannon firing the salute exploded, killing one man and injuring two others.[67]

From the vantage point of the present day, one is inclined to agree with the editor of the *Floridian* that Call had been "hardly dealt by" by the authorities at Washington. Yet in that day of slow communication his removal probably seemed to the people in Washington to be the only safe step they could take. In the absence of any word from Call and in the presence of reports indicating a disastrous withdrawal the administration was at a loss. Call might have been disabled or dead; so in the light of the available information the administration took the steps which seemed best calculated to protect the public interest.

Whatever his shortcomings, Call must be credited with having a clearer grasp of the problems faced in Florida than the succession of secretaries who paraded through the War Department. In his favor also was the vigor with which he pursued his frustrating task in the face of poor supply, petty bickering, War Department complacency, militia rebelliousness, navy hostility, and army suspicion. These same problems faced every other commander in the Florida War, and it is to Call's credit that none of them came off much better than he did. The names of some great figures in American military history were tarnished by their contact with the Seminoles: Winfield Scott, Zachary Taylor, Walker K. Armistead, William J. Worth, and Alexander Macomb. General Jesup had only praise for the governor's actions and told the Secretary of War that "no man could, under the circumstances in which he has been placed, have accomplished more than he has done. His plan of campaign was admirable."[68]

On March 6, 1837, Jesup concluded a treaty with the Indians under which they agreed to assemble near Tampa Bay for transportation to the West. He told Call: "If the citizens of the Territory be prudent, the war may be considered at an end, but any attempt to interfere with Indian Negroes, or to arrest any of the chiefs or warriors . . . would cause immediate resort to hostilities."[69] The citizens could not, however, be prudent. Slave hunters eventually began to appear to demand the return of alleged runaway slaves, and on June 2 most of the Indians melted into the wilderness. Until 1842 sporadic peace talks alternated with guerrilla warfare, with captive Indians being shipped to the West in groups as they could be rounded up. By this date about 3,800 Indians had been sent to Arkansas and the army estimated only about 300 remained in Florida. It officially declared the war at an end. For almost two more decades, however, the tiny band remaining caused occasional Indian scares. The seven-year war had cost almost $20,000,000 and the lives of about 1,500 soldiers.[70]

During the first administration of Governor Call the Indian troubles far overshadowed other local and national news to Floridians. On the national scene the surplus revenue was distributed among the states, the specie circular was issued, the Bank of the United States became a state bank, the Republic of Texas was organized, the Whig party was taking shape, Martin Van Buren became president, and the Panic of 1837 struck. Yet the intense Indian War took precedence over these important financial and political events in the newspapers and in the minds of most Floridians.

Despite the ravages of the war, and a severe freeze in 1835, Florida was slow to feel the effects of the financial panic. In mid-1836 Thomas Brown had written to John Parkhill, "You may tell the northern people that they need not be alarmed for Tallahassee. It is safe enough—*and their debts too.*"[71] During the thirties cotton remained above ten cents a pound in Florida and was fifteen and sixteen cents in the best years.[72] The severest phases of the depression came in Florida in the early forties. The banks were forced to suspend specie payment in the summer of 1837, but most of them resumed payment in 1838 and did not again abandon it until 1839. In his message of the latter year Call praised the banks as having been conducted with "distinguished integrity" and credited their liberal loan policy with having maintained the prosperity of Florida in the midst of the crisis. "Some of them may have been too liberal," he stated, "in relieving the wants and necessities of those who required relief; but this should not constitute a ground of complaint against them in that community which has experienced the advantages of this liberality."[73]

Though Call held no stock in the major banking corporations, he was close to the men who shaped the policies of the Union Bank. They were most cooperative in making funds available to the governor in emergencies during the Indian war when tax sources were not sufficient and when federal funds were slow in being provided. The bank also made loans to Call and his business partner George Walker, a somewhat unusual procedure since most of the funds went back to the stockholders as loans. At the severest point of the depression of the forties, Call and Walker were in debt to the Union Bank for over $90,000.[74]

Though Call was a friend of the local banks he had, as we noted, approved the triumph of Andrew Jackson over the Bank of the United States.[75] Call's ideas about banks and currency hovered between Jackson's "hard money" theories and the "easy money" philosophy of the state banking interests. His own railroad corporation issued "shinplasters" with little backing, yet he was aware of the danger to business and commerce which an unchecked inflationary issue of bank notes threatened. This awareness shows in his demands that the banks maintain adequate reserves to redeem their notes. In 1837 he vetoed the charter of a bank which made no provision for the redemption of bills in specie. "I am opposed," he told the 1839 Legislative Council, "to the policy of giving them [the banks] unbridled liberty to issue bills beyond their power of redemption, and believe that every charter should provide for its own forfeiture when the institution shall fail to redeem its notes according to their tenor." He cautioned that he would not abolish the banks "even if we had the power to do so" for they were indispensable agents in the promotion of commerce and in the ordinary transactions of business. "I regard them as having just claims to our favourable consideration and protection."[76]

Though Call believed that corporations could no more be deprived of their rights than could individuals, and thought that regulation beyond that provided for in the charter of a corporation was questionable, he was adamant in his insistence that what regulatory powers were exerted over state chartered corporations should be only in the hands of the state. He told the 1838 Legislative Council, "I am not prepared to admit the truth of the proposition . . . that a sovereign State has not the power to control the operations of any corporation which it has a constitutional right to create. Nor am I willing to subscribe to the doctrine that the Federal Government may create moneyed institutions, with the authority to control the operations of the State Banks."[77]

The working capital of the Florida banks had been obtained by the sale of bonds in the Northern and European money markets. In the cases of the Bank of Pensacola and the Southern Life Insurance and Trust Company the bonds were endorsed by the Territory of Florida. In the case of the Union Bank the bonds were actually Territorial bonds, bearing the official seal and signed by the governor, which the bank sold.[78] In all cases the territory pledged its faith and credit to the payment of the interest and principal on the bonds should the banks default; hence they came to be called "faith bonds." When the banks got into serious trouble after 1837 the anti-bank men made much of the fact that the taxpayers had been pledged to make good the debts of a private corporation. The men who had participated in the formation of these banks and in the granting of special privileges to them were saddled with the blame for the financial distress which impartially affected all classes. Since the Union Bank was the most important the men connected with it were seen as the biggest scoundrels. These men, many of them members of the old "Nucleus," became the scapegoats for the rising Democratic party of which Robert Raymond Reid, James D. Westcott, and David Levy were the guiding lights. Levy, a newcomer to the political scene with a brilliant mind for party organization, was from East Florida and later became famous as David Levy Yulee.

Call's friendy disposition to the banks did not endear him to the rising new political coalition. They looked with misgivings on his close cooperation with John Gamble and his Union Bank, and were outraged when Call continued to issue "faith bonds" to the Union Bank, as the law required him to do, during the financial crisis. As Levy saw it, Call was piling more and more indebtedness upon the heads of the people who, for the most part, received no direct benefits from the bank. This new issue of bonds which Call was signing had come as a consequence of an increase in the capitalization of the Union Bank in 1838.[79]

In the apportionment of new stock in the bank old subscribers were given preference to the disappointment of many would-be purchasers. Westcott's antipathy for the banks was perhaps heightened when his bid for a block of shares was turned down by the directors. The old subscribers made new purchases by a rather questionable manipulation. The property appraisers, appointed by Governor Call, reappraised all the mortgaged property which had been encumbered to buy their original shares, and increased its valuation. This increased valuation then became the basis for new mortgages which financed the purchase of more stock.[80]

At the conclusion of the second stock subscription, in 1838, Call proceeded to issue two thousand bonds valued at $1,000 each to the bank. The law authorized him to do this after the subscriptions had been secured by mortgages, but Call apparently acted prematurely in issuing these bonds before all the stock was secured. The Democrats charged that some of the bonds had even been sold abroad before some of the mortgages were completed. Thus was more fuel added to growing popular discontent with the financial institutions.[81]

In addition to Indian troubles and financial distress there was a third event of significance in Call's first administration. This was the convocation at St. Joseph in 1838 of a convention to write a constitution for a State of Florida. This convention resulted from Call's recommendation to the Legislative Council in 1837 that preparatory steps be taken looking toward statehood since, as Call said, "the wealth and number of our inhabitants, is now sufficient to enable us to assume a State Government."[82] The Council provided for a referendum on the convention at the election in May, 1837, at which time it was approved largely because of the overwhelming pro-statehood sentiment in Middle Florida. Opposition to the convention was strongest in East Florida, where many favored division of the territory into two parts so that the East might remain in territorial status.[83]

The election for convention members hinged on the bank and bond controversy, particularly in East Florida. There the issue loomed so large that the voters lost sight of the fact that the anti-bank delegates whom they elected were also proponents of statehood. Economic issues were less important than statehood in Middle Florida where the same voters sent both bank and anti-bank men to the convention. Overall, the anti-bank forces succeeded in electing a majority to the convention and much was done there to clarify party lines. Levy looked to the selection of the convention president as a test of strength between the pro and anti-bank factions but sectional issues clouded a clear-cut division on this issue. Reid, the anti-bank candidate, defeated DuVal, known as a bank man, by one vote. However, a constitution was produced which was sharply restrictive of banking institutions. The article on banks was approved by a vote of thirty-five to nineteen which clearly showed the dominance in the convention of the coalition that became the core of the Democratic party. Of the nineteen members who opposed the article, one was the director of a minor bank, twelve were stockholders in the Union Bank, and one owned stock in the Bank of Pensacola. Six of the thirty-five favoring the article owned stock in the Union Bank, but none of the remaining twenty-nine owned stock in any of the major banks.[84]

No criticism of the constitution by Call has been found. In his message of 1839 he warmly praised the banks and urged favorable consideration and protection for them. These words may have been aimed at the convention rather than the legislature, for there had been talk of using the power of the convention to intervene actively in the financial crisis. Call, however, could offer little criticism of the restrictions in the new constitution after his strong stand for state regulation. Many of Call's colleagues, DuVal, Richard C. Allen, George Ward, and Thomas Brown, had fought vigorously against the restrictive bank clauses, but a few of his friends had supported them. Leigh Read, Leslie A. Thompson, Benjamin D. Wright, and Joseph Sanchez all had joined the crusade against banks. After the convention adjourned, a large group from the majority element formally organized as the Jeffersonian Republican party of Florida. These were Florida's Democrats.[85]

During his first term Call was also interested in developing a system of internal improvements in Florida. He tried unsuccessfully to interest the Legislative Council in 1837 in buying half of the capital stock in the East Florida Railroad Company which projected a road from Jacksonville to St. Marks. He predicted that its revenues would pay the expenses of the projected new state government and lessen the need for taxation.[86] In 1838 he submitted to the Council a plan by James Gadsden for a cross-Florida railway and suggested that federal land grants be sought for its construction. Proceeds from the land sales would furnish the capital for a territorial bank which would undertake to finance the railroad.[87] Again, no action!

One topic close to the heart of Call as governor, was the reform of the militia system. He had seen its defects at first hand and urged upon the legislature a total overhaul aimed at restoring discipline and affording more adequate training. In 1839 the Legislative Council gave him a law setting forth in no uncertain terms the power of the governor to draft men into active service whenever necessary. Heavy penalities in terms of fines and dismissal were provided for officers who failed to produce the numbers of men called for by the governor, and those officers were empowered to use "any degree of force necessary" to compel the attendance of militia members when summoned. Officers failing to hold regular training periods were subject to dismissal and fine, and when called to active service all militia members were to be governed by the Articles of War as established by the United States Government.[88]

One of the more mundane administrative problems which plagued Call was the confused state of the revenue system of the territory. There was great laxity in the assessment and collection of taxes and in the disbursement of the revenue, and the power of the governor over the revenue officers was virtually nil, since they reported to the Legislative Council. At every legislative session during his administration Call urged the entire reorganization of the revenue department, but not until 1839 was anything done. In that year, however, the Council made the territorial treasurer and auditor each responsible to the governor. The governor was also empowered to appoint for each county a tax collector who should collect the taxes assessed by a justice of the peace, who was to be appointed by the county judge of each county. Property owners were to list and describe on oath to the justice of the peace their taxable property and were to be liable for double taxes on any property they failed to report. This law went far toward removing the evils of which Call complained, but still did not eliminate the inequities caused by differing standards of assessment in each county.[89]

Call also was concerned with the erection of a suitable capitol for the territory. The original log building had given way to an unfinished brick one which Call recommended should be completed. Funds for the building of the capitol came from the sales of land granted to the territory for that purpose by Congress. A commissioner was in charge of the sale of this land and the disposal and investment of the money thus raised. This sum became popularly known as the Tallahassee Fund. In 1839 Call reported it was impossible to get anyone to serve as commissioner of the fund because of the low salary and urged a higher one. He reported much injury to the territory from prior careless management of the fund and from careless conservation of the lands Congress had granted. The Council of 1839 followed his suggestion and set a $1,500 annual salary for the commissioner. He was also authorized to contract for the building of a capitol "agreeable to such plan as may be approved by the Governor, and in all matters relative to the building said Capitol and the payment or disbursement of money, the Commissioner shall be under the entire direction of the Governor."[90] Under this authorization the old capitol was demolished and a new one begun, which, however, was not finally completed until 1845. Assistance was received from Congress in the form of an appropriation provided in response to the request of the Legislative Council. This building still stands as the central unit of the present capitol.

Despite his removal from command of the federal forces in Florida, Call continued to offer advice and criticism to the Van Buren administration on the conduct of the war. When the army went into summer quarters Call would rout out what militia he could and take the field. Joel R. Poinsett, the Secretary of War, was annoyed that the energetic and caustic governor would not be quiet and let the government run the war in its own fashion. In 1837 Call's Kentucky relatives offered a mounted brigade for service in Florida on the condition that Call command it. Washington turned down both the brigade and Call's "valuable services."[91] In 1838 Call trudged off into the wilds of West Florida to collect straggling Creek refugees and send them off to the West. After he had won their confidence and gathered them together, malicious whites spread the rumor that they were to be executed, and all melted again into the wilderness. In the fall of the same year he went to Washington to urge personally more protection for Florida and material aid for citizens suffering from Indian depredations.[92] In 1839 he sent a commission of seven men having "extensive interests" in Florida to visit Van Buren again to seek aid for Florida.[93] When he met continued failure in his attempts to get more attention to the Florida Indian troubles, he threatened to organize an independent force and take the field to conduct his own forays.[94] Had the Secretary of War been an excitable man, he might well have been uncontrollable when that news arrived.

In 1839 events rapidly moved to a climax. Secretary Poinsett was becoming convinced that Call must be removed, and the Democrats in Florida were doing all in their power to assist him and President Van Buren in reaching that decision. Call had remained in Van Buren's eye not only because of his strictures on the war but also because of a petty controversy which he kept before the president for two years. He and the secretary of the territory were bitterly at odds, with the point of contention apparently little more important than a question of whether the governor or the secretary should remain in Florida during the "sickly season." This secretary, John P. DuVal, a brother of the former governor, had succeeded Call's cousin George Walker to the secretaryship in 1837. In the summers of 1837 and 1839 he had left the territory much against the wishes of Governor Call.[95]

Call deluged the Secretary of State with letters demanding that DuVal be ordered back or dismissed. Each time President Van Buren patiently requested and then ordered the secretary to return. Each time DuVal managed to remain absent until the summer was over. Call was particularly angered because DuVal was one of those who were undermining him among administration leaders. In May, 1839, hearing that DuVal was planning to leave, Call ordered him to remain. DuVal replied that he had not asked Call's consent to go and added, "I know not by what authority you write me a lecture in relation to my official duties. . . . I shall go to Va. You may renew your attacks on me, perhaps this time, they may recoil on yourself."[96] When DuVal returned to Florida in November Call ordered him from the capitol building and suspended him from office. The scene was a rowdy one, but as Call said, "I did not lay my hands on him until he drew a Pistol on me, and . . . I proceeded to disarm him without the least unnecessary violence."[97]

DuVal's remarks to Call indicate that he was, perhaps, aware of the fact that Call's removal was under consideration. David Levy had sent Van Buren an able analysis of the condition of the Democracy in Florida in 1839 in which he recommended that the governorship be placed in "thoroughly democratic hands." He told the president, "I can satisfy the Administration that it is not now in hands at all likely to advocate or advance its interests or to uphold the democratic movements." He assured Van Buren that the people of Florida were "radically Democratic."[98]

In 1839 Call issued four hundred bonds, "guaranteed by the Territory of Florida," to the Southern Life Insurance and Trust Company. Levy had feared this move and urged upon Poinsett the necessity for removing Call before he could issue them, but the administration had delayed action. Levy chided Poinsett, "Thus you will perceive that our public debt has been increased while the question of Call's removal was in suspense."[99] By November, however, Poinsett had decided that Call must go. He directed a letter to the president in which he declared that a bad state of affairs had long existed in Florida and that improvement could not be expected "so long as the present Governor remains in power." He blasted Call's plan to raise a territorial army and commented, "Such a measure would bring this department into direct collision with the civil authorities of the Territory & involve the Government in great immediate expense." Poinsett then asked Call's removal on grounds of disagreement on military policy. Martin Van Buren read this missive and scrawled on its back, "Let Gov. Call be superseded & Judge Reed appointed in his place."[100]

Call's removal was greeted in partisan fashion. The Democratic *Floridian* observed, "We have not for some time past found much cause of commendation in the course of Governor Call." The Washington *Metropolis* exulted, "There is nothing like having a *true* Democrat at the head of affairs in Florida. The *pretended ones* have done mischief enough."[101] In St. Augustine, *The News*, a new paper professing to support the Whig party, declared that "such a removal is more honorable than any office in the gift of the President." It asserted that Call had been removed because he strongly represented in Washington the sufferings of the people and pointed out "the utter inefficiency of Mr. Secretary Poinsett and his old women officers."[102]

Levy was supremely happy and congratulated Poinsett. He was relieved that the removal had been kept a closely guarded secret until accomplished. "Had intimation been given of the President's intention," he wrote, "I have no doubt that the whole interval between the intimation and removal would have been occupied in preparing and signing bonds."[103] As might be expected, Call was sent into one of his towering rages by the sudden dismissal, and he denied that differences over military policy were the reasons for the dismissal. He asserted that actually his removal was aimed at building up the president's political party in the territory. He ridiculed the Secretary of War and indirectly the president and scornfully charged, "The petty corporations of this Territory have claimed more paternal concern from the Federal Executive than the Seminole War, which is depopulating the country, consuming the substance of our people, and draining the last artery of the national Treasury."[104]

Call was unable to secure a Congressional investigation of his removal but he did succeed in getting his military correspondence with the government published by the Senate. Through an old army crony, Senator William S. Fulton of Arkansas, he got a public explanation from Poinsett of the cause for his dismissal. Poinsett wrote, ". . . no disgrace was attached to his removal—He thought proper to assume an attitude opposed to this Department, and his continuance in office, was, therefore, deemed incompatible with the interests of the public service."[105]

The explanation cleared Call of suspicion of misconduct, but he looked upon it as a contrived statement which hid the fact that only party machinations stood behind his removal. He was not mollified by the statement and grew bitter in his denunciation of the Democratic party. In a spirit of revenge, he made plans to give Van Buren cause to regret his removal.

8

The Austere Forties

FROM THE FINANCIAL DISTRESS of the late thirties and early forties, which had brought setbacks to the national Democratic party, came distinct gains for the Democrats of Florida. The fact of the insolvent banks, the defaulted "faith bonds," and the depreciated currency was plain evidence to many that the planting and business interests of the territory had exploited the people for selfish ends. Recognition of the fact that the territorial government had created corporations which were designed to assist the few but in which the risk was to be taken by the many provided a rallying point for the anti-monopolist movement that characterized the politics of the early 1840's in Florida. The class feelings stirred up by the driving new Democracy offended gentleman of the old school who, as did one St. Augustine newspaper, looked upon the new state of affairs as "an awful struggle between virtue and corruption."[1]

The old leaders, men of wealth and standing, seeing themselves assailed by a class-conscious group, reacted as conservatives often do in like circumstances. They denounced class distinctions as unpatriotic and ridiculed the idea that measures calculated for their benefit did not also benefit all other men. Unable or unwilling to grasp the realities of party organization—and often feeling that parties were demagogic, dishonorable, or even corrupting—the conservatives were slow to realize that they must organize and argue their cause before the electorate to fight this new movement. For years they had held to the view that they were the true Jeffersonians, the real inheritors of the old Republican party, the only political party of consequence since the War of 1812. Yet even when the conservatives began to organize they shook off the curse of factionalism with difficulty, and were reluctant even to agree upon a party name.[2]

Call shared this attitude toward party organization. In his forma-

[118]

tive years he had been imbued with the old Virginian notions about
public office, beliefs that family connections, judicious marriages,
and the winning of the favor of the few who held power was the
proper way for a gentleman to get ahead in politics, not by courting
the favor of the multitudes. Call never quite grew out of the idea
that gentlemen do not solicit votes. His political attitudes were not
only in line with Virginia practices but also with those of most of
the older seaboard states where close-knit caucuses named candidates and sponsored them before the electorate, while the candidates themselves remained aloof alleging that they were in the race
only at the insistence of their friends.[3]

Call's formative years had also been years in which the United
States lacked a healthy two-party system. The Federalists had lost
power in 1800 when Call was but eight years old, and had dwindled
away into a minority opposition party which during the War of
1812 had become tainted with disloyalty and disunionism. After
1816 the party vanished from national politics and a factional spirit
grew up which dominated until the election of 1832. It was in these
years that Call was initiated into politics. In Florida he had worked
with his cronies—other lawyers, planters, and men of affairs—to secure political ends. He often declared his unwillingness to stoop
to "ungentlemanly" acts to secure office, and when in Congress he
asserted that he served at personal sacrifice because the people had
requested his service. Undoubtedly he liked to think of himself as
a statesman, above "petty" party strife, serving the best interests of
all the people. Probably it did not occur to him that his conception
of the best interests of all was shaped by his heritage, limited by his
associations, and influenced, even if unconsciously, by his own interests.

When Jackson surged into office in 1829 Call was one of his
enthusiastic followers and acquiesced in and benefited from the
"spoils system." There is not, however, any indication that Call attempted to build a party in Florida through the instrument of the
patronage. Some of the replacements he sought to have Jackson
make in Florida were to provide for members of the "Nucleus"—
"our little caucus" as Benjamin Wright called it—but Call does not
appear to have embraced the idea basic to professional politicians of
the Martin Van Buren school that the patronage should be disposed
of primarily to build a great political organization. In Florida none
of the conservatives appreciated such uses of the appointive power

so well as did the radicals, David Levy and James D. Westcott. Perhaps it might be fairer to say that the radicals, lacking the prestige and command of material resources which their opponents had, did not believe that any dishonor was connected with use of the patron-age for such purposes.

When Call became governor in 1836 he did not use that position to build a political party. Conservative aversion to parties and to haranguing the electorate are not the only reasons for Call's neglect to organize a party on conservative principles, for a very important obstacle must have been indecision in his own mind as to the national group with which he could affiliate. He would not revive the Federalists, though many of their principles were attractive to him, for he associated them with treason, but would he be a Democratic Republican or a National Republican, a Democrat or a Whig? Until the late thirties Call never really had to concern himself with answering the question. It was enough that he was a Jackson man, and so it was that his allegiance was given not to a political party but to a political leader. So long as the principles of the Democratic party were those upon which Jackson stood, they were acceptable to Call. With the succession of Martin Van Buren to the presidency and the leadership of the party, however, submerged differences rose up.

Shaped by aristocratic ideals of politics and trained to a high sense of duty to absolute concepts of chivalry, truth, honor, and righteousness, Call's personality was not ideally suited to being a successful politician in a democracy. He lacked the qualities of pliability and willingness to give way on unessentials to secure ultimate goals, which mark the great politician. Compromise was equated in his vocabulary with dishonesty. He would not indulge himself in any laxity of duty, as he conceived it, and it was inconceivable to him that other men should expect tolerance from him when they were wanting in devotion to what he saw as their duty. His eldest daughter observed that trait in him and, sharing his attitudes, she was proud to boast that "he was particularly unfitted" for politics.[4]

Call's adherence to the Democratic party, as personified by Jackson, was sorely tried when Jackson removed him from military command in 1836. Never again were the relations between the two as cordial as they had been, and less than half a dozen letters now exist which were exchanged between them after 1836. Call's clear separation from the party of Jackson came in 1839 when Van Buren removed him from the governorship. By that year the Democratic party had become a power to be reckoned with in the Florida territory, but its opposition was still divided and impotent. Even in 1840 Call did not throw himself into the building of a Whig party in Florida. In part this was due to the fact that Florida was not yet a state and Van Buren, who was the object of Call's wrath more than was the Democratic party, could not be directly injured by political activity there. Instead, Call left Florida and took the stump in 1840 for William Henry Harrison. Call was not alone among prominent Floridians in his backing of the Whig candidate. William P. DuVal came out for Harrison as did Charles Downing, now Florida's delegate in Congress. Though Governor Reid told Secretary Poinsett that Call and Downing were working to establish Whig principles and Harrison newspapers all over Florida, Call's major efforts were reserved for the Northern states.[5]

The Van Buren administration did its best to cripple Call's contribution to the Whig cause. After his removal from the governorship, the government entered suit against him for an alleged shortage of more than $5,000 in his accounts as the Receiver at the Tallahassee land office. The Democratic press discussed the charges as though his guilt had already been determined, but Call announced that after an investigation he expected to recover a large sum from the government. He alleged that the discrepancies which the government charged against him were scattered over an eleven-year period and were on items "which have been suspended in consequence of technical informalities." He refused to comment on the justice and propriety of the government's action for, "I wish to create no prejudice in my favor."[6]

Suit was commenced against Call in February, 1840, in the federal court at Tallahassee. He entered pleas of *nil debit*, set-off, and payment. The court allowed his claim for extra services rendered in his capacity as receiver to go to the jury, to which the government objected on the grounds that the so-called extra duties were regularly prescribed by law. The jury, however, allowed $12,500 for the extra services, thus leaving a balance of over $7,000 in Call's favor. Government counsel moved for a new trial on the grounds the verdict was against the evidence, but the motion was denied.[7] The case was appealed by the government and the higher court awarded a writ of *venire facias de novo*, by which a new trial was ordered. Not, however, until 1847 did the second trial come to court. Again the verdict was in Call's favor, with the jury this time certifying him a balance of more than $8,500. After this trial the Treasury Department instructed the district attorney to drop the case.[8] The decision did not, however, come in time to affect the political contests of the forties, and the charge of having short-changed the government was hurled at Call in 1840 when he worked for Harrison and again in 1845 when he ran for Governor of the State of Florida.

Before leaving for the North to work for Harrison, Call did aid in efforts to build an anti-Democratic press in Florida. Tallahassee noted the arrival in 1840 of Cosam Emir Bartlett who took over the editorship of the *Star of Florida* in April, probably with the aid of $5,000 lent him by Call and Walker. Bartlett was a partisan of Harrison and the banks. His paper soon was known as the organ of the pro-bank party, which in 1840 in Tallahassee went under the name "Conservative party." In 1841 another faction of the anti-Democratic forces brought the *Quincy Sentinel* to Tallahassee as the *Florida Sentinel*. This paper became the organ of a group calling itself the "States Right Whigs" who, while not opposing banks, thought that it would be wise to allow the inflated Florida banks to die a natural death. This paper became the regular Whig organ in Tallahassee within a few years.[9]

By the middle of April, 1840, the Democratic *Floridian* complained that the opposition could muster to its banner the Tallahassee *Star*, the *Quincy Sentinel*, the *Pensacola Gazette*, the St. Joseph *Times*, the Jacksonville *Advocate*, and the St. Augustine *News*. The *Apalachicola Gazette*, it said, was "half way over." The only other important paper in the Democratic ranks was the St. Augustine *Florida Herald*. The *Floridian*, however, recognized the division among their opponents and remarked that it made for them difficult the distinguishing of "the counterfeit from genuine, the false from the true." It hailed the action of Bartlett, who had brought out the *Star* for Harrison, as a move toward drawing the line between parties "honestly differing in sentiment upon the great leading questions of political policy."[10]

Late in the summer Call began his speaking tour against Van Buren. Downing accompanied him during a portion of the tour, which took him to the District of Columbia, Maryland, Pennsylvania, New Jersey, and New York. On September 1 he spoke to the Young Men's Harrison Association of New York City at the "Central Log Cabin" on Broadway, and later at a great Harrison festival in Philadelphia. In the Pennsylvania metropolis his criticisms of the government's war policy in Florida brought thunderous applause and there he was toasted as: "A gallant hero in the defence of his country—his arm, uplifted in the cause of Harrison and Reform, has dealt mighty blows upon the bonds of corruption and misrule."[11] Everywhere he goes, reported the St. Augustine News, Call is hailed by the Whig party. "Gov. Call is a warm personal friend of Gen. Jackson. . . . But the friend of Jackson does not recognize in Van Buren the 'Hero's successor.' "[12] In this campaign Call exalted the nationalism of Americans, deriding Van Buren for being a Northern man with Southern principles. The South, he asserted, would disdain an executive governed by any sectional principles. The principles of the South, he maintained, were constitutional principles and those principles were American principles: "Who attacks the North attacks the South."[13]

The news of Call, and his old friend John H. Eaton, campaigning for Harrison was a jolt to Andrew Jackson. Many persons were urging him to take the stump for Van Buren and he threatened:

> I am determined to make the attempt particularly when I see that Genl Call and Major Eaton, have apostatised and taken the field with the piebald opposition of abolitionists, antimasons, and blue light Federalists. . . . I pity them sincerely, they can do us no harm, or at most but little. . . . I would infer that both these Gentlemen, from their apostacy, are broke or encumbered with debt, for we find all who are broke join the opposition and are in favor of Banks, wishing to pay their debts by a depreciated paper.[14]

Jackson, however, was able to make only a few speaking engagements in Tennessee and that could not help Van Buren's cause.

"Thank God! We are all delivered from the Phillistines," was the reaction of one of Call's correspondents in Florida to the news that Harrison had triumphed over Van Buren in the presidential race.[15] Call was jubilant at Van Buren's defeat and his own role in it. "I am satisfied," he wrote to Mrs. Kirkman, "that I have received quite as much attention and applause as I have merited. . . . I do not know what good, if any, I have done but I have at least annoyed the Administration and its friends and I have qualified my own feelings, I may say my *revenge*."[16]

With the defeat of Van Buren, the adherents of Harrison in Florida began to look about for someone to replace Reid in the governorship. One group supported William Wyatt, whom the *Sentinel* termed "unacceptable." Another group advocated Call for reappointment to the post, which the *Pensacola Gazette* said, "so appropriately belongs to him." The *Floridian* replied, "When the Whigs decide who other offices 'belong' to the people may be relieved of electing persons to them."[17] Nevertheless the office was to go to Call, and Downing joyfully wrote on March 8: "I have seen old Tip, & he says you shall be Gov. Bell told me so six weeks ago —every member Whig of Congress told me, if I wanted you, they would go for you."[18] Wyatt pressed his own claims and personally visited Harrison in Washington. Governor Reid viewed the entire matter philosophically and noted in his diary, "Harrison is *in a terrible fix,*—overrun by politicians and office-seekers. It would not be wonderful if the old fellow's steps to the grave were not hastened by such cares. . . . I expect the old hero will certainly send me *packing*."[19]

On March 19 Harrison fulfilled Reid's expectations and named Call to the governorship. The news was published in Florida on April 3, just two weeks before the news of Harrison's death was published.[20] According to Benjamin Putnam, St. Augustine greeted the news of Call's reinstatement with "a glorious salute of about 50 rounds, continued at intervals through the night, with hearty cheers from a large party of good fellows whose spirits were made buoyant at the prostration of a corrupt dynasty."[21] Despite the return of a Whig governor the division in the conservative camp was not ended as was made clear by the appearance of two opposition candidates for the post of Delegate in Congress. In East Florida the anti-statehood conservatives were supporting the incumbent, Downing, but in Middle and West Florida the pro-statehood conservatives were backing George Ward. Both were friends of Call and he took no active public part on behalf of either, although the *Star*, whose policy Call was reputed to influence, came out in favor of Ward.[22]

The Democrats united to favor David Levy for the congressional post and in the East his opponents were openly pessimistic about his defeat. Putnam told Call, ". . . that little *Jew politician* has been untiringly industrious through the Country, and I fear will get a very heavy support. There is but little doubt . . . that he will beat Downing in this County by a considerable majority, and in proportion through East Florida." Only a Middle Florida majority could save Downing, he pointed out, and Ward would take that from him.[23]

One anti-Democratic paper realized late in 1840 that division among the opponents of the Democrats could only continue to guarantee Democratic victories. The *Quincy Sentinel* urged the necessity of "a thorough, systematic organization" of Whigs to beat Levy and labored mightily to identify the Democrats as the hard money party opposed to all banks. It sought thus to rally and unify those who opposed such policies and favored a system of solvent banks and well-based paper currency. Its efforts, however, were productive of no high degree of party organization in 1841 and the local elections of that year resulted in a Democratic triumph. The constitution written by a Democratic convention had been ratified in 1839, and in 1841 a sweeping victory was won by that party in the Legislative Council and David Levy was sent to Congress. The pro-bank *Star* warned, ". . . if there is any virtue in the doctrine of loco focoism, we presume the people of Florida will have the full benefit of it during the present year."[24]

In 1842 the Whigs showed that they had learned something from the Democrats and exhibited more organization and an approbation for public opinion, shown in their disposition not to try to resurrect the banks. Under the leadership of the *Florida Sentinel* and the so-called States Right faction, they resumed control of the legislature and held it throughout 1843 and 1844. During the period from 1841 until 1844 Call again occupied the governor's chair, but he still did not use that position to build up a party. The faction to which he belonged, the "Conservatives," actually disintegrated during the period, some of its members becoming Whigs while others became Democrats. Judging from its stand for the local banks and its close cooperation with the Whigs, it apparently was a later Florida counterpart of the conservative movements of the Van Buren era in New York and Virginia under N. P. Tallmadge and William Cabell Rives, respectively. It was composed of those who were intent upon maintaining the Florida banks and who opposed the repudiation of the faith bonds, which measure the Democrats accomplished in 1842.[25]

The Conservative party ran its first slate in 1840 in Middle Florida. William P. DuVal was the most prominent nominee of that year and was elected to the Legislative Council. In addition to DuVal, Leslie A. Thompson, Robert Hayward, Thomas Brown, Charles H. Dupont, T. R. Betton, and R. A. Shine were among the prominent men connected with the movement. By 1842 the group was falling apart and its organ, the *Star*, was leaning towards support of John C. Calhoun. It refused to back the Whigs in that year reputedly because they had submitted to the "utter prostration" of the local banks.[26]

During Call's second administration the problems of overriding importance were economic in nature. The financial decline of the late thirties had become the depression of the early forties and the banks of the territory were having trouble meeting the interest payments on the "faith bonds." Cotton prices had begun the slow decline which was to carry them down to as low as 3½ cents per pound in 1845 and the stockholders of the bank, who were privileged to borrow from the banks up to two-thirds of the value of their stock, were unable to meet the interest on these debts. One observer estimated the debt of Leon County planters alone to be more than $3,000,000. All Middle Florida was said to be "literally shingled over with Judgements."[27]

Call felt the pinch of the depression years, though he was more favorably situated than those who were immediately involved in the failing banks. In 1839 he had owned almost 6,000 acres of land in Leon County alone, and town lots assessed at $10,000. By 1845 his town lots were valued at $1,500 and he owned only 3,250 acres of land in the county. His slaves, however, increased from eleven in 1839 to thirty-one in 1845. During the early forties judgments totalling over $20,000 were handed down against him and almost 1,000 acres of his land were sold at sheriff's sales.[28]

The Democrats expressed concern that Call might sign more territorial bonds for the banks, but their fears proved groundless. In his first message to the Legislative Council, delivered in 1842, Call reported that the mutual embarrassments of the banks and their debtors were affecting the entire community; he deplored the fact that the debtors found it easier to join in the denunciation of the banks than to pay their debts. In the preceding year he had been insistently petitioned by the representatives of Hope and Company of Amsterdam for the interest due on the bonds of the Bank of Pensacola, which payments the Bank had been unable to make. Call was no more disposed to accommodate the foreign bondholders than the Democrats were if it involved expense to the territory, but he would not accept the Democrats' solution of repudiation. Instead, he informed the bondholders that the territory stood in relation to the bonds only as a remote and contingent endorser. The territory could not be called upon for payment, he insisted, until after the creditors had exhausted all legal measures against the bank *and* individual stockholders. Though Hope and Company informed Call that they had no desire to enter into such involved legal operations and declared that his action endangered the good faith of the territory, the governor flatly refused to assume any responsibility for payment. Call felt that the bondholders wanted to get the territory to admit responsibility so that they might then proceed against the federal government, of whom the territory was a creation.[29] President Tyler admitted, "There appears to be a good deal of force in Gov. Call's views," and thought it would be wise for the bondholders to proceed against the bank and its stockholders.[30]

Call admitted that the territory was bound to pay both the principal and interest on the bonds if the bank and its stockholders could not do so for, he said, "Our honour must be vindicated." He recommended, however, to the 1842 legislature the passage of a resolution which would deny the bondholders any relief until they had made every legal effort to get redress from the banks and their stockholders. The Council did not pass such a measure. Brushing aside the governor's views, the legislators repudiated all territorial responsibility for the bonds and passed acts calling for the cancellation of the bonds and forbidding the issuance of more. These acts were passed over the governor's veto.[31]

In the Legislative Council of 1842 the Democrats also put through three bills severely restricting the note-issuing powers of the banks and facilitating the collection of debts owed by the banks. Call vetoed all three and sent them back with a defiant message that the measures violated the chartered privileges of the banks. He held that the measures had not been aimed at alleviating financial distress but were intended for the "utter annihilation of the banking institutions of the Territory."[32] James D. Westcott, the leading Democrat in the Council, denounced Call's veto as bringing "incalculable evils" upon the people. He declared that it was "only those deeply immersed in bank and corporation speculations, stocks, and who owe the banks large sums, that the veto can benefit."[33] Call gave his support to a stay law as the best means of combatting the unsettled economic conditions, and such an act was approved by the Council. Westcott ridiculed that measure, saying that it struck only at the effects of the economic distress, but that the acts the Democrats had sponsored aimed at the cause of the trouble.[34]

The year 1842 was one of the worst years of the depression. In January of 1843 Call told the Council, "The tide of prosperity which once flowed over our land has receded, and has been followed by a universal derangement of business, a depreciated currency, prostration of credit, and the general embarrassment of the whole community." He painted a dark picture of the indebtedness of the people and of the sacrifices involved in the sale of property under execution. The picture seemed to him to be one which offered "an impressive appeal to the Legislature to interpose its conservative power to prevent in future the recurrence of such evils."[35]

The governor told the lawmakers that since the principal source of the depression was past legislation of the Council the people had an especial right to claim protection at the hands of their representatives. Past legislatures, he said, had incorporated banking houses without capital, having extraordinary privileges to raise money on the faith of the territory. These institutions had expanded their note issues far beyond their capacity to redeem them, had afforded too easy credit to individuals, and had "seduced even the most prudent and cautious into wild and hazardous speculations." He recommended the extension of the stay law, which the Council effected, the establishment of a minimum price for property sold at execution, and provision for debtors redeeming their property within certain limits. Neither of the latter two recommendations was carried out. Again he declared his opposition to repudiation of the bonds, and he reaffirmed that the bondholders should get no relief from the territory until they had prosecuted the banks and stockholders.[36]

Governmental revenue was also a problem during these depression years. Most taxes had been suspended during the worst distress, and in 1843 Call recommended that the Council increase taxes again or cut expenditures. He informed the legislators that there was $26.79 in the treasury and that claims upon the government amounted to $16,483.41. They responded by reviving the land tax and levying a $250 annual tax on all bank agencies operating in Florida. Salaries of the treasurer and auditor of the territory were cut to $300 annually and the commissioner of the Tallahassee Fund had his salary cut to $400 annually. The collection of the tax on auctioneers, which apparently was a major source of income, was tightened up.[37]

In 1844 Call was able to report the return of peace to the territory though the economic scene still was depressed. The three major banks had ceased to function, although the Union Bank was still in process of liquidation and had missed five installments of interest on the faith bonds. Call suggested that the Council compel it to pay them, but praised the efforts of the officers of the bank. The legislature took no action on this recommendation. Call noted the initiation of a new bank under an old charter, the Bank of Florida, and praised its conservative management as having afforded many facilities in the transaction of business.[38]

Throughout Call's administrations he had been concerned with education. The Congress had granted two townships to the territory for seminaries, and the sixteenth section of every township for the support of schools. The conservation of these lands was one of Call's prime interests. The management of the lands had varied from time to time, but by 1844 trustees had been provided for their management. The governor and Council named the trustees of the Seminary lands and the citizens of each township chose the trustees of the school lands. The trustees were empowered to provided for the conservation and rental of the lands and the expenditure of the income from them. Trustees of the Seminary lands were empowered to lend out the income at 8 per cent interest. Though Call recommended the establishment of a public school system, virtually nothing was done about the matter until after the Civil War.[39]

During the hard times of Call's second administration a religious revival began to sweep Middle Florida. Frequent services and camp meetings were held and in this atmosphere the temperance movement flourished in Tallahassee. George W. Call, the governor's brother, was elected president of the Tallahassee Temperance Society in 1842 and in 1843 was named head of the Total Abstinence Society. Richard Call was not disposed to engage in such activity, but he recommended to the Legislative Council in 1843 that these organizations be commended to "the encouragement and support of the friends of morality and virtue."[40]

Many a timid soul may have believed that the temperance and religious movements were long overdue. In the late thirties visitor Castelnau recorded that intemperance was the most common vice in Tallahassee. He asserted that he saw men of responsible position rolling in the streets until their slaves came to carry them home in their arms. Gambling was rampant, according to the French visitor, and gave rise to frequent brawls and murders. The continental observer also declared that every man was armed and that hostile planters meeting on horseback in the streets would start fighting on sight, their slaves and friends joining in.[41]

Despite the hard times, liquor was plentiful and cheap during the forties. Whiskey could be had at thirty-five cents per gallon; New England rum was forty cents per gallon; and real, hard-to-get old rye was eighty cents. With the great reliance on strong drink in election campaigns, the dinners with round upon round of toasts, not to mention the day-to-day opportunities for imbibing, perhaps it was not so strange that it was said that half the men who settled in Tallahassee died drunkards.[42]

Yellow fever, however, proved a more mortal enemy to the populace of Middle Florida than did strong drink, and Call's second administration was ushered in by a serious epidemic of that disease. Pensacola, St. Joseph, and Tallahassee were the hardest hit areas. Many prominent men were carried away by the plague, including Robert Raymond Reid and two successive editors of the *Floridian*.[43] Call had dashed off to the national capital when he heard that attempts might be made to defeat the confirmation of his appointment and thereby missed the worst part of the epidemic. His daughters were also out of the danger zone, Ellen being in school in Philadelphia and Mary being with her grandmother in Nashville.[44]

The worst year of the depression had both bright and dark spots in Call's personal life. His old friend DuVal was fading into obscurity but he found time to encourage the governor. "I have great confidence in your judgement, management, and perseverance," he once wrote. "No man will hail with more sincere joy, your deliverance from all your difficulties, personal and political, than myself." The spirits of the former governor were sinking however, and he confided that he was often seized with melancholy "when

I look to Tallahassee and think of the days of life and joy that once shed there happy influences around me."[45]

At the Hermitage, ailing old Andrew Jackson was thinking of his place in history and wrote Call for his accounts of several events in which they had participated. They were, he said, to go to Amos Kendall for "the Biography." The old general had softened in his feelings toward his rebellious former protégé and, thanking Call for his efforts to accommodate him, Jackson wrote, "It will give us pleasure to see you at the Hermitage, and believe me *as usual* your friend."[46] The two old friends, however, did not meet again.

Renewed attempts of David Levy to undercut him with the Tyler administration were dark spots in these years for Call. Both of the anti-Democratic papers in Tallahassee praised his administration as being "above" party politics. The *Star* jovially asserted that, indeed, Call's administration had been too impartial to suit it.[47] The Democrats were hard put to find an issue serious enough to demand the removal of the governor. The best opportunity came when Call pardoned Michael Ledwith, a convicted accessory to the murder of Leigh Read. Read had been a staunch Democrat and foe of the banks and popular feeling ran high about his death. He had been killed from ambush by Willis Alston, who had made two previously unsuccessful efforts to kill him. Alston was seeking to avenge the death of his brother Colonel Augustus Alston whom Read had killed in a duel. The latter Alston had been a leading Whig and exponent of the banks, and the quarrel which led to the duel stemmed from bitter political differences. Legend has it that Alston's sisters cut Read's bullets from their brother's body and sent them to Willis Alston in Texas, with a plea to use them against Read.[48]

At any rate Willis came to Tallahassee, and after two unsuccessful attempts to kill Read he hid in the home of Ledwith. It was from this house that he made the fatal attack on Read. Alston promptly escaped from Florida and Ledwith was tried as an accessory and convicted. The jury recommended mercy and a petition was presented to Call for his release. Levy and the Democrats, however, chose to see political partisanship in Ledwith's pardon. Levy conversed with President Tyler about the event and the president showed every disposition to placate the Florida Democrat. Tyler insisted, however, that there was no ground on which he could act against Call since the pardoning power was a discretionary one which the governor had a right to exercise upon his own responsibility. The president did assure Levy, nonetheless, that if Call were to pardon a murderer that he would be removed. He also told Levy that if the choice of a governor had been his to make, it would not have been Call.[49]

As Call's second term drew near its close insistent rumor had it that he would not be reappointed. On March 30, 1844, he inquired of the Postmaster General if this were true and asked to be allowed to defend himself if he should be removed for any but party reasons. As it developed, the rumor was true and party reasons apparently were the explanation. Call proved to be too much inclined to Whiggery to suit Tyler, and in August John Branch was named to succeed him when his term expired in that month. Call afterward made no effort to conceal his support for Tyler's enemy, Henry Clay, and his opposition to Tyler's project for the annexation of Texas.[50]

Call did not campaign in the presidential canvass of 1844 as he had in 1840, but he was as strongly opposed to the Democrats as he had been in the latter year. He stated that the success of Polk would jeopardize the Union, he asserted his preference for preserving the national honor rather than annexing Texas, and he gave his endorsement to the views of Van Buren and Clay on the Texas question. At this time he was a defender of the protective tariff, and summarized his sympathy for Clay as being based on the belief that he would preserve the Union and maintain the tariff.[51]

Meanwhile, factionalism was on the wane as the Florida Whigs became better organized. They had begun the practice of holding county and district conventions to nominate candidates. Call's brother was active in these meetings, as were his two cousins George K. and David S. Walker. The latter had come to Florida in 1837 and was a practicing lawyer. In 1844 Dr. George W. Call had presided over both the Leon County and the Middle District Whig conventions. Control of the Legislative Councils of 1843 and 1844 was in part a result of this Whig organization.[52]

Meanwhile in Congress, David Levy and other Democratic leaders had waged a vigorous campaign to get Florida admitted to the Union. Their efforts met with success in 1845, and on March 1 the United States Senate approved a bill from the House of Representatives admitting both Iowa and Florida into the Union. Governor Branch proclaimed May 26 as the date for the election of a governor, congressman, and members of the legislature. The Democrats

met in state convention on April 14 and named William D. Moseley
for governor and David Levy for Congress. The Whigs, less well
organized, got off to a slow start, but their convention in Tallahassee
nominated Call for governor and Benjamin Putnam for Congress
on April 21. Both slates were geographically balanced.[53]

When first approached by Whig leaders Call had declined to
make the race, but an appeal from a group of Middle Florida Whigs
prevailed upon him to make the campaign. In part they said, "You
grew up at a time when it was fashionable for men to be patriots,
not partisans. . . . and we ask of you your services now, not as a
mere partisan Governor, for we know you would not grant them on
these terms. But we ask you to serve us as the *Governor of Florida*;
administering the Government for the best interests of the *whole
people*."[54] Call accepted this bid, declaring it the paramount duty
of a citizen to serve when his country called. As if to assure his Whig
friends he wrote, "I am not a democrat in the signification in which
that term is used by the demagogues of the present day."[55]

Ellen Call Long declared that her father considered himself a
Democrat of the Madisonian school who had been forced out of
the Democratic party by the radicalism of Martin Van Buren. Call
himself often made similar statements and denied that he could be
a repudiator of the public faith or a "disorganizer of the moral
foundation of society." He stated, "I am not in favor of the banding
together of partisans under any name or creed, to divide among
themselves the spoils of conquest, acquired by any means to attain
their ends."[56] Under the appeal, however, to serve the whole people Call agreed to head up the Whig band of partisans.

In the campaign which followed, the brunt of the speechmaking
was borne on the opposing sides by Call and Levy. Both Moseley
the Democrat and Putnam the Whig were relatively unknown. Insistently the Whigs summoned Call to the East to combat the vigorous and skilful Levy. Many felt that Putnam was not well enough
versed in Florida politics nor able enough to "expose in a public
speech the cunning trickery and sophistry of Mr. Levy."[57] In the
brief time available before the election Call tried to meet as many
of the demands upon his time as possible.

By 1845 newspaper opposition to the Democrats was waning. In
Tallahassee the *Star of Florida* maintained strict neutrality. In St.
Augustine *The News*, oldest Whig paper in Florida, was acquired
by the Democrats. Yet with the loss of these two papers the Whigs

still managed a hot campaign. Democratic papers attacked the
Whigs, particularly Call, as bank men. *The News* charged Call was
pledged to serve the banks and to make the people pay off the
faith bonds. The *Pensacola Gazette* dissented saying, "He is poor.
He has lost all but his honor. . . . this will go with him untarnished
to the grave."[58] Generally the Whigs advocated a policy of unity
and the subordination of party politics to the welfare of the new
state; they were eminently unsuccessful. When the returns were in
it was seen that the Democrats had won the governorship, the seat
in the House of Representatives, and majorities in both houses of the
state legislature. Among the Whig minority in the legislature were
such prominent men as David S. Walker, Benjamin D. Wright, and
Thomas Brown.[59]

Levy readily took most of the credit for the scope of the Democratic victory. He had gotten Moseley elected, he asserted, by
drawing strict party lines, even risking losing some votes for him-
sel, and making his supporters adhere to them. "By this means I
secured for the whole ticket my own vote—and by attacking Call
I secured for Moseley all the additional vote which prejudice
against C. would give him."[60] Thus did Florida come into the
Union under the Democratic party, and Richard Call end his career
as an aspirant for public office.

6

The Lord of the Lake

IN 1845 CALL was fifty-three years old. Around him the world in which he had grown up was gradually being transformed. The United States had grown from a small Atlantic coast country to a great power expanding relentlessly westward toward the Pacific. In the South the centers of wealth and population were shifting from the seaboard and upper South to the western and lower South, and inventions which had fantastically increased the demand for cotton had fastened upon the region a labor system which forty years earlier had seemed on the point of decay. In Florida the rugged, Indian infested territory to which Call had come in 1821 had become the youngest state of a still young Union and early centers of wealth, power, and influence were losing their predominance.

By 1845 Call's personal relationships had undergone some change. His beloved wife Mary had been gone almost a decade. Before the year was out Andrew Jackson died at the Hermitage. In the previous year Call's daughter Ellen had married Medicus A. Long and a young Richard Call Long joined the family circle in 1846. Medicus Long was a young Tallahassee lawyer in partnership with Call's cousin George Walker, and the fact that he also was a Democrat did not unduly cloud family relationships. George W. Call had three boys approaching maturity and two were becoming close political associates of their father and their uncle. Young Wilkinson Call was a great admirer of his uncle and remained a loyal Whig and Unionist throughout the fifties. He achieved fame in the post-Civil War era as a rare bird in Florida politics—an anti-corporation liberal Democrat. Wilk, as he was called, was authorized by special act of the legislature in 1846 to practice law at the age of seventeen.[1]

As Florida achieved statehood Call more and more turned from his busy legal and political life to the more leisurely and satisfying life of the planter. From land purchases in the rich area north of

Tallahassee between Lake Jackson and the Ochlockonee River he carved a plantation which was called Orchard Pond. There he spent much of his time after 1845 teaching his young grandson the lore of the woods, taking pride in productions of the soil, and in developing and improving his livestock. Among the more novel of his activities there was his experimentation with the fibers of various plants in an attempt to find a substitute for hemp which could be profitably raised in Florida. He was quite enthusiastic about results from a species of yucca called bear grass. From this plant he prepared a product which he termed Florida hemp.[2]

Some of Call's old promoter spirit flared as he told Governor William Moseley about his experiments. He assured the governor that "there is no staple of our country which will yield so great a profit to planters as the Florida Hemp." He revealed that he had performed similar experiments using Spanish Bayonet instead of bear grass and that its fiber was just as good but not so long as that of bear grass. Bear grass was also preferable because planters had found it to be almost indestructible; hence it would need but one planting and would give continuous yield. Its cultivation would be a great boon to the poor man who could not afford the Negroes necessary to raise cotton and sugar, Call pointed out, and in addition it would attract more white labor to the South to reap the rich rewards of its production. It would, he thought, "be the source of the greatest wealth and prosperity to the Southern Country."[3] He presented George Bancroft, the Secretary of the Navy, with a sample of the hemp and asked that the Navy Department evaluate it. If they could use it for cordage, it would, he assured Bancroft, speedily be cultivated in great quantity.[4]

Call's enthusiasm for the potentialities of the bear grass hemp proved excessive. The fiber found no ready market and he apparently abandoned his experiments with it. The United States Department of Agriculture years later reported that its uses were very limited. It stated in 1911, "The fibers of the various species of yuccas, generally known as bear-grass, . . . are often suggested as fibers for binder twine, but they are too short and otherwise unfit for the purpose."[5]

For a number of years Call's planting activities were on a minor scale. Until 1853 the number of his slaves varied between thirty and forty and his land holdings dwindled to a low point of 861 acres in 1849, yet in this same period his investment in cattle increased, and by the latter year he had built up a herd of about one hundred head. The slave figures, based on the Leon County tax rolls, vary from the census figures which credit him with 143 slaves in 1850. The discrepancy is probably explainable by the fact that the census takers probably designated the slaves of the Tallahassee Railroad as belonging to Call. There is no evidence that he held slaves in any other county.[6]

By 1853 Call was planting on a large scale and had given over his Tallahassee residence to his eldest daughter Ellen in 1851 for her own home. By 1853 he had acquired 141 slaves and over 4,000 acres of land, while his town lots were valued at $6,000 and he sported an expensive pleasure carriage.[7] Withdrawn from the press of active politics, surrounded by his family, and engrossed in the operations of his plantation community, Call became more philosophic, more reflective, and more patriarchal in his outlook and actions. He took much interest in the poorer whites of the Lake Jackson region, counselled them in their problems, aided them in their distress, and influenced their decisions in political matters. His daughter stated that his neighbors came to him "from miles around with the confidence of children to a parent." He advised them in domestic matters as well as in agricultural, political, and religious affairs, and to the younger generation he became known as a matchmaker.[8]

Since early youth Call had been a Mason. He had joined the organization in Clarksville, Tennessee, in 1814 and his certificate of membership bears the signature of a Junior Warden by the name of Sam Houston. Call was instrumental in the organization of the Tallahassee lodge, became its Grand Master, and later was a founder and first master of a lodge at Concordia, a few miles from his plantation. In religion he was an Episcopalian and had been prominent in St. John's Church in Tallahassee. At Lake Jackson, however, he built and maintained a wooden church building which was alternately used by Methodists and Baptists. After the city pulpit became another platform from which Southern extremists held forth, Call joined the country folk at the Lake Jackson church and listened with relief to their simple sermons. Daughter Ellen was convinced that had it not been for the danger to the Union Call would have been content to shut out the world beyond Lake Jackson and devote himself to agricultural pursuits and literary enjoyments.[9]

The agricultural pursuits of his plantation were rather diversified. Cotton was the great staple crop and received the major attention, as in most areas of the South. Call also raised his own provisions, which indicates that a diversified vegetable garden was maintained to feed the slaves and family. Call was among those who had ventured to raise sugar cane when the cotton prices became so depressed, as had many Middle Florida planters who hoped it might become an alternate staple. Corn was also raised on a large scale for both humans and livestock.[10]

Through the fifties a large number of varying types of livestock were accumulated at Orchard Pond. Call became quite proud of his mules, and though he never condescended to enter the competitions at county fairs he did exhibit his prized animals. At the time of his death the livestock inventory of his plantation showed twenty mules and eight "fine mules." The inventory also indicated the importance of hogs, sheep, and cattle on his place. There were 220 sheep, 200 cattle, and over 300 hogs; 4 yokes of oxen, 10 asses, and 14 horses completed the list. The division of slaves after his death indicates that Call had owned 197, of whom 66 had been deeded to daughter Ellen before his death.[11]

Call showed considerable interest in the agricultural societies and conventions of his district. In 1852 he was named to the executive committee of the State Central Agricultural Society and had been the chief sponsor of a meeting of Leon County cotton planters in 1851 to consider cooperative action to keep cotton prices up. He was also one of forty delegates named to a cotton planters' convention in Macon in that year. He was, in 1852, one of sixty delegates named from Florida to a preliminary convention looking to an industrial exhibition to be held in New Orleans in 1853.[12]

It is to be regretted that we do not know more about the "literary enjoyments" to which Call devoted himself in the seclusion of his plantation. Presumably they were not out of line with the conventional Southern literary tastes in the forties and fifties. Repeated references in his public statements during the fifties to incidents in Greek history would make it a reasonable assumption that he read the Greek classics. Probably Sir Walter Scott was prominent among the authors whom he read. The writings of Scott permeated all literary circles in the old South, and evidence of his influence may be seen in the reference to Call by some of his friends as the "Lord of the Lake," a name suggested perhaps by Scott's *The Lady of the Lake* or *The Lord of the Isles*.[13]

The chivalric theme was the most pervasive one from Scott to

influence the old South. Florida was as receptive to the appeal of
the Age of Chivalry as were other regions of the South, even to
the extent of holding tournaments patterned after the jousting
matches of the medieval era. One such tournament in Tallahassee
featured the usual feats of horsemanship, all performed by bachelor
contestants bearing the names of knights. This event was closed by
a night of dancing, with one of the local belles presiding as the
Queen of Love and Beauty. In Florida, Scott and the chivalric ideal
were modified by frontier influences, as attested by the fact that
the winner of the tournament was the Knight of Miccosukie, who
was dressed as an Indian. However, Ellen Call Long tells us that
Scott's heroes and heroines were discussed as vividly as though they
lived in the next town.[14]

Call never formulated a systematic philosophy, but the philosophic ideals which emerge from his writings show a passionate
attachment to conservatism. He was a vigorous defender of the
status quo and of the Southern institutions which many were willing
to defend by upsetting the political *status quo*. He abhorred all radicalism whether that of the Southern particularist or of the Northern
abolitionist. His attachment to the established order, his aversion to
radical change, his reverence for old and familiar institutions, and
his devotion to the somewhat mystical ideal of a unity in history
binding past, present, and future generations in a partnership put
him in the classic stream of conservative thought well defined in
the writings of Edmund Burke.[15]

There is no concrete evidence upon which we may conclude that
Call actually studied Burke. Circumstantial evidence indicates that
he read Greek classics and history, Edward Gibbon's work on the
Roman Empire, and perhaps the novels of Walter Scott. As a lawyer
he might be expected to have read some of the works of Blackstone,
Chancellor Kent, and John Marshall. From all these, as well as from
the conservative circles in which he moved, Call may have imbibed
the precepts of Burkean conservatism without ever having read
Burke.

Despite a nationalistic bent and his contempt for the more radical
Southern fire-eaters, Call did not differ from most other Southerners
in his defense of slavery and his belief in the natural inferiority of the
Negro. The most complete exposition of his philosophy in regard
to the Negro and slavery was made in a letter published and circulated in the North in 1861. In it Call described the Negro as "A

wild barbarian, to be tamed and civilized by the discipline of slavery." He portrayed the Negro as "an animal in the form of man," having great capacity to labor and endure hardship but lacking capacity of mind or spirit to regard slavery as degradation. In the exploitation of the resources of the New World European and Indian labor had both proved unsatisfactory, according to Call's history, and every colonial nation had substituted the labor of the African. "Nobly has this race done the great work required," he asserted, adding: "they have been elevated in the scale of human beings."[16]

Call saw the history of African slavery as an important part of our history and he claimed that slavery had done more to better the world than any other institution. He believed, however, that the Negro was so inherently inferior, so patently designed by the Creator for slavery, that he would ever remain a slave so long as there was a superior race willing to be his master. He viewed American Negro slavery as a historical and national problem, not a peculiar minority problem of the South. He saw it as an American institution, the inheritance of a past generation, protected by the Constitution.[17]

Despite the fact that he was a man of mercurial temperament who often sounded harsh in his defense of slavery, Call was as beneficent a master as the ideal of the patriarchal system could have required. Some of his house servants were literate, and one who went to war with Call's nephew wrote back to his relatives of their encounters.[18] One unusual set of letters among the Call papers also tells the story of a free Negro residing in Canada who purchased his daughter from Call. The Negro, John Jenkins, lived in Hamilton in what is now Ontario province and first wrote to Call in the summer of 1858, appealing to him as a father to understand the grief of another father at separation from his daughter. He revealed that the owner of another daughter had sold her to him and expressed a burning desire to grant to the daughter in Call's possession the same great benefit, exclaiming: "its name is *Liberty!*"[19]

Call immediately replied to Jenkins, consenting to sell the girl for $400, a fraction of her market value. By June, 1859, she was reunited with her father, who addressed an effusive, grateful letter to Call, inviting him to visit Canada and conveying regards to Call, his family, and his servants. The daughter herself appended a note to her former master informing him of the progress of her education and the novelties of her new home. She also included the rather intimate news that her sister's husband was "as Dark as myself."[20]

The sectional tension centering around slavery was increased by the Mexican War which began in May, 1846. That war was greeted with little enthusiasm in Florida, which had recently been drained of martial spirit by seven years of Indian warfare. Yet even among many of the older Southern States there was opposition to the war, as well as in the North particularly in abolitionist circles. Southern Whigs who had opposed annexing Texas, and some who had favored it, looked upon the Mexican War as an unjustified conflict. Southern Whigs did not, however, carry their opposition to the war into opposition to the expansion of slavery into the lands secured from Mexico.[21]

Call's view of the war was that of most Southern Whig leaders. It was in his opinion "the little war we have so wantonly provoked with Mexico." To his mother-in-law he confided, "Certainly a more unnecessary war was never brought about between civilized nations. . . . The conquest of all Mexico, would add little to the glory of our arms, or our national wealth, while it must be attended with great expense, and injury to our commerce." Since the war was under way, however, he saw nothing to do but support it, right or wrong. "I have no idea of going into service myself," he wrote. "The country has able men enough in the field."[22]

The Mexican War, though opposed by many Whigs, provided them with a successful presidential candidate in the person of General Zachary Taylor. Call had been an ardent supporter of Henry Clay and had not been disposed to generous praise of Taylor's war record in Florida, so it is not too surprising that he remained secluded on Lake Jackson and kept a discreet silence in the election of 1848. Locally, the Whig success in 1848 brought into office a Whig governor to join the Whig legislature elected the year before, and a Whig representative in Congress. Thomas Brown, as governor, was representative of the established large slave-holding, commercial, and banking interests of Florida. He was as staunch a Unionist and as opposed to radicalism as was Call. The representative in Congress, young Edward Carrington Cabell, was a real sparkplug in the revitalization of the Florida Whigs. He represented a newer generation, less committed to old ideas and causes and more willing to compromise. He was the best vote-getter the Whigs ever had in

Florida and the last important Whig to hold on to office in Florida.

Call's political silence was maintained through the exciting events of 1849 when the propriety of Calhoun's proposed convention of Southern states at Nashville to consider their position in the Union was being discussed. This probably can be explained by his pre-occupation with his plantation and his complete satisfaction with the manner in which Thomas Brown met the critical events of 1849 and 1850. Brown vigorously opposed the Nashville Convention and refused to appoint delegates to it.[23] After passage of the Compromise of 1850, which killed the Nashville Convention and, so many thought, settled the sectional controversy for all time, Call and most leading Florida Whigs gave their full support to this comprehensive settlement. During the 1850 campaign for Congress Call emerged from his silence to speak often for Cabell and Compromise. A heated rivalry developed between Call and John Beard, the Democratic nominee. Beard preferred disunion to "submission" to the Compromise and at one Democratic barbecue the aging Call took on Beard, soundly berating him in an emotional nationalistic talk. Though not unobjectionable the Compromise was infinitely preferable to the horrors of disunion, Call declared. "Where," he asked, "would enslaved humanity throughout the earth, turn for succor, hope or comfort, if the Great God of nations should withdraw his protecting arm, and permit this sun of liberty to sink in a night of strife and fraternal blood."[24] To his listeners it was not necessary to explain that "enslaved humanity" referred only to white humanity.

Beard was not the only fire-eater among the Florida Democrats. Call's old adversary, the senior United States Senator David Levy Yulee, had been a vigorous opponent of the Compromise in the Senate. Yulee was up for re-election in the legislature of 1850-1851 in which the Democrats had a slight majority, but was defeated in that body by the moderate pro-Compromise Democrat Stephen Russell Mallory. The election of Mallory was the work of twenty-four Whigs and seven Democrats and has been traditionally interpreted as a rebuke to the radicalism of Yulee.[25] Recent researches, however, suggest that conflicting interests of rival railway promoters may have been an equally important factor. This thesis holds that Yulee's defeat came from a coalition of Whigs who wished to see a cross-state railroad built under Whig auspices and Democrats from South Florida who were opposed to any railroad at all. Yulee was the active promoter of a projected Fernandina to Cedar Key railroad while Whig leaders were prominent in a projected Jacksonville to Pensacola road.[26]

Call was vitally interested in the Whig project and had made several recommendations for such a railway while he was territorial governor. In 1851 he presented to Governor Brown proposals for a cross-state railway which Brown transmitted to the legislature with a recommendation for the creation of an internal improvement board to draw plans for a general system of improvements to eliminate "local disorganized projects," possibly meaning Democrat Yulee's project. The legislature created the board and Call became one of its members. By the close of Brown's administration, however, Call was sixty years old and more interested in devoting his remaining energies to the fight to preserve the Union. After the sale of his interest in the Tallahassee Railroad in 1855, he took no prominent part in the promotion of internal improvement measures.[27]

After the crisis of 1850 a briefly promising Union party movement which developed in Georgia, Alabama, and Mississippi attracted Call's interest. It was composed for the most part of Whigs and Democrats who feared both Northern and Southern extremists, but it found little support in Florida. In 1851 Call visited the North and came back full of enthusiasm for the perpetuity of the Union. He saw the material advance of the country and the rapid extension of improved modes of transportation as inevitably binding the Union more tightly together. Admittedly he saw elements of disunion in the North among abolitionists, but he believed that they were only a well-organized minority and that a great Union party would guarantee that they would remain a minority. To this end he urged Southern men to support the Union party movement, to give up their local prejudices, and to sacrifice their old party ties upon the altar of country. Said he, "The man who loves party more than he loves his country, who contracts his patriotism and whose affections cannot embrace his whole country with its distant boundaries and great resources, is unworthy the name of 'American citizen.' "[28]

Call hoped for a national Union party, yet he conceded that old party ties might be too strong for such a development, in which case Whigs and Democrats of the South should merge their differences in a Southern Union party. This organization could then act with whichever of the Northern parties would disavow abolitionism. Thus, he argued, the South would be united to preserve the Union rather than to destroy it. Among other things, the scheme demonstrates Call's lack of grasp of the workings of a democratic party system and indicates that he underestimated the popular moral drive behind the abolition movement. Democrats laughed at his proposal and the Tallahassee party organ wrote, "We should have thought much better of Gen. Call's views . . . if he had advanced them when the whig party had something besides a *name* to dispose of. . . . Evidently, whiggery is in a most fearful decline."[29]

The election of 1852 was the last presidential election which the Whigs contested in Florida and the entire Call family played leading roles in it. In June George W. Call, Jr., was a delegate to the Whig National Convention in Baltimore. In July Richard Call and his brother George were delegates from Leon County to the State Whig Convention and Richard was elected its presiding officer. This state convention named for governor an old Whig of the Call-Brown school, George T. Ward. Edward C. Cabell was renominated for Congress, and George W. Call, Jr., was named an alternate presidential elector.[30]

Despite the rebellious opposition of some Southern Whigs, the party nominated General Winfield Scott for the presidency at the Baltimore National Convention. Florida's young Congressman Cabell had vigorously opposed Scott even to the point of declaring that he would not support him if he were nominated. Cabell's stand caused George Ward to refuse to run on the same ticket with the congressman. Party leaders, however, induced Cabell to "acquiesce" in Scott's selection and Ward was satisfied.[31] Call attempted to rally sagging spirits in the state convention to Scott's banner. He lavishly praised the military accomplishments of the general despite the fact that he had been critical of Scott's conduct in the Florida Indian warfare. Nevertheless, Scott proved particularly vulnerable in Florida because of his odious general order during the Indian war in which he criticised the conduct of the citizenry. Despite the efforts of Call and other Whig orators Scott proved a millstone around the necks of Florida Whigs. The gubernatorial and congressional candidates were defeated by slim majorities but Scott was overwhelmingly defeated, carrying only three small and sparsely populated counties.[32]

The Whig party disintegrated rapidly after 1852. The planters in many instances began to look to the Democrats as the only party strong enough the protect the institution of slavery. It is ironical that the Democratic party, largely because of actions of its Northern

wing, came to be regarded as the party which stood on the Compromise of 1850, while the Whigs, largely because of their Northern
wing, became identified with repudiation of the Fugitive Slave Law,
a basic part of the Compromise. In Florida, many of the more flexi-
ble Whigs of the stripe of Cabell retired from the political scene
or became Democrats, and the withered remnants of the Whig organization came almost completely under the dominance of the
ultra-conservative element typified by Call, Brown, and Ward.

◯ 10 ◯

Defender of the Union

T HE DECISIVE DEMOCRATIC VICTORY of 1852 left
the Whigs in Florida in a depressed and spiritless state.
The party made no effort to contest state elections after
1854, though here and there a few die-hards held to the Whig name.
During the early fifties the leadership of the state shifted from the
moderate Democrats, such as Moseley and Westcott, and the conservative Whigs, such as Cabell and Brown, to a new school of politicians imbued with the radicalism of the "South Carolina school."
These new leaders were often actually South Carolinians by birth
and included such persons as James E. Broome, Madison S. Perry,
and John C. McGehee. Yulee was in accord with this group and
was returned to the United States Senate in 1855.[1] Throughout this
decade Call devoted his energies to fighting the extremists at home,
as typified by the new Democratic leadership, and the extremists
at the North, typified by the abolitionists.

Call's efforts through the fifties were directed toward urging the
suppression of issues which might upset the finality of the Compromise or tend to renew sectional passions. The stand which he took
was a logical consequence of the line of action pursued by the
South in defense of its rights after 1850. That new line of action
involved an abandonment of the policy of the "concurrent voice,"
which hinged upon the control of one of the three departments of
government by the South, and a shift to reliance upon the guarantees of the Constitution for the protection of Southern rights. When
the old power-checks-power concept was abandoned, many of the
radicals, such as Yulee in Florida, despaired for the safety of Southern institutions within the Union. They were political realists and
recognized that a powerless minority enjoys only the rights which
a majority is tolerant enough to permit it to enjoy.[2]

On the conservative side the power alignments were viewed differently and perhaps less realistically. Ultra-conservatives such as

Call refused to admit that the South was fighting a losing sectional battle with the North, and they still insisted on viewing the struggle as one in which the conservative interests were national not sectional in character. Until the very eve of the Civil War, Call's statements revealed his assumption that he spoke for a non-sectional majority of conservative men who would uphold constitutional guarantees. He charged that neither Southern radicals nor Northern extremists were sufficiently attached to either the Union or its Constitution.

Those who placed their faith in constitutional guarantees, however, were faced with the necessity of maintaining a public opinion which would respect those guarantees. Respect for law had to be fostered and an attitude of reverence for the sanctity of the Constitution had to be created and perpetuated. The founding fathers had to be placed upon an exalted plane and the mystic continuity of history which militated against rapid or far-reaching change had to be invoked. The Union must be cloaked with a religious reverence and the Constitution endowed with the infallibility of revealed truth. Yet the younger generation of Southerners, born and educated since the Missouri Compromise and impressed with the differences between North and South, was inflamed with the romantic vision of a great Southern nation. It was usually from the older, more conservative generation that there stemmed the greatest respect for constituted authority and from them that there came the romantic glorification of the old order, raising the Constitution and Union to the level of Bible and Cross. Call excelled in the use of the mystic and emotional weapons of romanticism, and as the fifties wore on he increasingly abandoned logic and reason in his defense of the existing order in favor of emotionalism.

In the year 1854 the Whig party in Florida named Thomas Brown as its last nominee for Congress. The most important political issue on the national scene in that year was the Kansas-Nebraska bill, which applied the formula of popular sovereignty to the Kansas territory and repealed the Missouri Compromise, thus opening all the territories to slavery in law if not in fact. Brown campaigned on the theme that this act had been unwise because it had reopened the slavery controversy.[3] Call campaigned for Brown, but even before the campaign began he had expressed opposition to the Kansas-Nebraska act. He stated that the repeal of the Missouri Compromise ought not to be considered by Southerners from a strictly legalistic point of view, but should be examined from the viewpoint of the practicality and expediency of running a risk of injury to the Union which might stem from disturbing that Compromise. He doubted that any practical advantage or benefit could be secured to the country as a whole, or the South in particular, by its repeal, and expressed doubt that the territory in question could ever support slavery. He advised that the continuation of good feeling between North and South was more important than a fruitless victory. "The repeal," he said, "would disturb the steady, sober political men of the North." He cautioned: "There are many gentlemen at the South who may not care what consequences may flow from such a course."[4]

After the defeat of Brown in 1854, the rapid rise of the "Know Nothings" began to receive sympathetic attention in the old Whig press. The *Sentinel* called it the "greatest wonder of the age," and expressed amazement at "the unexpected success of the infant and mysterious organization."[5] Beginning as a secret society, the movement was dedicated to anti-Catholicism and native Americanism, and first attracted great strength in the Northeast. Conservatives in the South saw in the movement an organization which might be used to succeed the dying Whig party. Its anti-foreign principles appealed to the slaveholders who believed that the ranks of the abolitionists and the power of the North were being swelled by the influx of foreigners. Its emphasis on the Catholic Church as unAmerican and subversive was seen by some as an emotional issue which might divert attention from the even more explosively emotional issue of slavery.

Call's daughter asserted that her father had been cognizant of the danger of "the foreign vote that has proved so pernicious to the country" since 1832.[6] One of his Boston friends wrote to him about the Native American movement in 1837 in an attempt to enlist his influence in the cause. This friend told him, ". . . 'tis the only political topic, being purely American, *sui generis*, on which I mean through my remaining days, to feel & express an interest."[7] Though Call did not show any public interest in the movement at that time, he threw himself into it in the fifties with all his characteristic vigor.

By 1855 the movement was well advanced in Florida where the "Know Nothings" won the Jacksonville city elections while "the outsiders had no idea that there was a K.N. ticket in the field."[8]

During the first week in April a state convention was held and secrecy was abandoned. The name "American party" was adopted and a central committee of correspondence was formed with subsidiary committees in each county. A state council, with Call as its president, was chosen to direct the party. In the nominations for the 1856 state elections Call's cousin David S. Walker was named for governor and James M. Baker for Congress. The leadership of the new party was predominantly composed of old Whigs.[9]

After presiding over a June session of the state council Call went to Nashville, where he joined with A. J. Donelson in speaking to a great American party Fourth of July mass meeting and barbecue. Donelson had deserted the Democrats and was working for the same ends for which Call labored. Call's speech was an impassioned appeal for the Union and a partisan endorsement of the principles of the American party. He sought to link the party with the principles of Andrew Jackson, showing that Jackson's maxims and those of the American party were the same: support of the Constitution and defense of the Union.[10]

Call placed greater emphasis on the anti-foreign than the anti-Catholic aspects of the party. He saw the foreign vote as an element of corruption tainting the purity of American institutions. Immigrants were seen to be particularly hostile to slavery, not because they loved liberty, but because they wished to displace the slaves. Call deplored the fact that the immigrants no longer came from "the intelligent class . . . who understood our institutions" but from "the lowest orders of Europeans" banished from their homes by want or crime, and he charged that for political purposes the Catholic portion of them could be marshaled and directed like an army.[11]

Call maintained that the American party would not put curbs upon religious freedom or impose religious tests for office but would, instead, urge that Americans vote against foreigners and Catholics in order to exclude their "corrupting" influence from our system. He linked Protestantism with liberty and depicted the Catholic Church as the worst despotism on earth. "Your government," he warned, "is in danger of subversion by the power of foreign influence, against which you have been warned by Washington and Jackson."[12] Heedless of the parallels which could be drawn, Call showed how improved transportation facilities had made Catholic monarchies virtual neighbors of republican America.

They could not live in such proximity, he claimed, because of the antagonism between liberty and slavery: "Liberty . . . must have freedom of thought and action—freedom from want, from ignorance, vice and superstition. She must have unity of support and defence." Call said that he could never vote for any man who owed allegiance to the Pope of Rome, "or any other Prince or earthly power, higher than the allegiance he owes to the Constitution and Government of the United States." He called patriots to unite, saying "its the genius of your country which calls you. Let us unite in the name of God and Country to save our liberty and institutions."[13]

The *Sentinel* reported that Call's speech "gave unmixed delight to the vast concourse assembled to hear it."[14] Democrats reacted differently, claiming that Call had slandered Andrew Jackson. The *Floridian* declared, "Protestant as we are, we can join in no such infamous *un*-American proscription." It pointed out that Roger B. Taney had been a Catholic and that Jackson had been the son of a foreigner. As for foreigners in government, every administration in history had had them.[15]

Call rebutted his Democratic critics throughout the fall of 1855 in the press. Many of his charges have a familiar ring in the political atmosphere of the mid-twentieth century. Attacking foreign and papal influence Call charged that twenty-seven of twenty-eight subordinate officers of the State Department were Roman Catholics. This to him was a fact to excite grave apprehension. "It could not be accidental," he asserted. Democrats had sought them out to fill government posts, not because Democrats were more liberal or tolerant than other men, he said, but because Catholics and foreigners were on their side. Genuine patriots should break away from party bondage and unite to expel foreign influences from the government. Few foreigners, he charged, were even entitled to the friendship and regard of native citizens.[16]

As Call continued his attempt to identify Jackson with the principles of the American party and disassociate him from the Democratic party, his efforts became interwoven with his attempt to disassociate himself from the Democratic party. He denied that he had left the party because Van Buren had removed him from office and then claimed that he had never owed his office to the party, but to Andrew Jackson. He owed nothing to the Democratic party except a series of wrongs, slanders, and persecutions. He minimized Jackson's domestic policies and asserted that the old hero's great

kinship with the American party was his overriding desire to preserve the Union.[17]

During the fall of 1855 Call also spoke at gatherings throughout
Middle Florida despite the fact that his old bodily ailments were
afflicting him again. These talks were usually lengthy emotional
appeals described, as the *Sentinel* pictured one three-hour speech,
as the appeal of a patriot "his heart o'erflowing with feeling for his
country."[18] Everywhere he hammered home the theme, Americans
only must govern America. In the campaign Wilk Call was a staunch
supporter of his uncle, though he claimed that he was still a Whig
and not a member of the American party. George W. Call, however,
deserted his uncle and became a Democrat, denouncing American
party principles as "wicked in their tendencies." His position as
secretary of Yulee's railroad company was thought by some to have
influenced his political stand.[19] At one political gathering in December Call was opposed in debate by George Call and Medicus
Long.[20]

At the December American State Convention in Florida, Call,
Edward Hopkins, and L. W. Rowley were selected to represent
Florida at the American National Convention in Philadelphia in
February, 1856. Only Call attended, however. Call was also a mem-
ber of the National Council of the party which met on Monday,
February 18. The purpose of this meeting was to try to iron out
differences over the slavery portions of the platform. Passions ran
high at the meeting and confusion and bitterness were rampant.
Call used his influence and eloquence in behalf of harmony and
unity.[21]

On the fourth day a new platform less explicit in its defense of
slavery than the one the Council had drawn up the previous June
was finally adopted. It upheld the reserved rights of the states, and
favored non-interference by Congress and other states in matters
of purely state concern, as well as popular sovereignty in the territories and the admission of states when they had population enough
for one representative, provided that only those who were American citizens should take part in forming the state government. Amid
many objections the new platform was adopted and the Council
adjourned. Call had voted for the new platform.[22]

On February 22 the convention opened with about three hundred delegates present. On the second day O. E. Small of the Pennsylvania delegation moved the repudiation of all platforms drawn

by the Council and offered a five-point platform which provided no suitable protection for slaveholders. The chair ruled the motion out of order, after which various motions were made, to the bewilderment of the chairman, who became unable to understand the position of affairs. Ultimately the impasse was resolved by declaring Small's motion in order. At that point Call took the floor and declared himself an ultra-Union man who had fought radicals at the South for twenty years. Then he turned upon the Northern delegates crying, ". . . you bring Black Republicans here from Congress to sit with me. You will yield nothing to the South; the South must yield everything to you." He proceeded at length, attributing the differences between the North and South to the aggressiveness of the North. "I am satisfied that this amalgamation of different parties cannot save this Union," he declared, "and I have determined therefore to withdraw from this convention."[23]

At this, Small interjected his willingness to compromise and asserted that he would alter his motion, if Call would agree to abide by it, to put forth the Bible and the Constitution as the only platform. His offer brought great applause, but Call was adamant in his adherence to the platform adopted by the Council and reiterated his determination to walk out. Wild excitement prevailed in the hall with twenty delegates clamoring for the floor. Delegates from Tennessee, Alabama, and Virginia were getting up and preparing to leave with Call. Delegates from New York and Pennsylvania shouted encouragement to Call while the convention president, E. B. Bartlett of Kentucky, vainly tried to pound order with his gavel. When partial order was restored Bartlett made a dramatic appeal, as "tears coursed down his cheeks," to the Southern men not to leave the convention. When his words had no effect, Bartlett moved the convention adjourn until July 3. From the extreme confusion which followed there emerged a motion to table the motion. After a six and one-half hour roll call, it was tabled.[24]

On the beginning of the third day, while Call was still absent from the convention, an attempt was made to incorporate into the platform a plank favoring re-establishment of the Missouri Compromise line, but it was defeated. At this point many Northern delegates from New Hampshire, Connecticut, Rhode Island, Massachusetts, Pennsylvania, Ohio, Iowa, and Illinois walked out. They called for cooperation with the Republicans and did not return. After the names of Millard Fillmore and W. R. Smith had been presented for

HON. WILKINSON CALL.

Wilkinson Call, nephew of Richard K. Call, was an adherent of his uncle in the fruitless fight against secession in the late 1850's. After the Civil War, he won fame as a United States Senator.

Built in the 1830's, the Call mansion still holds its place in Tallahassee as a home of architectural distinction.

(Red Kerce Photography)

A French visitor to America, the Comte de Castelnau, sketched this impression of a Tallahassee street scene in the 1830's.

Capt Call

Hermitage

Dear Sir I am disappointed in not seeing you

previous to your out set — permit me to
you my best wishes for your prosperity
I had many things to say which Capt Carn
with this pen. suffice it to say farewell with
going out and coming in is the[y] your friends &—

Rachel Jackson

October 3rd — 1820.

N.W. view of Fort Mellow Lake Monroe E.F. 1837

A typical fort of the second Seminole War period as sketched in 1837. This location is only a few miles south of Volusia, on the St. Johns River, where Richard Call was relieved of the command of U. S. forces in November of 1836.

A "faith bond" sold by the Territory of Florida to provide capital for the Union Bank of Florida located in Tallahassee. Signed by R. K. Call as territorial governor.

the presidential and vice-presidential nominations, respectively, a recess was taken. In the afternoon session William G. "Parson" Brownlow proposed to welcome back into the convention Call of Florida, Percy Walker of Alabama, "and all others who had been going astray." The motion was carried by acclamation and the Southerners returned.[25]

> Mr. Brownlow, amid great applause, advanced toward General Call, and embraced him.
> The greatest merriment was occasioned by this fond embrace, and Mr. Brownlow took his seat, with his brow radiant with joy, amid the joy of all present.
> General Call said he had given his hand to his brother, and he now gave his heart to the Convention. He was truly happy to be enabled to return without the least inconsistency, and resumed his seat, now that peace and harmony was restored.[26]

After the seating of the Southern delegates Fillmore's nomination was made unanimous and a demonstration took place. In the midst of the enthusiasm a Virginia delegate took the stand and placed in nomination for the vice presidency Richard Keith Call, whom he described as "Old Hickory's" well-tried friend on the battlefield and right-hand man in council. Three cheers were then given for Call and scores of voices summoned him to the stand. Sincerely flattered by the demonstration, Call responded, voicing his deep gratitude but declining the nomination, which he said he particularly appreciated, for in refusing it he could show that he sought no office for himself from the party. He then proposed for the nomination Andrew Jackson Donelson, who was unanimously selected.[27]

Happy that the extremists had left the convention, Call still professed to believe that conservative men were in a majority, ignoring the fact that the slavery issue had as effectively split the new American party as it had the old Whig party. He was convinced that there was still patriotism and conservatism enough in the land to save American institutions from the rage of faction and fanaticism. The American party, he declared, "is now the only pure national conservative party in the United States."[28]

Call penned a bright enthusiastic letter to Donelson in the spring of 1856, offering suggestions for the campaign and encouraging him to the hopeless task. "You have not left behind you the maxims of Jefferson, Madison, and Jackson," he wrote, "you have carryed them with you." However, he advised: "Attack the traditions of Democracy! Undeceive the people, the honest people, who sincerely believe that modern democracy is the legitimate descendant from the republican principles of Jefferson and Madison." He regretted that this was widely believed "among the honest working men" and was a tower of strength to the Democratic party. "Now you and I know this to be a blind unfounded faith," he continued. "You and I know that Martin Van Buren and Thomas H. Benton, and not Jefferson, Madison, & Jackson, are the fathers of Democracy."[29]

In June, 1856, the Democrats held their State Convention in Florida and named George W. Call, Jr., and Medicus A. Long as two of their three presidential electors and both spent much time on speaking tours for the party. Wilkinson Call, still claiming to be a Whig, showed great zeal and enthusiasm in the cause of Fillmore and Donelson. Richard Call was somewhat hampered in the stump speaking by a recurrence of his old fever and a bad lung condition. David Walker was the American gubernatorial candidate so the family was well represented on both sides of the canvass of 1856.[30]

The Democrats made a clean sweep of the elections and the existence of the American party in Florida was decisively ended. Call retired to his plantation to nurse his health and reflect upon the course of events. Until the advent of the campaign for the election of 1860 he remained a silent observer. He was, nevertheless, seriously disturbed by the rapid rise to prominence of the new Republican party in the North, based upon what he viewed as subversive principles. In the summer of 1859 he gave his first important public address since the campaign of 1856—and it was a ringing appeal to American patriotism. The occasion was a meeting in Tallahassee of a ladies' association raising money to help in the purchase of Mount Vernon, that the first president's home might be turned into a national shrine. The speech shows Call's growing mysticism and his increasing identification of patriotism with religion. Mount Vernon he ranked in importance with the holy sepulchre, and the conquests of Washington were likened to the conquests of the Cross. The Constitution was described as the "highest warrant of civil and religious liberty known to the nations of the earth." The fact that the Union was the "palladium of our safety" was likened to "the truth of revelation." Still he placed his faith in conservative men: "There is a conservatism in the American heart and mind—there is a strength and power in the yeoman's arm, which will come to the rescue when-ever our glorious Union shall be placed in danger."[31]

Weighing political developments in the light of 1859, Call made a decision to return to the ranks of the Democrats to fight the Re-publican party. He noted that the Democrats were acting in har-mony with the Constitution, that they were a national party, and that they were opposed to abolitionists. "I am an old-line Whig," he wrote, "and opposed to secession—but in a choice between the Democratic party and the Black Republican or Abolition party, I must be a decided, determined and energetic Democrat."[32] Yet he was still at odds with Florida Democrats.

In early 1860 Call began excoriating the Republican party in frequent public letters with all the vigor at his command. He charged that the party was in rebellion and insurrection against constitutional government and asked, "Can you believe for one moment, sir, that the conservative men of the North and the South constituting a majority of the men of the nation, will permit the progress of this incipient subversion of the government without re-sistance?"[33] By 1860 he also had sharp words for many Southern Democrats because he had ceased to believe that secession was the right of a state. So long as the federal government observes the basic law, he said, so must the states. The South must make its stand in the Union, under the stars and stripes, but should "Black Republicans" ever use the Union to oppress the South a resort to arms would be the answer of Southerners.[34]

When Democrats interpreted this statement to mean Call would favor dissolution rather than "submit" to the election of Abraham Lincoln he at first merely replied, "I have never had a local feeling or affection strong enough to combat my patriotism. . . . I love my whole country."[35] Yet after the Democrats had split and Lincoln's election seemed quite likely he became more specific and denied that such an event should cause a breakup of the Union. "I should not despair of this glorious Union," he wrote. "It is the . . . govern-ment of a great people." He admitted that should conditions become oppressive under Lincoln then he might favor an internal rebellion, but "no thought or feeling favorable to secession ever entered into my heart or mind."[36]

Until after the Charleston convention, Call continued to pin his hopes on the Democrats, favoring Stephen A. Douglas for the nomination. He expressed hopes that the South and West would stay together in 1860 as they had in 1812 against the fanaticism of the North. Abolitionism was but the old "hereditary treason coming up in another generation which appeared in the Hartford convention." Jackson had led the South and West to victory in New Orleans on the eighth of January, and Call hoped that "the gallant Douglas" might lead them to another before the eighth of November.[37]

In April, however, the Democratic National Convention at Charleston split into Northern and Southern factions with Northerners favoring Douglas and Southerners favoring John C. Breckenridge. Call, declaring that he would have supported any man the convention named, lost faith in the Democrats and turned in despair to the new Constitutional Union party. On June 16 a county convention of the new group was held in Tallahassee with Thomas Brown presiding. Call and his nephew Wilk both were present and spoke, as did George Ward. The leaders in the party were virtually the same men who had led the "Nucleus," the Whig party, and the American party. The State Convention was held at Quincy on June 27 and there, on Call's nomination, Brown was elected by acclamation to preside. Nephew Wilk was prominent in the Quincy convention and was named a Bell-Everett presidential elector. Meanwhile, nephew George had been named to the National Committee of the States Rights Democratic party.[38] As was his nature Call threw himself wholeheartedly into the fight for his new party, denouncing the bolt of Southern Democrats at Charleston as directly aimed at fomenting secession. He declared with disgust that the Southern Democrats could have done more to get Lincoln elected only by voting for him.[39]

On November 1, 1860, Call submitted to the press a statement outlining his attitude toward many leading questions. He again denied that he would favor resistance to the inauguuration of Lincoln or that he would favor any measure which would lead to war. The situation, he warned, was not one which called for rash or hasty action but one that required firmness and calm deliberation. "The fate of this union with its past successes, its present progress, its future glory . . . all depend on the result of our deliberation."[40]

In this statement Call also revealed that he shared the lack of faith of most Southerners of his generation in the universal human rights philosophy of the Declaration of Independence. He repudiated the theory of universal human freedom as "the mad offspring of delusion and passion, and not the result of enlightened reason. Liberty is the refinement of blessing to enlightened people." He declared the Republicans perverted the Declaration by applying its philosophy to the Negro when it had been "intended by our fathers to apply only to the white man, to our own Anglo Saxon race." He saw their design as the destruction of the Southerner's right of property in his slaves and then the elevation of the former slave to social equality.[41]

Call brought under fire one specific plank in the Republican platform, the promise of a Homestead Act. He saw it as another weapon aimed at the South in that under its auspices the Republicans could invite what Call referred to as all the paupers and criminals of Europe to emigrate to the Western territories and receive land at the expense of the government. From these territories new free states would thus be formed until there were enough to amend the Constitution and emancipate the slaves.[42]

Call hoped that conservative men could delay events long enough for a reaction to set in in their favor. Thus it was that he urged Southern extremists to sit out Lincoln's administration should he be elected to see if he would injure Southern interests. As a further concession to the radicals, Call suggested that the South suspend all commercial intercourse with the North and that Southerners decline to hold federal office as a demonstration to fanatics that slavery was indispensable. The *Floridian*, voice of the radicals, chided Call for his half-way measures saying, "General, you must advance a step or two."[43]

As Call had foreseen the election of Lincoln was inevitable and with it he saw the radical measures which he would have forestalled achieving reality. On November 26 Governor Madison S. Perry appeared before the new session of the legislature to ask the convocation of a state convention at an early date to protect the rights of the people of Florida. The radicals prevented efforts in the legislature to have the convention submitted to a popular referendum, and its convocation was set for January 3, 1861. Governor Perry proclaimed that the election for delegates should be held on December 22, leaving scarcely three weeks to campaign. By this time popular opinion had become so inflamed that the Unionists felt it wiser not to oppose secession publicly, but rather to seek to delay it in the hope that a conservative reaction would come. In Leon County the Unionist slate for the convention called itself the "People's ticket" and pledged that they would fight to submit the acts of the convention to the people for ratification. Wilk Call, George Ward, M. D. Papy, George W. Parkhill, and D. P. Hogue composed this group.[44]

The bluntest and most outspoken opposition to secession came from Richard Call. In a pamphlet published on December 1 Call termed secession "high treason against our constitutional government," and asked: "Is it not a fact that the present disunion movement in Florida is not because of the election of Mr. Lincoln but from a long cherished hatred of the Union by the leading politicians of the State?" He believed that the assembling of a convention would produce "the most fatal consequences," and he appealed again to the patriotism, the calm judgment, and the conservatism of the people. Fervently he wrote, "I pray that in the hour of death, the Stars and the Stripes may still wave over me, and wave forever over our whole united country."[45]

On election day Call visited the polling places in Leon County and in nearby Gadsden County, and reported that the people seemed bewildered at having to decide the fate of a great system of government, "almost without a moment's reflection." He hoped that the people would yet not be rushed into rebellion and treason and that the convention would not strike the American flag without submitting its action to the people. Before the convention met Call announced a great celebration at Lake Jackson to celebrate the anniversary of the battle of New Orleans. He stated that all were invited "whose hearts beat time to 'the music of the Union'—true hearted American citizens."[46]

In the convention the conservatives, led by George Ward, A. K. Allison, and Jackson Morton, unsuccessfully tried to delay the passage of the secession ordinance and on January 10 it was adopted. On the eleventh it was publicly signed on the east portico of the capitol by sixty-four of the sixty-nine members of the convention and Florida was declared an independent state.[47] On that day a number of jubilant men accosted aged Richard Call.

"Well, Governor," they shouted, "we have done it!"

"And what have you done?" asked the old man, waving his cane over his head. "You have opened the gates of Hell, from which shall flow the curses of the damned which shall sink you to perdition!"[48]

For a time Call looked to the border states to stay the tide of secession bringing America to the brink of "the most stupendous ruin . . . the world has ever known." He looked to them to retain their senses and act to bind the extremities together which had gone astray in "idolatrous worship of their local and sectional divinities." He still insisted "Disunion must be fatal!"[49] The events of 1861 soon shattered his last hopes. Even nephew Wilk gave up and admitted, "The present movement in the South has now become a sentiment in which all classes share."[50]

Call was but one of a group of ultra-conservative Southern men who fought for the preservation of the Union, believing to the last that the interests of the South could better be served in the Union than out of it. Most of them were, like Call, old men shaped in their beliefs by the nationalism of the War of 1812 and by old Southern concepts of an aristocracy of talent and means devoted to public service. Most of them were men with a stake in the great vested property interest of the South. They included such leading figures as John Bell of Tennessee, Sam Houston of Texas, Alexander H. Stephens of Georgia, Benjamin F. Perry of South Carolina, Herschel V. Johnson of Georgia, and William Cabell Rives of Virginia. Some, such as John M. Berrien of Georgia and Joel Poinsett of South Carolina, had not lived to see the climax of the secession movement.

Representing respectable property interests, these men had much to lose from revolutionary movements. They were intent upon preserving old institutions, old ideals, and old values. Some of them stood in awe of the majesty of the Union and, like Call, thought in "big" terms encompassing continents and generations. Theirs was the vision of a great and powerful America, united and vigorous, standing as an example to the world of the qualities they most admired in her society. In the mid-fifties Call had dreamed dreams of an America which should be "the center of the world" and predicted that from it, "the Gospel will be sent to the 'far ends of the earth.' "[51]

These Unionists fought the secessionists, the men who thought in "little" terms and who feared the power of a mighty America in which they and their interests were declining to a minority element of lesser and lesser importance. The secessionists would conserve Southern traditions and institutions, but they were without the Unionists' attachment for the system in which they lacked any real power to conserve those traditions and institutions. The Unionists and secessionists fought the doctrinaires, the fanatics, and the moral crusade forces of the North which dreamed "big" dreams of an

America in which the precepts of the Declaration of Independence would be taken seriously and all men should live in Christian brotherhood, in freedom and equality.

Whose was the nobler vision? The Southerners would have conserved all the bad features of the system as well as the good. They would have fastened on their section a system of labor which would have become increasingly burdensome as technology advanced. They would have conserved the features so incompatible with the generous idealisms of the followers of Thomas Jefferson. The abolitionists would have achieved freedom for the slaves even at the cost of shattering the good features of the American system to eradicate the bad. The laws which safeguard liberty—as well as those which sheltered slavery—might have been lost to the "higher law" approach that would have substituted the narrow consciences of the reformers for the guarantees of the Constitution. Perhaps we may borrow a term from Burke and observe that the result was testimony to the "genius" of the American tradition. Neither side prevailed, and from the great conflict and its aftermath emerged a composite: a great powerful American Union which has become "the center of the world" and a degree of freedom and equality approaching that dreamed of by the crusaders for abolition, but within the structure of law and the Constitution. Even the concept of state rights still lives on, transformed and emasculated, but not dead.

In the remaining days of Call's life, however, all cause for optimism seemed to fade away. In the first surge of Southern nationalism after secession, Call appeared to some zealots to be a dangerous subversive whose loyalty to the South was questionable. The suspicion and resentment of his critics wounded and embittered the old man. Though he had fought secession, when he became convinced his cause was lost he had resigned himself to it and had offered his military services to the state. They were not accepted. Sourly he claimed that he had been denied any part in the struggle, "owing to the influence and opposition of such reptiles as would now Sting me in the back, and cover me with their malignant slime." Any man who questioned his fidelity to the South was branded "a fool, or a willfully malicious lying scoundrel."[52]

Suspected by his neighbors, rejected by his government, and growing daily more infirm, the old general retired to his Lake Jackson plantation to occupy his mind with his crops and slaves. He followed the war news with interest, and in the summer of 1862 he confided to his eldest daughter, "The withdrawal of troops from the Mississippi is significant. It indicates . . . the approach of the death struggle at Richmond. It will be terrible and fatal. Then the short and brilliant military course of the Southern Confederacy will end, like the going down of the Sun. . . . My heart sickens in the contemplation."[53]

During the spring of 1862 George Call, Jr., died in battle and the old general began to fail rapidly. As he grew worse he was brought into town to the mansion which he had built years before for a Nashville belle. There he received what medical science could do to relieve his suffering. On Sunday, September 14, 1862, a dark sky clouded Tallahassee and a noisy wind buffeted the countryside. In the afternoon his daughters became concerned lest the noise of the storm disturb him, but he relieved their anxiety with the quiet words that the sound of the wind was comforting to him. All that he asked was to be let alone to sleep. Between four and five o'clock on that stormy Sunday afternoon, Richard Call slept out the last minutes of his life.[54]

It was a life which had spanned some of the most important years in American history, the years from George Washington to Abraham Lincoln. It was a life passed for the most part among the people of his adopted state, Florida, to whose upbuilding and growth he contributed much. In the dark days of Civil War he came to believe that it was a life that had lasted too long, for it had embraced "the disruption of the great American Union, . . . the ruin of this once mighty empire."[55] His personal tragedy was that of the staunch, national-minded Southerners of his generation who could not give up or compromise either slavery or the Union.

A man of strong beliefs and great courage, Call had been as tenacious in his friendships as he had been in his enmities. He was authoritarian and demanding in his own right, but he never hesitated to question authority and hurl defiance at vested power when he believed that his cause was right. A gentleman, striving to remember his obligations as well as his privileges, jealous of his reputation, chivalrous in personal conduct, possessed of the courage to fight to the end against overwhelming odds for his convictions—he was representative of a passing generation and a vanishing class.

Notes

1

Soldiering on the Southern Frontier

1. Marquis James, *Andrew Jackson: The Border Captain* (Indianapolis, 1933), 163, 166; James Parton, *Life of Andrew Jackson*, 3 volumes (New York, 1859-1861), I, 412-421; "The Journal of Governor Richard K. Call," 15, Ms. in the Florida Historical Society Library, Gainesville, Florida. Referred to hereinafter as "Call Journal." All citations from this journal refer to a bound copy made by Ellen Call Long from the original. Discrepancies have been resolved in favor of the original manuscript which is in Call's hand. The first page in the bound copy cited here is numbered 12.
2. "Call Journal," 15-16; Parton, *Andrew Jackson*, I, 422.
3. Parton, *Andrew Jackson*, I, 422-425.   4. "Call Journal," 17.
5. *Ibid.*   6. *Ibid.*, 18.   7. *Ibid.*, 13.
8. *Biographical Directory of the American Congress, 1774-1949* (Washington, 1950), 937.   9. "Call Journal," 13.
10. Avery Odelle Craven, *Soil Exhaustion as a Factor in the Agricultural History of Virginia and Maryland, 1606-1860* (Urbana, Ill., 1926), 118-119, 162-163.   11. "Call Journal," 13-14.   12. *Ibid.*, 14.
13. *Biographical Directory of Congress*, 1965, 1966.
14. "Call Journal," 14-15.
15. *Ibid.*, 15; Mary Jane Seymour (ed.), *Lineage Book National Society of the Daughters of the American Revolution*, 166 volumes (Washington, 1895-1939), VII, 115; Edgar E. Hume, "The Virginia Society of the Cincinnati's Gift to Washington College," *Virginia Magazine of History and Biography*, XLIII (January, 1935), 55; "The Home Life of Chief Justice Marshall," *William and Mary Quarterly*, series 2, XII (January, 1932), 68.
16. "Call Journal," 15.   17. *Ibid.*, 18.
18. James, *Andrew Jackson: Border Captain*, 166-167.
19. "Call Journal," 23.   20. *Ibid.*, 26-30, 36-38.   21. *Ibid.*, 38.
22. *Ibid.*, 60, 62-67; James, *Andrew Jackson: Border Captain*, 176-179.
23. "Call Journal," 70-71; James, *Andrew Jackson: Border Captain*, 180.
24. Jackson to Call, January 30, 1814, in John Spencer Bassett (ed.), *Correspondence of Andrew Jackson*, 7 volumes (Washington, 1926-1933), I, 454.
25. Call to the Adjutant General, August 8, 1814, Misc. letters recd., Adjutant General's Office, War Department, National Archives; "Call Journal," 72, 77-78; William A. Gordon, *Compilation of Registers of the Army of the United States* (Washington, 1837), 42; James, *Andrew Jackson: Border Captain*, 186.
26. "Call Journal," 78-80; James, *Andrew Jackson: Border Captain*, 210.
27. James, *Andrew Jackson: Border Captain*, 192-193, 195.

28. "Call Journal," 77.
29. *Ibid.*, 81-82; James, *Andrew Jackson: Border Captain*, 210-211; Albert James Pickett, *History of Alabama and Incidentally of Georgia and Mississippi, from the Earliest Period* (Sheffield, Ala., 1896), 608.
30. "Call Journal," 83-84; James, *Andrew Jackson: Border Captain*, 211, 213.
31. Jackson to A. P. Hayne, January 25, 1815, in Parton, *Andrew Jackson*, II, 275; Gordon, *Army Register*, Appendix, 5.
32. James, *Andrew Jackson: Border Captain*, 287-288; Gordon, *Army Register*, 65, 71.
33. Call to Daniel Parker, June 23, 1815, August 31, 1816, Call to Edmund P. Gaines, October 16, 1817, Misc. letters recd., Adjutant General's Office, War Department.
34. L. Cross to Call, February [?], 1818, in Caroline Mays Brevard, *History of Florida from the Treaty of 1763 to Our Own Times*, 2 volumes (De-Land, Fla., 1924), I, 255; "Testimony of R. K. Call," in *State Papers*, 15 Congress, 2 Session, No. 100.
35. Call to Don José Masot, February 24, 1818, Call papers, Southern Historical Collection, University of North Carolina Library, hereinafter cited as Call papers, UNC; Masot to Call, February [?], 1818, in Brevard, *History of Florida*, I, 256-257.
36. Calhoun to Jackson, December 26, 1817, in *State Papers*, 15 Congress, 2 Session, No. 14.
37. Jackson to Calhoun, March 25, 1818, in *ibid.;* "Testimony of R. K. Call," in *State Papers*, 15 Congress, 2 Session, No. 100; Mark F. Boyd, "Events at Prospect Bluff on the Apalachicola River, 1808-1818," *Florida Historical Quarterly*, XVI (October, 1937), 89-90.
38. Jackson to Calhoun, April 8, 1818, in *State Papers*, 15 Congress, 2 Session, No. 14.
39. Masot to Jackson, April 15, 1818, in Bassett, *Jackson Correspondence*, II, 359; "Report of the Senate Committee to inquire into the advance of United States troops into West Florida," *State Papers*, 15 Congress, 2 Session, No. 100.
40. James, *Andrew Jackson: Border Captain*, 307, 314.
41. Jackson to Calhoun, June 2, 1818, in Bassett, *Jackson Correspondence*, II, 379.
42. Jackson to James Monroe, June 2, 1818, in *ibid.*, II, 377.
43. Jackson to Call, August [?], 1818, in Ellen Call Long, "Call Journal," 156. Call's personal journal ends with the Battle of New Orleans in 1814-1815. In later years his daughter Ellen Call Long sought to complete it, primarily from letters and her memory. To distinguish this portion of the journal from that written by Call himself, it will be designated as Ellen C. Long, "Call Journal." See also Jackson to the Senate of the United States, March 6, 1820, in *State Papers*, 16 Congress, 1 Session, No. 73.
44. Jackson to Call, August 5, 1818, in Ellen C. Long, "Call Journal," 155-156.
45. Jackson to Call, August [?], 1818, in *ibid.*, 156; James, *Andrew Jackson: Border Captain*, 316-317.
46. Parton, *Andrew Jackson*, II, 533, 549-551.
47. Deposition by Call, July 30, 1819, Jackson papers, Library of Congress.
48. James C. Bronaugh to Call, March 18, 1820, Call papers, Florida Historical Society Library, hereinafter cited as Call papers, FHS; Parton, *Andrew Jackson*, II, 557.

49. Deposition by Call, July 30, 1819, Jackson papers; Parton, *Andrew Jackson*, II, 565, 568; James, *Andrew Jackson: Border Captain*, 324-326.
50. Bronaugh to Call, March 18, 1820, Call papers, FHS; Ellen C. Long, "Call Journal," 157.
51. Call to Andrew Erwin, September 4, 1819, Call papers, FHS; Call to Jackson, November 15, 1819, in Clarence Edwin Carter (ed.), *The Territorial Papers of the United States*, 22 volumes (Washington, 1934-19--), XVIII, 736.
52. Jackson to Calhoun, July 9, 1820, Bassett, *Jackson Correspondence*, III, 29.
53. Call to Jackson, July 8, July 12, July 16, and August 17, 1820, Jackson papers; Commission of Captain R. K. Call, August 10, 1820, Call papers, UNC.
54. Ellen C. Long, "Call Journal," 163, 167; Marquis James, *Andrew Jackson: Portrait of a President* (Indianapolis, 1937), 84.
55. Rachel Jackson to Call, October 3, 1820, Ms collections, Virginia Historical Society, Richmond, Virginia.

2

From Military to Political Life

1. James Monroe to Jackson, January 24, 1821, Bassett, *Jackson Correspondence*, III, 38; James, *Andrew Jackson: Border Captain*, 336-337. For a detailed account of the transfer negotiations and Jackson's days in Florida see Herbert J. Doherty, Jr., "The Governorship of Andrew Jackson," *Florida Historical Quarterly*, XXXIII (July, 1954), 3-31, and Doherty, "Andrew Jackson v. the Spanish Governor," *ibid.*, XXXIV (October, 1955), 142-158.
2. John Quincy Adams to Jackson, March 12, 1821, Jackson to Adams, April 12, 1821, in *Senate Papers*, 17 Congress, 1 Session, No. 1.
3. Parton, *Andrew Jackson*, II, 615-616; Claude M. Newlin, "Henry M. Brackenridge," *Dictionary of American Biography*, ed. Allen Johnson *et al.*, 21 volumes (New York, 1928-44), II, 543-544.
4. Jackson to Adams, July 30, 1821, Jackson papers; Jackson to Adams, May 1, 1821, Bassett, *Jackson Correspondence*, III, 52.
5. Jackson to Call, May 11, 1821, in Brevard, *History of Florida*, I, 260.
6. Call to Jackson, May 21, 1821, Callava to Call, May 14, 1821, in *Senate Papers*, 17 Congress, 1 Session, No. 1; Ms. diary fragments, Call papers, UNC.
7. Call to Jackson, May 21, 1821, *loc. cit.*; Jackson to Gadsden, May 21, 1821, Call papers, UNC.
8. Gadsden to Call, June 5, 1821, Call papers, UNC.
9. Jackson to James C. Bronaugh, June 9, 1821, Bassett, *Jackson Correspondence*, III, 65.
10. Monroe to Jackson, May 23, 1821, in Stanislaus M. Hamilton (ed.), *The Writings of James Monroe*, 7 volumes (New York, 1902), VI, 184-185.
11. A. J. Donelson to [?], n.d., cited in Ellen C. Long, "Call Journal," 176; Rachel Jackson to [a brother], August 25, 1821, cited in Parton, *Andrew Jackson*, II, 610.

12. Jackson to Bronaugh, June 9, 1821, Bassett, *Jackson Correspondence*, III, 65.   13. Callava to Jackson, June 10, 1821, *ibid.*, 66.
14. Jackson to Callava, June 12, 1821, *ibid.*, 67; Jackson to Call, June 12, 1821, *ibid.*, 69-70; Adams to Jackson, March 23, 1821, *ibid.*, 45; Call to Jackson, June 23, 1821, *ibid.*, 78; Call to Callava, June 15, 1821, Ms. letter in P. K. Yonge Library of Florida History, University of Florida.
15. Ms. diary fragments, Call papers, UNC; Jackson to Adams, June 29, 1821, in *Senate Papers*, 17 Congress, 1 Session, No. 1; Parton, *Andrew Jackson*, II, 600.
16. Ms. diary fragments, Call papers, UNC; Pensacola *Floridian*, August 18, 1821; Rachel Jackson to Eliza Kingsley, June 23, 1821, in Parton, *Andrew Jackson*, II, 605-606; William G. Dodd, "Theatrical Entertainment in Early Florida," *Florida Historical Quarterly*, XXV (October, 1946), 125.
17. Jackson to Adams, July 17, 18, 1821, in *Senate Papers*, 17 Congress, 1 Session, No. 1; James, *Andrew Jackson: Border Captain*, 344-345.
18. Jackson to W. G. D. Worthington, July 26, 1821, Jackson papers.
19. Jackson to John C. Calhoun, July 29, 1821, Jackson papers; David Y. Thomas, *A History of Military Government in Newly Acquired Territory of the United States* (New York, 1904), 69.
20. Pensacola *Floridian*, August 18, September 1, 1821, June 1, 1822; William G. Dodd, "Theatrical Entertainment in Early Florida," *loc. cit.*, 126.
21. Rachel Jackson to Eliza Kingsley, July 23, 1821, in Parton, *Andrew Jackson*, II, 604, 605, 606.   22. Pensacola *Floridian*, August 18, 1821.
23. The documentary story of the Vidal case is found in *State Papers*, 17 Congress, 1 Session, No. 42. See also James, *Andrew Jackson: Border Captain*, 349-355.
24. Call to the People of Florida, April 17, 1833, Call papers, FHS.
25. Ellen C. Long, "Call Journal," 177; Long, *Florida Breezes; or, Florida, New and Old* (Jacksonville, 1882), 80.
26. Pensacola *Floridian*, October 15, 1821; Parton, *Andrew Jackson*, II, 610.
27. Call to Jackson, October 14, 1821, Bassett, *Jackson Correspondence*, III, 129n.   28. Jackson to Call, November 15, 1821, *ibid.*, 130.
29. Jackson to Call, November 4, 1821, Call papers, UNC.
30. Jackson to Call, December 14, 1821, *ibid.*; Jackson to Call, November 15, 1821, *loc. cit.*, 131.
31. Rachel Jackson to Call, December 15, 1821, Call papers, UNC.
32. Call to Jackson, November 26, 1821, Jackson papers.
33. Mary L. Kirkman to Mrs. Thomas Kirkman, November 7, 1821, Call papers, UNC.   34. Call to Jackson, November 19, 1821, Jackson papers.
35. Brackenridge to Caesar A. Rodney, December 20, 1821, Ms. collections of the Historical Society of Pennsylvania, Philadelphia.
36. Jackson to Monroe, October 5, 1821, Call to Jackson, October 30, 1821, Jackson papers; Thomas, *Military Government*, 98.
37. Book of Consular and Miscellaneous Officers, 1789-1868, 353, State Department, National Archives.
38. Special Order No. 5, Headquarters Western Department, January 15, 1822, and Daniel E. Burch to Call, May 25, 1822, Call papers, UNC.
39. Call to Rachel Jackson, February 2, 1822, Jackson papers.
40. Call to Jackson, November 26, 1821, Jackson papers.
41. Long, *Florida Breezes*, 142. See also Tallahassee *Floridian*, March 30, 1833; Apalachicola *Florida Journal*, March 17, 1841.

42. "Junius" to the *Floridian*, n.d., Tallahassee *Floridian*, March 9, 30, 1833.
43. Pensacola *Floridian*, June 15, 1822.
44. *Ibid.*, August 10, 1822; Call to the People of Florida, April 17, 1833, Call papers, FHS.   45. Jackson to Call, May 20, 1822, Jackson papers.
46. Daniel Call to R. K. Call, n.d., cited in Ellen C. Long, "Call Journal," 179.   47. Pensacola *Floridian*, July 20, 27, 1822.
48. Commission of R. K. Call, January 28, 1823, Call papers, UNC; Brackenridge to Jackson, February 4, 1824, Jackson papers.
49. Pensacola *Floridian*, April 26, 1823; St. Augustine *East Florida Herald*, June 7, 1823.   50. *Ibid.*, May 31, June 7, 21, 1823.
51. *Ibid.*, September 27, 1823; James, *Andrew Jackson: President*, 61.
52. Call to Jackson, October 2, 1823, Jackson papers; Jackson to Rachel Jackson, November 19, 1823, Bassett, *Jackson Correspondence*, III, 215.
53. Jackson to Rachel Jackson, December 7, 1823, *ibid.*, 215.
54. Jackson to Rachel Jackson, March 2, 1824, *ibid.*, 233.
55. *Journal of the House of Representatives of the United States*, 18 Congress, 1 Session, 40, 163, 574.   56. *Ibid.*, 73, 337, 602.
57. *Annals of Congress*, 18 Congress, 1 Session, 292, 294.
58. Call was supported in debate by John Cocke of Tennessee, David Trimble and Robert P. Henry of Kentucky, Henry H. Gurley of Louisiana, Peter Sharpe of New York, and Joseph Hemphill of Pennsylvania. *Annals of Congress*, 18 Congress, 1 Session, 926-930, 932.
59. *Ibid.*, 2585, 2600-02. Congressmen who opposed Call's amendment were Mark Alexander and William McCoy of Virginia, John Brown of Pennsylvania, and Christopher Rankin of Mississippi. The latter favored a money grant to the canal company rather than a land grant.
60. *U.S. House Journal*, 18 Congress, 1 Session, 363, 587.
61. *U.S. Statutes at Large*, III, 656.
62. Memorial of the Legislative Council in *State Papers*, 17 Congress, 1 Session, No. 53.
63. *U.S. Statutes at Large*, IV, 45-46; *U.S. House Journal*, 18 Congress, 1 Session, 166, 281, 602.
64. Commission of Benjamin D. Wright, May 27, 1824, Misc. Permanent Commissions, Book E, State Department, National Archives.
65. *U.S. Statutes at Large*, IV, 47; *U.S. House Journal*, 18 Congress, 1 Session, 199, 602.
66. *State Papers*, 17 Congress, 2 Session, No. 53, and 18 Congress, 1 Session, No. 36.
67. Alfred J. Hanna, *A Prince in their Midst* (Norman, Okla., 1946), 59.
68. Ms. diary fragments, Call papers, UNC.
69. James, *Andrew Jackson: President*, 71.
70. Meade Minnigerode, *Some American Ladies, Seven Informal Biographies* (New York, 1926), 254, 258.
71. Ben Perley Poore, *Perley's Reminiscences of Sixty Years in the National Metropolis*, 2 volumes (Philadephia, 1886), I, 120, 123.
72. [Call to Jackson], July 23, 1829, Call papers, UNC. This is an eight-page fragment of a letter in Call's hand, giving his version of the events of 1824 and later controversies regarding Eaton and his wife. Internal evidence makes it plain that it was directed to Jackson, though it may never have been sent.
73. *Ibid.*, and Call to Jackson, April 28, 1829, Jackson papers.
74. [Call to Jackson], July 23, 1829, Call papers, UNC.

75. Jackson to William B. Lewis, September 10, 1829, Bassett, *Jackson Correspondence*, IV, 72-73; Jackson to Call, July 5, 1829, *ibid.*, 50-53.
76. [Call to Jackson], July 23, 1829, Call papers, UNC.
77. Martin Van Buren, *The Autobiography of Martin Van Buren*, ed. John C. Fitzpatrick (Washington, 1920), 344, 408.
78. John Floyd, *The Life and Diary of John Floyd*, ed. C. H. Ambler (Richmond, 1918), 149; J. Franklin Jameson, "Preface," *Jackson Correspondence*, ed. Bassett, IV, iii.
79. [Call to Jackson], July 23, 1829, Call papers, UNC; Lewis to Jackson, July 2, 1829, Bassett, *Jackson Correspondence*, IV, 51n.
80. Ellen C. Long, "Call Journal," 191; James, *Andrew Jackson: President*, 84.   81. *Ibid.*, 84-85.
82. Call to Calhoun, September 17, 1824, Consolidated file, Quartermaster General, War Department, National Archives; Call to Southard, September 17, 1824, Misc. letters recd. 1824, Book 5, Navy Department, National Archives; Ellen C. Long, "Call Journal," 191.
83. *Pensacola Gazette*, September 25, 1824.
84. *Ibid.*, October 9, 1824; Ellen C. Long, "Call Journal," 191.
85. James, *Andrew Jackson: President*, 100.
86. Call to John P. Van Ness, February 4, 1828, in *United States Telegraph —Extra*, I (May 10, 1828), 196.
87. Thomas Jesup to Call, January 14, 1825, Letters sent, Book 7, Quartermaster General, War Department, National Archives; *U.S. House Journal*, 18 Congress, 2 Session, 128, 313.
88. *Ibid.*, 281, 317; *Register of Debates in Congress*, 18 Congress, 2 Session, 738.
89. Edgar Macon to Call, February 2, 1825, copy in Ms. "Florida Territorial Records," Territorial Records Office, National Archives.
90. *Register of Debates in Congress*, 18 Congress, 2 Session, 438-440; *U.S. House Journal*, 18 Congress, 2 Session, 197-198.
91. *Reports of Committees of the House of Representatives*, 18 Congress, 2 Session, No. 87.
92. Joseph L. Smith to the Public, March 3, 1825, in *Pensacola Gazette*, April 30, 1825.
93. *Acts of the Legislative Council of the Territory of Florida: Passed at their Second Session, 1823* (Pensacola, 1823), 136-137.
94. Call to Smith, n.d., in *Pensacola Gazette*, May 7, 1825.
95. *Pensacola Gazette*, January 1, 1825.   96. *Ibid.*, February 5, 1825.
97. *Ibid.*, January 8, 22, 1825.   98. *Ibid.*, January 29, 1825.
99. *Ibid.*, January 22, February 25, 1825. See also White to the People of Florida, n.d., in *ibid.*, June 4, 1825.   100. *Ibid.*, February 5, 1825.
101. "A Citizen of Jackson County" to Call, March 12, 1825, in *ibid.*, April 2, 1825.
102. "Plain Truth" to the Editor, n.d., in *ibid.*, February 26, 1825.
103. "A Citizen of Jackson County" to Call, March 12, 1825, *loc. cit.*
104. Andrew Stewart to Call, February 19, 1825, Call papers, FHS.
105. Quoted in *Pensacola Gazette*, June 25, 1825.
106. *Ibid.*, March 19, 1825; George Graham to Call, February 28, 1825, Misc. letters sent, Book 14, General Land Office, National Archives.

3

Reaping the Unearned Increment

1. *Pensacola Gazette,* April 23, 30, 1825; Jackson to Call, May 26, 1825, in Ellen C. Long, "Call Journal," 192.
2. John Lee Williams to Call, November 20, 1823, Call papers, UNC; Call to Jackson, October 2, 1823, Jackson papers; *Pensacola Gazette,* September 24, 1825.
3. *Ibid.,* October 23, November 13, 1824, April 9, 1825; Butler to George Graham, November 15, 1824, Letters recd. from Surveyors General, General Land Office, National Archives. For a more detailed treatment of the growth of the "Nucleus" see Doherty, "Andrew Jackson's Cronies in Florida Territorial Politics," *Florida Historical Quarterly,* XXXIV (July, 1955), 3-29.   4. *Pensacola Gazette,* April 9, June 4, 1825.
5. Call to the People of Florida, n.d., Call papers, UNC.
6. Jackson to Call, July 24, 1825, Call papers, UNC.
7. *Pensacola Gazette,* September 24, 1825.   8. *Ibid.,* December 24, 1825.
9. Call to Jackson, September 23, 1825, Jackson papers; Ellen C. Long, "Call Journal," 192.
10. Call to Jackson, September 23, 1825, Jackson papers; Dorothy Dodd, "The Florida Census of 1825," *Florida Historical Quarterly,* XXII (July, 1943), 36.
11. Testimony of John H. Eaton in *State Papers,* 15 Congress, 2 Session, No. 100, 43-44; *State Papers,* 18 Congress, 2 Session, No. 111, 87; *Niles' Register,* July 10, 1819.
12. Williams to Call, November 1, 1823, Call papers, UNC.
13. Kathryn T. Abbey, "The Story of the Lafayette Lands in Florida," *Florida Historical Quarterly,* X (January, 1932), 115-121.
14. George Graham to Robert Butler, March 2, 1825, Letters to Surveyors General, General Land Office, National Archives.
15. Lafayette to Call, January 9, 1831, Ms. collections, Virginia Historical Society. See also Graham to Lafayette, March 9, 1825, Misc. letters sent, Book 14, McKee to Graham, April 21, 1825, Misc. letters recd., Book M, General Land Office, National Archives; Ms. diary fragments, Call papers, UNC; Tallahassee *Florida Advocate,* January 29, 1829.
16. Lafayette to Call, January 1, 1826, in Caroline M. Brevard, "Richard Keith Call," *Florida Historical Quarterly,* I (July, 1908), 10-11; Call to Graham, August 3, 1830, Misc. letters recd., General Land Office, National Archives; Abbey, "Story of the Lafayette Lands," *loc. cit.,* 126.
17. Graham to Call and Butler, December 16, 1826, Misc. letters sent, Book 18, General Land Office, National Archives.
18. Call to Jackson, September 23, 1825, Jackson papers.
19. Jackson to Call, March 9, 1826, Bassett, *Jackson Correspondence,* VI, 481. See also Call to Graham, December 2, 1825, Misc. letters recd., General Land Office, National Archives.
20. Jackson to Call, April 9, July 25, September 30, 1826, Call papers, UNC.
21. Edwin H. Ewing to [?], August 20, 1847, Call papers, UNC.

22. Call to Jackson, November 8, 1826, Jackson papers; Jackson to Call, July 1, 1827, Bassett, *Jackson Correspondence*, VI, 495; Edwin H. Ewing to S. W. Carmack, November 25, 1846, Call papers, UNC.
23. *U.S. House Journal*, 19 Congress, 1 Session, 93, 129, 177, 233.
24. Elias B. Gould to Adams, January 9, 1826, Henry Clay to Macon, April 6, 1826, Macon to Clay, April 25, 1826, in Ms. "Florida Territorial Papers," Territorial Records Office, National Archives.
25. Burch to Call, April 19, 1826, Call papers, FHS.
26. Ramage to Call, August 3, 1826, Call papers, FHS; *Pensacola Gazette*, September 22, 1826.
27. Call to White, n.d., Call papers, FHS.
28. White to Ramage, September 28, 1826, Ramage to Call, October 16, 18, 1826, Call papers, FHS.
29. Tallahassee *Florida Intelligencer*, October 27, 1826.
30. Henry Yonge to W. Hasell Hunt, December 10, 1826 in *Pensacola Gazette*, December 21, 1826.
31. Jackson to Call, n.d., in Ellen C. Long, "Call Journal," 165.
32. John Quincy Adams, *Memoirs of John Quincy Adams*, ed. Charles Francis Adams, 12 volumes (Philadelphia, 1874-77), VII, 220.
33. Call to Jackson, November 8, 1826, Jackson papers.
34. "Georgian" to the Editor, n.d., in Tallahassee *Floridian and Advocate*, December 21, 1831.
35. Jacob Robinson to the Editor, March 25, 1833, in Tallahassee *Floridian*, April 6, 1833.
36. Call to Graham, March 20, 1827, Misc. letters recd., Graham to Call, February 25, 1827, Misc. letters sent, General Land Office, National Archives.
37. "Q in a Corner" to the Editor, n.d., in Tallahassee *Floridian*, February 9, 1833.
38. Green to Call, December 11, 1828, Duff Green papers, Library of Congress.
39. White to the Editor, June 4, 1829, in Tallahassee *Florida Advocate*, June 13, 1829.
40. Leon County Deed Books, County Courthouse, Tallahassee, Fla.; Receipt Book Public Land Sales, 1825-31, Tallahassee, Florida, in Records of the States of the United States of America, ed. William S. Jenkins, microfilmed by the Library of Congress, 1949.
41. *U.S. Statutes at Large*, IV, 126; *Senate Documents*, 26 Congress, 1 Session, No. 449.
42. White to DuVal, n.d., in Tallahassee *Floridian and Advocate*, February 24, 1831.   43. Call to Jackson, September 5, 1827, Jackson papers.
44. Jackson to Call, May 3, 1827, Bassett, *Jackson Correspondence*, III, 354-355.   45. George W. Call to Jackson, July 11, 1827, Jackson papers.
46. Reverdy Johnson to Call, n.d., copy in Call papers, UNC; Call to Editor, *United States Telegraph*, n.d., copy in Call papers, FHS.
47. *Niles' Register*, January 5, 1828.
48. Call to Van Ness, February 4, 1828, in *United States Telegraph—Extra*, May 10, 1828; Call to Wickliff, February 19, 1828, Personal papers: R. K. Call, Library of Congress.
49. Jackson to Call, August 16, 1828, Bassett, *Jackson Correspondence*, III, 426-427.

50. Call to Jackson, August 19, 1828, Jackson papers; Parton, *Andrew Jackson*, III, 155-156, 165.
51. *Ibid.*, 185-186; James, *Andrew Jackson: President*, 210, 212-213.
52. [Call to Jackson], July 23, 1829, Call papers, UNC.
53. James, *Andrew Jackson: President*, 210-211; Parton, *Andrew Jackson*, III, 186.
54. Jackson to Ezra Stiles Ely, April 10, 1829, in Parton, *Andrew Jackson*, III, 192-195.   55. Call to Jackson, April 28, 1829, Jackson papers.
56. Jackson to Call, May 18, 1829, Bassett, *Jackson Correspondence*, IV, 34-36.   57. Jackson to Call, July 5, 1829, *ibid.*, 50-53.
58. [Call to Jackson], July 23, 1829, Call papers, UNC.   59. *Ibid.*
60. Call to Joseph M. White, n.d., in *Niles' Register*, June 13, 1829.
61. Berrien to Jackson, March 28, 1829, Attorney General Letterbook A, Justice Department, National Archives.
62. Call to Jackson, July 13, 1829, Jackson papers. See also Jackson to Call, July 31, 1829, and Green to Call, June 20, 1832, as cited in Call to the People of Florida, n.d., in Tallahassee *Floridian*, April 13, 1833.
63. Branch to Call, October 15, 1829, Call papers, FHS.

4

Defending the Public Domain

1. Leon County Tax Book, 1829, Florida State Library, Tallahassee, Fla.; W. H. Carter, "History of St. John's Church, Tallahassee," *Semi-Centennial of the Diocese of Florida Held in Tallahassee: January 18 and 19, 1888* (Jacksonville, Fla., 1889), App. C, 4, 8; T. Frederick Davis, "Pioneer Florida," *Florida Historical Quarterly*, XXIV (April, 1946), 293.
2. George Graham to Call, March 26, 1829, Misc. letters sent, General Land Office, National Archives; *U.S. Statutes at Large*, IV, 284-286.
3. Wirt to Adams, July 26, 1828, Attorney General's Opinions, Book C, Justice Department, National Archives.
4. White to Graham, August 14, 1828, Letters from the Sec. of the Treasury to the General Land Office, Treasury Department, National Archives.
5. Graham to White, August 28, 1828, Misc. letters sent, General Land Office, National Archives; White to Graham, August 14, 1828, *loc. cit.*
6. Graham to Jackson, March 9, 1829, Graham to Call, March 26, 1829, Misc. letters sent, General Land Office, National Archives.
7. Berrien to Jackson, March 28, 1829, Attorney General Letterbook A, Justice Department, National Archives.
8. Jackson to Berrien, March 30, 1829, in Tallahassee *Floridian*, May 11, 1833.
9. Call to Graham, March 30, 1829, Misc. letters recd., General Land Office, National Archives; Hamilton to Call, March 30, 1829, Instructions to U. S. Ministers, Vol. 12, State Department, National Archives.
10. Call to Hamilton, March 27, 1829, Misc. letters, State Department, National Archives; Alfred J. Hanna, "Diplomatic Missions of the United States to Cuba to Secure the Spanish Archives of Florida," *Hispanic American Essays*, ed. A. Curtis Wilgus (Chapel Hill, 1942), 209-214.

11. Hamilton to Call, March 30, 1829, *loc. cit.;* Thomas Douglas to Graham, August 5, 1829, Misc. letters recd., General Land Office, National Archives.
12. Call to Jackson, April 28, 1829, Jackson to Call, June 13, 1829, Jackson papers.
13. Call to Van Buren, July 26, 1829, Misc. letters, State Department, National Archives; Call to Graham, July 26, 1829, Misc. letters recd., General Land Office, National Archives.
14. Call to Van Buren, March 28, 1830, Florida Archives, envelope 7, State Department, National Archives. William Shaler was Jackson's replacement for Thomas M. Rodney, whose removal Call had recommended. Call had suggested Vincent Gray for the post. Call to Jackson, April 28, 1829, Jackson papers. 15. Call to Van Buren, March 28, 1830, *loc. cit.* 16. *Ibid.*
17. *Ibid.;* Call to Graham, March 20, 1830, Misc. letters recd., General Land Office, National Archives; Call to Van Buren, March 23, 1830, Florida Archives, envelope 7, State Department, National Archives; Ms. diary fragments, Call papers, UNC.
18. Call to Van Buren, March 28, 1830, *loc. cit.;* D. Hunter Miller (ed.), *Treaties and Other International Acts of the United States of America,* 8 volumes (Washington, 1931-48), III, 9.
19. *Mitchel et al. v. United States,* 9 Peters, 716; Alfred J. Hanna, "Diplomatic Missions of the United States to Cuba to Secure the Spanish Archives of Florida," *loc. cit.,* 219.
20. Gustavus Myers, *History of the Supreme Court of the United States* (Chicago, 1925), 340. Obvious errors in the treatment of these land cases suggest that Myers' work should be used with caution.
21. Charles Warren, *The Supreme Court in United States History,* 2 volumes (Boston, 1937), I, 783.
22. *Ibid.,* 782; *United States v. Arredondo,* 6 Peters, 705.
23. *Ibid.,* 705-706.   24. *Ibid.,* 745-746, 749.
25. *Ibid.,* 721-723, 725-726, 734; Warren, *The Supreme Court,* I, 782-783.
26. Call to Elijah Hayward, November 1, 1832, Misc. letters recd., General Land Office, National Archives.
27. Call to Graham, June 2, 1829, Call to Elijah Hayward, March 13, 1831, Misc. letters recd., General Land Office, National Archives.
28. *Mitchel et al. v. United States,* 9 Peters, 719-722, 730-731. See also Call to Van Buren, March 28, 1830, Florida Archives, envelope 7, State Department, National Archives.
29. Livingston to R. K. Kall [*sic*], May 7, 1832, Domestic letters sent, State Department, National Archives; *Mitchel et al. v. United States,* 9 Peters, 723-724.
30. Robinson to Call, May 28, 1832, Call to Robinson, June 3, 1832, in "Jeremy Robinson Journal," II, 39-43, Florida Archives, State Department, National Archives.
31. Alfred J. Hanna, "Diplomatic Missions of the United States to Cuba to Secure the Spanish Archives of Florida," *loc. cit.,* 220, 222-223, 228-230, 232.
32. Taney to Jackson, May 22, 1832, Attorney General Letterbook A, Justice Department, National Archives.
33. *United States v. George J. F. Clarke,* 8 Peters, 451; Butler to Louis McLane, February 15, 1834, Misc. letters sent, Book A2, Justice Department, National Archives; Tallahassee *Floridian,* February 15, March 8, 1834.

34. *United States v. George J. F. Clarke,* 8 Peters, 468-469.
35. *United States v. Frances Richard, United States v. Antonio Huertas, United States v. Eusebio M. Gomez, United States v. George Fleming's heirs, United States v. Moses Levi, United States v. Philip R. Younge, United States v. Joseph H. Hernandez, United States v. John Huertas, United States v. Francis P. Fatio's and Louisa Hallowes's Heirs, United States v. William Gibson et al.,* 8 Peters, 470-494.
36. Call to Butler, December 11, December 25, 1834, Misc. letters recd., Justice Department, National Archives.
37. "Parochial Records of St. John's Episcopal Church, Tallahassee, Florida, 1832-1880," 11, 36, typescript copy in P. K. Yonge Library of Florida History, University of Florida; Ellen C. Long, "Call Journal," 198.
38. Butler to Call, January 19, 1835, Misc. letters sent, Book A2, Justice Department, National Archives.
39. Butler to Levi Woodbury, January 21, 1835, Butler to William H. Cabell, January 16, 1835, Misc. letters sent, Book A2, Justice Department, National Archives.
40. *Mitchel et al. v. United States,* 9 Peters, 724.   41. *Ibid.,* 725-761.
42. *Ibid.,* 730-732; see also Call to Levi Woodbury, November 4, 1835, in *Executive Documents,* 24 Congress, 1 Session, No. 14, 6-32.
43. Call to A. J. Donaldson [*sic*], March 23, 1835, Donelson papers, Library of Congress. (Throughout his life Call misspelled the name Donelson.)
44. Call to Levi Woodbury, November 4, 1835, *loc. cit.* Gustavus Myers reprints much of this letter in his *Supreme Court,* 347-354, but he was under the delusion that Call was Assistant Attorney General.
45. *Mitchel et al. v. United States,* 9 Peters, 724.   46. *Ibid.,* 728, 761.
47. Call to Butler, April 17, 1835, Letters recd., Butler to Call, March 31, 1835, Misc. letters sent, Book A2, Justice Department, National Archives.
48. Myers, *Supreme Court,* 353-354. 49. Warren, *The Supreme Court,* I, 782.
50. Ernest Sutherland Bates, *The Story of the Supreme Court* (Indianapolis, 1936), 135.
51. Call to Butler, June 8, 1834, Misc. letters recd., Justice Department, National Archives.   52. Call to Woodbury, November 4, 1835, *loc. cit.*

5

To the "Nucleus" Go the Spoils

1. DuVal to Jackson, April 21, 1829, copy in Ms. "Florida Territorial Papers," in Territorial Records Office, National Archives.
2. Adams, *Memoirs,* VIII, 172, 176-177. See also White to Van Buren, February 28, 1830, Misc. letters recd., State Department, National Archives.
3. *Niles' Register,* April 3, 1830; Tallahassee *Florida Advocate,* February 7, 1829; James Owen Knauss, *Territorial Florida Journalism* (DeLand, Fla., 1926), 23-25.
4. Tallahassee *Floridian and Advocate,* December 28, 1830.
5. *Ibid.,* January 6, February 24, 1831.
6. Knauss, *Territorial Florida Journalism,* 25-26, 65-66.
7. Van Buren to Samuel Brents, June 2, 1829, Domestic letters sent, State Department, National Archives; *Journal of the Senate of the United States of America,* 22 Congress, 1 Session, 494; *Niles' Register,* March 28, 1829.

8. Tallahassee *Floridian and Advocate,* October 26, 1830.
9. *Ibid.,* November 9, 16, December 21, 1830.
10. "Orlando" to Editor, n.d., in *ibid.,* November 30, 1830; "Georgian" to Editor, n.d., in *ibid.,* February 3, 1831.
11. *Ibid.,* February 3, March 3, 17, 1831.   12. *Ibid.,* May 19, June 2, 1831.
13. White to Van Buren, March 16, 1831, in *ibid.,* April 14, 1831; R. C. Allen to H. L. White, February 3, 1831, in *ibid.,* July 28, 1831; Wyatt to the Public, n.d., in Tallahassee *Floridian,* September 18, October 23, 1832, January 5, 1833.
14. R. C. Allen to H. L. White, February 3, 1831, *loc. cit.*
15. Tallahassee *Floridian and Advocate,* July 7, August 10, 1831.
16. Tallahassee *Floridian,* September 25, 1832; Dorothy E. Hill, "Joseph M. White, Florida's Territorial Delegate 1825-1837," unpublished M.A. thesis (University of Florida, 1950), 96-97.
17. *U. S. Senate Journal,* 22 Congress, 1 Session, 497, 510-511; Tallahassee *Floridian,* September 18, October 23, 1832.
18. Notes made by Robinson in Tallahassee, June 3, 1832, envelope 6, Florida Archives, State Department, National Archives.
19. Wright to Call, May 27, 1832, Call papers, FHS.
20. Tallahassee *Floridian,* May 4, 1833.   21. *Ibid.,* April 6, 1833.
22. Call to the People of Florida, April 17, 1833, copy in Call papers, FHS.
23. Tallahassee *Floridian,* June 12, 1832, February 9, 1833.
24. *Ibid.,* April 13, 1833.   25. *Ibid.,* March 23, 1833.
26. *Ibid.,* March 2, 1833.   27. *Ibid.,* April 27, 1833.
28. "A Floridian" to Editor, April 15, 1833, in *ibid.,* April 20, 1833.
29. Long, *Florida Breezes,* 97-98.
30. White to Call, April 12, 1833, Call papers, FHS.
31. Call to the People, n.d., in Tallahassee *Floridian,* April 13, 1833.
32. Jackson to Call, July 14, 1833, in Ellen C. Long, "Call Journal," 197-198.
33. Gadsden to Call, October 11, 1833, Call papers, FHS; J. Fred Rippy, "James Gadsden," *Dictionary of American Biography,* VII, 83-84.
34. Daisy Parker, "R. K. Call: Whig Leader," *Tallahassee Historical Society Annual: 1939* (Tallahassee, 1939), 17; Reginald C. McGrane, *Foreign Bondholders and American State Debts* (New York, 1935), 224.
35. *Executive Documents,* 26 Congress, 2 Session, No. 111, 278, 293-296.
36. Tallahassee *Floridian,* June 12, 1832.
37. Henry M. Brackenridge, *Judge Brackenridge's Letters* (n.p., n.d.), 1-3.
38. Statement of Joseph L. Smith, January, 1832, copy from House files in Ms. "Florida Territorial Papers," Territorial Records Office, National Archives.
39. Stephen F. Miller, *The Bench and Bar of Georgia: Memoirs and Sketches,* 2 volumes (Philadelphia, 1858), I, 201-203.
40. White to William Wilson, May 28, 1832, in Tallahassee *Floridian,* June 12, 1832.
41. "Diary of Robert Raymond Reid 1833, 1835," 2 volumes (transcript by Historical Records Survey, W. P. A., 1939), I, 1.   42. *Ibid.,* 2.
43. *Ibid.,* 1.   44. *Ibid.,* II, 2.   45. *Ibid.,* I, 37.
46. *Ibid.,* 2-3.   47. *Ibid.,* 18; II, 6, 8.
48. Murat to Gadsden, n.d., in Hill, "Joseph M. White," 118.
49. Tallahassee *Floridian,* May 17, 1834.
50. *Ibid.,* December 13, 1834, March 14, April 11, 1835.
51. "Reid Journal," II, 2-3.   52. *Ibid.*

6

A Frontier Entrepreneur

1. Call to George Graham, August 3, 1830, Misc. letters recd., General Land Office, National Archives.
2. Lafayette to Call, January 1, [1826], in Brevard, "Richard Keith Call," *loc. cit.*, 10-11.
3. Lafayette to Call, January 9, 1831, Ms. collections, Virginia Historical Society.
4. Abbey, "Story of the Lafayette Lands," *loc. cit.*, 127-128.
5. John P. Kennedy, *Memoirs of the Life of William Wirt*, 2 volumes (Philadelphia, 1850), II, 201, 335.
6. Wirt to Laura Randall, December 7, 1827, in *ibid.*, 206-207.
7. Wirt to William Pope, March 23, 1828, in *ibid.*, 211.
8. Wirt to Louis Goldsborough, March 30, 1833, in *ibid.*, 342.
9. Wirt to Mrs. Wirt, January 31, 1833, in *ibid.*, 337.
10. Wirt to Goldsborough, February 15, 1833, in *ibid.*, 339. Either Wirt was according Call an honorary title or the word "General" was miscopied "Governor" in transcribing this letter into the *Memoirs*, for Call did not become Governor of Florida until 1836.
11. Wirt to Goldsborough, July 18, 1833, in *ibid.*, 343; *ibid.*, 335.
12. Wirt to Randall, July 29, 1833, in *ibid.*, 344.
13. Albert H. Roberts, "Wilkinson Call, Soldier and Senator," *Florida Historical Quarterly*, XII (January, 1934), 95.
14. Kennedy, *William Wirt*, II, 202.
15. Rowland H. Rerick, *Memoirs of Florida*, ed. Francis P. Fleming, 2 volumes (Atlanta, 1902), I, 218.   16. Tallahassee *Floridian*, April 17, 1832.
17. Leon County Deed Book C, 657, Book I, 36, 253, County Courthouse, Tallahassee, Fla.; Marshall D. Haywood, "John Branch, Secretary of the Navy in the Cabinet of President Jackson, etc.," *The North Carolina Booklet*, XV (October, 1915), 92-93; William Whatley Pierson, "John Branch," *Dictionary of American Biography*, II, 597.
18. Tallahassee *Florida Advocate*, November 11, 1828; Tallahassee *Floridian*, February 15, 1834.
19. *Senate Documents*, 24 Congress, 1 Session, No. 346.
20. George W. Parkhill to John Parkhill, January 16, 1845, Parkhill papers, Southern Historical Collection, University of North Carolina.
21. Dorothy Dodd, "The Tallahassee Railroad and the Town of St. Marks," *Apalachee*, IV (1956), 3.
22. Call to George Graham, March 13, 1829, Misc. letters recd., General Land Office, National Archives.
23. Graham to Call, March 24, 1829, Misc. letters sent, General Land Office, National Archives; Tallahassee *Floridian and Advocate*, April 20, 1830; Dodd, "Tallahassee Railroad and St. Marks," *loc. cit.*
24. Tallahassee *Floridian and Advocate*, January 20, 27, 1831.
25. George W. Pettengill, *The Story of the Florida Railroads, 1834-1903* (Boston, 1952), 11; Dorothy Dodd, "Railroad Projects in Territorial Florida," unpublished M.A. thesis (Florida State College for Women, 1929), 27.
26. *Ibid.*, 27-28.   27. Tallahassee *Floridian*, March 29, June 14, 28, 1834.

28. Tallahassee *Florida Sentinel*, November 6, 1855; Dodd, "Railroad Projects,"
    27-28.   29. Tallahassee *Floridian*, October 4, 1834.
30. *Senate Documents*, 23 Congress, 2 Session, No. 38.
31. *U. S. Statutes at Large*, V, 778.
32. Tallahassee *Floridian*, August 1, 1835; Articles of agreement between Tal-
    lahassee Rail Road Company and John D. and William Gray, May 16,
    1835, Florida State Library; see also Dodd, "Tallahassee Railroad and St.
    Marks," *loc. cit.*, 6-7.
33. Articles of agreement between Tallahassee Rail Road Company and John
    D. and William Gray, May 16, 1835.
34. Tallahassee Railroad Company *v.* John D. and William Gray, Law file No.
    1945, Clerk of the Circuit Court, Leon County, Florida.
35. Tallahassee *Floridian*, December 30, 1837.
36. Call to Ellen Kirkman, January 4, 1838, Call papers, UNC.
37. Tallahassee *Floridian*, December 23, 1837, April 28, 1838.
38. Call to Ellen Kirkman, June 29, 1841, Call papers, UNC.
39. Comte Francis de Castelnau, "Essay on Middle Florida, 1837-38," tr. A.
    R. Seymour, *Florida Historical Quarterly*, XXVI (January, 1948), 215-
    216.
40. John S. Tappan to Benjamin French, December 13, 1841, in *Florida His-
    torical Quarterly*, XXIV (October, 1945), 108-111.
41. Earnest Malvern, "A Visit to Wakulla Spring," in Tallahassee *Florida
    Sentinel*, March 13, 1855.   42. Dodd, "Railroad Projects," 29-30.
43. Slave Schedules, Leon County, Florida, Sixth Census, 1840, National
    Archives.
44. Tallahassee *Floridian*, January 11, 1840; Dodd, "Tallahassee Railroad and
    St. Marks," *loc. cit.*, 10-11.
45. Call to Ellen Kirkman, May 25, 1840, Call papers, UNC.
46. *Ibid.* and Tallahassee *Floridian*, June 6, 1840.
47. Tallahassee *Florida Sentinel*, September 19, 1843.
48. *Ibid.*, October 10, 1843.
49. Dodd, "Tallahassee Railroad and St. Marks," *loc. cit.*, 11-12.
50. *Acts and Resolutions of the General Assembly of the State of Florida,
    Passed at its Third Session* (Tallahassee, 1848), 56; *Acts and Resolutions
    of the General Assembly of the State of Florida, Passed at its Fifth Session*
    (Tallahassee, 1851), 76, 317.

7

War and Politics

1. Mary Call to Call, October 14, 27, 1835, Call papers, UNC; Jackson to
   Andrew Jackson, Jr., September 12, 1835, Bassett, *Jackson Correspondence*,
   V, 364.   2. Reid to Call, November 11, 1835, Call papers, FHS.
3. John T. Sprague, *The Origin, Progress, and Conclusion of the Florida War*
   (New York, 1848), 17-20.   4. *Ibid.*, 20-25, 73.
5. *Ibid.*, 74-79.   6. *Ibid.*, 79.   7. *Ibid.*, 82-83.
8. Call to Jackson, June 1, 1836, in *Senate Documents*, 26 Congress, 1
   Session, No. 278, 55-56.

9. Mark F. Boyd, "The Seminole War: Its Background and Onset," *Florida Historical Quarterly*, XXX (July, 1951), 56, 73. This article is an excellent account of the background of the Indian troubles.

10. Reid to John Forsyth, December 3, 1835, Ms. collections, P. K. Yonge Library of Florida History, University of Florida. Jackson's order is an endorsement on the back of this letter.

11. Tallahassee *Floridian*, December 12, 1835.

12. Call to Jackson, December 22, 1835, *Senate Documents*, 26 Congress, 1 Session, No. 278, 29-30.   13. Sprague, *Florida War*, 89-90.

14. Call to Eaton, January 8, 1836, in *Senate Documents*, 24 Congress, 2 Session, No. 224, 208-209; Clinch to R. Jones, January 4, 1836, in Boyd, "The Seminole War," *loc. cit.*, 76-77.

15. Call to Eaton, January 8, 1836, *loc. cit.*; Sprague, *Florida War*, 92.

16. Call to Eaton, January 8, 1836, *loc. cit.*; Tallahassee *Floridian*, January 9, 1836.

17. Call to Jackson, January 9, 1836, in *Senate Documents*, 26 Congress, 1 Session, No. 278, 30-31.

18. Lewis Cass to Scott, January 21, 1836, Cass to Eaton, January 22, 1836, Misc. letters sent, War Department, National Archives; Tallahassee *Floridian*, February 6, 1836.

19. James W. Silver, *Edmund Pendleton Gaines, Frontier General* (Baton Rouge, 1949), 171-172.   20. *Ibid.*, 176.

21. *Ibid.*, 177.   22. *Ibid.*, 182   23. *Ibid.*, 181, 183.

24. Ellen C. Long, "Call Journal," 199; Tallahassee *Floridian*, February 27, 1836.   25. Cited in Ellen C. Long, "Call Journal," 200.

26. Tallahassee *Floridian*, March 5, 1836; "Parochial Records of St. John's Episcopal Church, Tallahassee, Florida, 1832-1880," 36, typescript copy in P. K. Yonge Library of Florida History, University of Florida.

27. Call to Mrs. Kirkman, March 3, 1836, Call papers, UNC; Call to James Kirkman, March 19, 1836, Call papers, FHS.

28. Commission of R. K. Call as Governor of Florida, March 16, 1836, Call papers, UNC.   29. Tallahassee *Floridian*, April 2, 1836.

30. Call to A. J. Donaldson [*sic*], April 4, 1836, Call papers, UNC.

31. Tallahassee *Floridian*, April 9, 1836.

32. *Ibid.*, April 23, 1836; Call to Cass, April 20, 1836, in *Senate Documents*, 26 Congress, 1 Session, No. 278, 33-34.   33. *Ibid.*

34. See Governor Call Letterbook, 1836, Florida State Library, Tallahassee.

35. Tallahassee *Floridian*, April 30, 1836.

36. *Ibid.*, May 14, 1836.   37. *Ibid.*, June 4, 1836.

38. Call to Scott, May 26, 1836, in *Senate Documents*, 24 Congress, 2 Session, No. 224, 366-367.

39. Call to Cass, May 10, 1836, Governor Call Letterbook, 1836.

40. Call to Jackson, May 12, 1836, in *Senate Documents*, 26 Congress, 1 Session, No. 278, 45.   41. Call to Cass, May 14, 1836, in *ibid.*, 46.

42. Call to Donaldson [*sic*], May 16, 1836, Donelson papers.

43. Cass to Call, May 14, 1836, *Senate Documents*, 26 Congress, 1 Session, No. 278, 232.   44. Call to Cass, May 24, 1836, *ibid.*, 48-49.

45. Call to Jackson, June 1, 1836, in *ibid.*, 55-56.

46. White to Jackson, May 28, 1836, in *Senate Documents*, 24 Congress, 2 Session, No. 224, 367.   47. Tallahassee *Floridian*, July 8, 1836.

48. Call to Jackson, May 30, 1836, in *Senate Documents*, 26 Congress, 1 Session, No. 278, 54-55.   49. Call to Cass, June 21, 1836, in *ibid.*, 56.

50. Dallas to Call, July 2, 1836, in *ibid.*, 72; see also Call to Dallas, June 25, 1836, Governor Call Letterbook, 1836.
51. B. K. Pierce to Call, September 13, 1836, in *Senate Documents*, 26 Congress, 1 Session, No. 278, 82; Call to Jackson, September 22, 1836, in *ibid.*, 81.
52. R. Jones to Call, July 25, 1836, in *ibid.*, 27-28.
53. Cass to Call, June 18, 1836, in *ibid.*, 4.
54. Call to Jackson, June [?], 1836, Jackson papers.
55. Call to Cass, July 5, 1836, in *Senate Documents*, 26 Congress, 1 Session, No. 278, 59; Call to Thomas S. Jesup, September 8, 1836, in *ibid.*, 77-78.
56. Call to Jesup, September 8, 1836, in *ibid.*, 77-78; Call to Cass, September 18, 1836, in *ibid.*, 77.   57. Tallahassee *Floridian*, September 17, 24, 1836.
58. Call to the Secretary of War [unnamed], October 10, 1836, in *Senate Documents*, 26 Congress, 1 Session, No. 278, 86.
59. Call to Benjamin F. Butler, December 2, 1836, in *ibid.*, 98-108.
60. Butler to Call, November 4, 1836, in *ibid.*, 11-12.
61. Call to the Secretary of War [unnamed], November 27, 1836, in *ibid.*, 92-98.   62. Call to Butler, December 2, 1836, *loc. cit.*
63. Butler to Call, January 14, 1837, in *ibid.*, 16.   64. *Ibid.*
65. Tallahassee *Floridian*, December 10, 1836.   66. *Ibid.*, December 31, 1836.
67. *Ibid.*, December 31, 1836, and January 7, 1837.
68. Jesup to Butler, December 5, 1836, Misc. letters recd., War Department, National Archives.
69. Jesup to Call, April 18, 1837, in Ellen C. Long, "The Discovery and Occupation of Florida," 252, unpublished Ms. in Call papers, UNC; Tallahassee *Floridian*, March 18, 1837.
70. Kathryn Abbey Hanna, *Florida Land of Change* (Chapel Hill, 1948), 211-217.
71. Brown to Parkhill, June 25, 1836, Parkhill papers, Southern Historical Collection, University of North Carolina.
72. Dorothy Dodd, "Florida in 1845," *Florida Historical Quarterly*, XXIV (July, 1945), 9.   73. *Florida House Journal* (1839), 7.
74. Leon County Deed Book E, 91, Book G, 329, Leon County Courthouse; Call to John Gamble, February 9, 1838, Call papers, FHS.
75. Call to B. F. Butler, December 11, 1834, Misc. letters recd., Justice Department, National Archives.
76. *Florida Legislative Council Journal* (1837), 98-99; *Florida House Journal* (1839), 7.   77. *Florida Legislative Council Journal* (1838), 7.
78. *Ibid.*, (1842), 21; Kathryn T. Abbey, "The Union Bank of Tallahassee," *Florida Historical Quarterly*, XV (April, 1937), 209.
79. Levy to Joel R. Poinsett, January 19, 1839, in Arthur W. Thompson, "David Yulee: A Study of Nineteenth Century American Thought and Enterprise," unpublished Ph.D. dissertation (Columbia University, 1954), 239-241.
80. McGrane, *Foreign Bondholders*, 227; *House Executive Documents*, 26 Congress, 2 Session, No. 111, 307-316.
81. "Report of the Committee on Banks," *Florida House Journal* (1840), Appendix, 33.   82. *Florida Legislative Council Journal* (1837), 9.
83. Dorothy Dodd (ed.), *Florida Becomes a State* (Tallahassee, 1945), 35, 37-38.
84. *Journal of the Proceedings of a Convention of Delegates to Form a Constitution for the People of Florida* (St. Joseph, 1839), 7, 113. A list of

stockholders in the three major banks is in *House Executive Documents,* 26 Congress, 2 Session, No. 111.

85. St. Augustine *Florida Herald,* February 21, 1839.
86. *Florida Legislative Council Journal* (1837), 46-47.
87. *Ibid.,* (1838), 16-17.
88. *Florida Senate Journal* (1839), 12; *Acts of the Legislative Council of the Territory of Florida* (1839), 8-10.
89. *Florida Senate Journal* (1839), 6; *Acts of the Legislative Council of the Territory of Florida* (1839), 12-14.
90. *Ibid.,* 20; see also *Florida Senate Journal* (1839), 13.
91. Poinsett to Call, September 5, 1837, *Senate Documents,* 26 Congress, 1 Session, No. 278, 23; see also Call to Poinsett, August 23, 1837, in *ibid.,* 131.
92. Tallahassee *Floridian,* March 17, July 21, August 25, December 15, 1838.
93. Call to Van Buren, July 28, 1839, in *Senate Documents,* 26 Congress, 1 Session, No. 278, 185.
94. Poinsett to Van Buren, November 29, 1839, Van Buren papers, Library of Congress.
95. Call to John Forsyth, June 3, 1837, June [?], 1839, Misc. letters recd., State Department, National Archives.
96. DuVal to Call, June 1, 1839, Misc. letters recd., State Department, National Archives; see also Call to Forsyth, August 16, 1837, Misc. letters recd., Forsyth to Call, June 16, 1837, A. Vail to DuVal, August 21, 1839, Domestic letters sent, State Department, National Archives.
97. Call to Van Buren, November 24, 1839, Misc. letters recd., State Department, National Archives.
98. David Levy, "Brief remarks concerning the Democratic cause in Florida, with a suggestion, respectfully submitted to the President," Van Buren papers.
99. Levy to Poinsett, January 19, 1840, in Thompson, "David Yulee," 240.
100. Poinsett to Van Buren, November 29, 1839, Van Buren papers.
101. Tallahassee *Floridian,* December 28, 1839, and Washington *Metropolis* cited in *ibid.*   102. St. Augustine *News,* January 24, 1840.
103. Levy to Poinsett, January 19, 1840, *loc. cit.*
104. "Memorial of Richard K. Call," *House Executive Documents,* 26 Congress, 1 Session, No. 136, 2, 12-14.
105. Poinsett to Fulton, January 18, 1840, copy in Ms. "Florida Territorial Papers," Territorial Records Office, National Archives. See also *Biographical Directory of the American Congress, 1774-1949,* 1188.

8

The Austere Forties

1. St. Augustine *News,* September 11, 1840.
2. *Ibid.,* May 8, 1840; Tallahassee *Florida Sentinel,* October 21, 1841.
3. Charles S. Sydnor, *The Development of Southern Sectionalism* (Baton Rouge, 1948), 52, 281.
4. Long, *Florida Breezes,* 142, and "Florida," unpublished essay in Call papers, FHS.

5. Reid to Poinsett, April 15, 1840, in Thompson, "David Yulee," 245.
6. Call to the Editor, n.d., in Tallahassee *Floridian*, April 18, 1840; *ibid.*, April 11, 1840.　　　　7. *Senate Reports*, 46 Congress, 2 Session, No. 648.
8. *Ibid.*
9. Tallahassee *Floridian*, April 18, 25, 1840; Leon County Deed Book F, 487, Book G, 273, Leon County Courthouse; Knauss, *Territorial Florida Journalism*, 27; Herbert J. Doherty, Jr., "The Florida Whigs," unpublished M.A. thesis (University of Florida, 1949), 24-25, 28-29.
10. Tallahassee *Floridian*, April 25, 1840; *ibid.*, April 18, 1840.
11. *Quincy Sentinel*, September 18, 1840; see also Adam Lee to Call, September 16, 1840, Call papers, FHS, and G. A. Halsey to Call, August 28, 1840, H. Addison to Call, October 17, 1840, Call papers, UNC.
12. St. Augustine *News*, October 2, 1840.
13. Speech of Call at Philadelphia, cited in A. B. Norton, *Reminiscences of the Log Cabin and Hard Cider Campaign* (Dallas, 1888), 313-316.
14. Jackson to Francis P. Blair, September 26, 1840, Bassett, *Jackson Correspondence*, VI, 78.
15. Benjamin A. Putnam to Call, March 26, 1841, Call papers, FHS.
16. Call to Mrs. Kirkman, n.d., Call papers, FHS.
17. Tallahassee *Floridian*, February 13, 1841; *Quincy Sentinel*, February 19, 1841.　　　　18. Downing to Call, March 8, 1841, Call papers, FHS.
19. "Diary of Robert Raymond Reid," cited in Miller, *Bench and Bar of Georgia*, II, 225-226.
20. Tallahassee *Floridian*, April 3, 17, 1841.
21. Putnam to Call, March 26, 1841, Call papers, FHS.
22. Tallahassee *Floridian*, December 19, 1840.
23. Putnam to Call, March 26, 1841, Call papers, FHS.
24. Tallahassee *Star of Florida*, January 7, 1842; see also *Quincy Sentinel*, October 30, November 20, 1840.
25. Tallahassee *Star of Florida*, February 10, 1842; Doherty, "Florida Whigs," 30-31.
26. Tallahassee *Star of Florida*, October 6, 1842; *ibid.*, August 18, September 1, 1841.
27. Samuel J. Douglas to Daniel Webster, February 12, 1842, copy in Ms. "Florida Territorial Papers," Territorial Records Office, National Archives; see also Dodd, "Florida in 1845," *loc. cit.*, 9.
28. Leon County Tax Rolls, 1839, 1845, Florida State Library; Leon County Deed Book I, 277, 333, 354, Leon County Courthouse.
29. Tallahassee *Floridian*, May 1, 1841; Call to Hope and Co., June 28, 1841, Henry J. Williams to Call, October 13, 1841, Call to Edmund J. Forstall, November 12, 1841, in *Florida House Journal* (1842), Appendix, 16-18, 20-22, 26-27; Governor's Message, in *ibid.*, 13.
30. Tyler to Webster, January 4, 1842, Misc. letters recd., State Department, National Archives.
31. *Florida House Journal* (1842), 16, 19-20, 21; *Acts and Resolutions of the Legislative Council of the Territory of Florida* (1842), 45, 53.
32. *Ibid.*, 257.　　　　33. *Ibid.*, 285.　　　　34. *Ibid.*, 292, 308.
35. *Ibid.* (1843), 10.　　　　　　　　　　　　36. *Ibid.*, 10, 11, 12.
37. *Acts and Resolutions of the Legislative Council of the Territory of Florida* (1843), 25, 34, 42; *Florida Senate Journal* (1843), 19-20.
38. *Florida House Journal* (1844), 9, 10, 13.

39. *Acts and Resolutions of the Legislative Council of the Territory of Florida* (1843), 36; *ibid.* (1844), 61-65; *Florida Senate Journal* (1843), 25.
40. *Florida Senate Journal* (1843), 27; Tallahassee *Florida Sentinel,* November 11, 1842, January 20, 1843; Dodd, "Florida in 1845," *loc. cit.,* 20.
41. Comte Francis de Castelnau, "Essay on Middle Florida, 1837-38," tr. A. R. Seymour, *Florida Historical Quarterly,* XXVI (January, 1948), 236-237.   42. Dodd, "Florida in 1845," *loc. cit.,* 20.
43. Tallahassee *Floridian,* July 10, September 11, 25, 1841.
44. Call to Mrs. Kirkman, July 5, 1841, Call papers, UNC; Tallahassee *Floridian,* July 10, 1841.
45. DuVal to Call, September 5, 1842, Ms. collections, P. K. Yonge Library of Florida History, University of Florida.
46. Jackson to Call, October 3, 1842, Call papers, UNC; see also Jackson to Francis P. Blair, October 3, 1842, Bassett, *Jackson Correspondence,* VI, 171.
47. Tallahassee *Star of Florida,* July 7, November 3, 1842; see also Tallahassee *Florida Sentinel,* November 1, 1842.
48. Tallahassee *Floridian,* May 1, 1841; Long, *Florida Breezes,* 214-215.
49. Levy to James D. Westcott, May 6, 1842, in Thompson, "David Yulee," 249; Tallahassee *Florida Sentinel,* February 18, 1842.
50. Call to C. A. Wickliff, March 30, 1844, Call papers, UNC.
51. Call to James L. Seward and others, September 12, 1844, Call papers, FHS.
52. Tallahassee *Florida Sentinel,* July 18, 1843; Tallahassee *Star of Florida,* August 16, 30, 1844.
53. St. Augustine *News,* March 29, 1845; Tallahassee *Star of Florida,* April 25, 1845.
54. Committee of Twenty to Call, April 22, 1845, Call papers, FHS.
55. Call to the Committee of Twenty, April 24, 1845, Call papers, FHS; see also *Pensacola Gazette,* May 3, 1845.
56. Call to Joseph Clisby, [July, 1845], Call papers, UNC.
57. H. C. Wilson to Call, April 20, 1845, Call papers, FHS; Ellen C. Long, "Richard Keith Call," unpublished sketch in Call papers, FHS.
58. *Pensacola Gazette,* May 24, 1845; see also St. Augustine *News,* May 10, 1845, and Tallahassee *Star of Florida,* April 25, 1845.
59. *Ibid.,* June 20, 1845.
60. Levy to Westcott, May 29, 1845, in Thompson, "David Yulee," 262.

9

The Lord of the Lake

1. Albert H. Roberts, "Wilkinson Call," *loc. cit.,* 96-97; see also Call to Mrs. Kirkman, May 25, 1846, Call papers, UNC; "Parochial Records of St. John's Episcopal Church, 1832-1880," typescript copy in P. K. Yonge Library of Florida History, University of Florida.
2. Call to William C. Mosely [*sic*], November 8, 1845, Call papers, FHS; Call to Mrs. Kirkman, May 25, 1846, Call papers, UNC.
3. Call to Mosely [*sic*], November 8, 1845, Call papers, FHS.

4. Call to Bancroft, November 16, 1845, Call papers, UNC.
5. Lyster H. Dewey, "Fibers used for Binder Twine," *Yearbook of the United States Department of Agriculture, 1911* (Washington, 1912), 200.
6. Leon County Tax Rolls, 1845-1853, Florida State Library; Slave Schedules, Seventh Census, Leon County, Florida, 581-583, and White Population, Seventh Census, Leon County, Florida, 99, National Archives.
7. Leon County Tax Rolls, 1853, Florida State Library; Deed, conveying land from Call to Ellen Call Long, October 23, 1851, Call papers, UNC.
8. Ellen C. Long, "Richard Keith Call," unpublished sketch in Call papers, FHS.
9. *Ibid.;* R. K. Call Masonic Certificate, September 14, 1814, Call papers, FHS.
10. Estate of Richard K. Call, filed September 30, 1862, County Judge's Court, Leon County, Florida.
11. *Ibid.;* Tallahassee *Florida Sentinel,* September 28, November 30, 1852.
12. Tallahassee *Floridian and Journal,* July 12, August 2, 1851; Tallahassee *Florida Sentinel,* April 20, December 14, 1852.
13. Ellen C. Long, "Richard Keith Call," unpublished sketch in Call papers, FHS; Rollin G. Osterweis, *Romanticism and Nationalism in the Old South* (New Haven, 1949), 41.
14. Long, *Florida Breezes,* 131; Osterweis, *Romanticism and Nationalism,* 42-43; Tallahassee *Floridian and Journal,* February 21, 1852.
15. John MacCunn, *The Political Philosophy of Burke* (London, 1913), 71-72, 83-84, 92.
16. Call to John S. Littell, February 12, 1861, in Brevard, *History of Florida,* II, 221-222.   17. *Ibid.,* 223-224.
18. Edmond Powell to Cloe, Edmond's mother [*sic*], March 14, 1862, Call papers, UNC.   19. Jenkins to Call, July 5, 1858, Call papers, UNC.
20. Jenkins to Call, September 2, 1858, June 7, 1859, Call papers, FHS.
21. Sydnor, *Development of Southern Sectionalism,* 328; Arthur C. Cole, *The Whig Party in the South* (Washington, 1913), 118-119.
22. Call to Mrs. Kirkman, May 25, 1826, Call papers, UNC.
23. Brown to Yulee, Jackson Morton, and Cabell, February 22, 1850, in Jacksonville *Florida Republican,* March 7, 1850; see also Herbert J. Doherty, Jr., "Florida and the Crisis of 1850," *Journal of Southern History,* XIX (February, 1953), 32-47.
24. Tallahassee *Florida Sentinel,* September 10, 1850.
25. Doherty, "The Florida Whigs," 167-168; Cole, *Whig Party in the South,* 193-194.
26. Arthur W. Thompson, "The Railroad Background of the Florida Senatorial Election of 1851," *Florida Historical Quarterly,* XXXI (January, 1953), 181-193.
27. *Ibid.,* 187; Tallahassee *Florida Sentinel,* December 24, 1850, January 28, 1851.
28. Call to Joseph Clisby, November 20, 1851, in Tallahassee *Floridian and Journal,* December 6, 1851; see also Cole, *Whig Party in the South,* 213-215.
29. Tallahassee *Floridian and Journal,* December 27, 1851; see also Call to Clisby, November 20, 1851, *loc. cit.*
30. Tallahassee *Florida Sentinel,* June 1, 8, July 20, 1852; Tallahassee *Floridian and Journal,* July 17, 1852.
31. *Pensacola Gazette,* July 24, 1852; see also Cole, *Whig Party in the South,* 260.

32. Tallahassee *Floridian and Journal,* July 17, 1854; Tallahassee *Florida Sentinel,* July 20, November 23, 30, December 7, 1852.

10

Defender of the Union

1. Edwin L. Williams, Jr., "Florida in the Union, 1845-1861," unpublished Ph.D. dissertation (University of North Carolina, 1951), 524.
2. Jesse T. Carpenter, *The South as a Conscious Minority* (New York, 1930), 5, 84.   3. Jacksonville *Florida Republican,* September 28, 1854.
4. Notes of a speech delivered March 3, 1854, Call papers, FHS.
5. Tallahassee *Florida Sentinel,* November 28, 1854.
6. Ellen C. Long, "Florida," unpublished essay in Call papers, FHS.
7. George W. Boyd to Call, October 10, 1837, Call papers, UNC.
8. Unidentified letter to E. L. L'Engle, April 8, 1855, L'Engle papers, Southern Historical Collection, University of North Carolina.
9. W. Darrell Overdyke, *The Know Nothing Party in the South* (Baton Rouge, 1950), 76.   10. Tallahassee *Florida Sentinel,* August 7, 1855.
11. *Ibid.*   12. *Ibid.*   13. *Ibid.*   14. *Ibid.,* July 24, 1855.
15. Tallahassee *Floridian and Journal,* August 18, 25, 1855.
16. Call to Charles E. Dyke, September 18, 1855, in Tallahassee *Florida Sentinel,* September 25, 1855.
17. Call to Dyke, August 27, 1855, in *ibid.,* September 4, 1855.
18. *Ibid.,* September 25, 1855.
19. *Ibid.,* October 2, 16, 1855; Jacksonville *Florida Republican,* September 20, 1855.   20. Tallahassee *Floridian,* December 11, 1855.
21. Tallahassee *Florida Sentinel,* December 11, 1855; Washington *Daily National Intelligencer,* February 21, 22, 1856.
22. *Ibid.,* February 22, 23, 1856.
23. Tallahassee *Floridian,* May 3, 1856; Washington *Daily National Intelligencer,* February 28, 1856.   24. *Ibid.*   25. *Ibid.*
26. Jacksonville *Florida Republican,* March 6, 1856.
27. *Ibid.;* Call to Ellen C. Long, February 25, 1856, Call papers, FHS.
28. Call to the Editor, April 14, 1856, in Tallahassee *Floridian and Journal,* May 3, 1856; Jacksonville *Florida Republican,* April 9, 1856.
29. Call to Donaldson [*sic*], April 23, 1856, Donelson papers.
30. Tallahassee *Floridian and Journal,* June 28, July 19, 1856; Jacksonville *Florida Republican,* September 3, 1856.
31. Richard K. Call, *Address of Past Grand Master R. K. Call, delivered at the Capital of Florida, by request of the Most Worshipful Grand Lodge, on the 24th of June, 1859* (Tallahassee, 1859), 1-24.
32. Call to [a N.Y. friend], November 24, 1859, in Tallahassee *Floridian and Journal,* December 3, 1859. Described as a letter to a friend in New York who was a follower of Seward.
33. Call to [a N.Y. friend], January 15, 1860, in *ibid.,* February 11, 1860.
34. *Ibid.*   35. Tallahassee *Floridian and Journal,* March 24, 1860.
36. Call to the Editor, August 23, 1860, in *ibid.,* September 1, 1860.
37. Call to [a N.Y. friend], March 10, 1860, in *ibid.,* March 24, 1860.
38. *Ibid.,* June 23, 30, July 7, August 11, 1860.
39. Call to the Editor, August 23, 1860, in *ibid.,* September 1, 1860.

40. Call to Edwin A. Hart, November 1, 1860, Call papers, UNC. Hart was editor of the *Florida Sentinel*.
41. *Ibid.;* see also Sydnor, *Development of Southern Sectionalism*, 334; Call to John S. Littel, February 12, 1861, in Brevard, *History of Florida*, II, 228. 42. Call to Hart, November 1, 1860, Call papers, UNC.
43. Tallahassee *Floridian and Journal*, November 3, 1860; see also Call to Hart, November 1, 1860, Call papers, UNC.
44. Williams, "Florida in the Union," 558-560; Roberts, "Wilkinson Call," *loc. cit.*, 99.
45. Richard K. Call, *An Address to the People of Florida from General R. K. Call* (Tallahassee, 1860), passim.
46. Call to Hart, December 22, 1860, Call papers, UNC.
47. Williams, "Florida in the Union," 576-578, 581.
48. Long, *Florida Breezes*, 306-308.
49. Call to Littel, February 12, 1861, in *loc. cit.*, 219-220.
50. Wilkinson Call to John J. Crittenden, March 4, 1861, Crittenden papers, Library of Congress.
51. Call to Charles E. Dyke, n.d., in Tallahassee *Florida Sentinel*, October 30, 1855.
52. Call to Thomas J. Perkins, March 19, 1862, Call papers, FHS.
53. Call to Mrs. Long, May [?], 1862, Call papers, FHS.
54. Tallahassee *Florida Sentinel*, July 8, September 16, 1862; Call obituary clipping from unidentified newspaper, Call papers, UNC; Brevard, "Richard Keith Call," *Florida Historical Quarterly*, I (October, 1908), 20.
55. "Call Journal," 13.

Bibliography

Manuscript Collections and Unpublished Records

THE MOST VALUABLE TWO COLLECTIONS of manuscripts for this study were both collections of Call papers, one in the possession of the Florida Historical Society Library at the University of Florida, the other in the possession of the Southern Historical Collection, University of North Carolina Library. Both collections include letters, articles, speeches, newspaper clippings, political broadsides, and pamphlets. The North Carolina collection includes fragments of a diary, and a scrapbook. The Florida collection contains "The Journal of Governor Richard K. Call." This journal is a valuable source for the early years of Call's life, giving information not to be found elsewhere. It is copied, with a few alterations, from a manuscript in Call's own hand which is in the same collection. The portion from 1815 to the end is entirely the work of Ellen Call Long. In her portion there are copies of letters not found elsewhere. An item of unusual interest in the Florida collection is a lock of Call's hair.

Probably second in importance to the Call collections were the Andrew Jackson papers in the Library of Congress. This is a vast collection of personal and political papers, pamphlets, speeches, memorandum books, etc. Letters to and from Call were most numerous in the period from the War of 1812 to the first presidential term of Jackson. Several other collections in the Library of Congress contained scattered items of significance to this study. They include the Andrew J. Donelson papers, the Martin Van Buren papers, the Duff Green papers, the John J. Crittenden papers, and a collection of miscellaneous personal papers.

Scattered items of interest were also found in the Southern Historical Collection at the University of North Carolina among the papers of William H. Branch, Edward M. L'Engle, and John Parkhill. The Leon County, Florida, tax rolls for 1829, 1839, 1843-1854, and 1861 were found in the Florida State Library in Tallahassee, as was also the letterbook of Call while governor in 1836. Scattered items of Call correspondence were also used from the manuscript collections of the Virginia Historical Society, the Historical Society of Pennsylvania, and the P. K. Yonge Library of Florida History at the University of Florida. A typescript copy of portions of the "Diary of Robert Raymond Reid" was found in the library of the Florida Historical Society.

The greatest single collection of public records used was that of the National Archives, whose vast holdings constitute a gold mine of historical source materials. In the Archives records, mostly letters, were used from the Bureau of the Census, the General Land Office, the Justice Department, the Navy Department, the State Department, the Treasury Department, the War Department, and the Territorial Records Office. The holdings of the latter office were of extreme importance in this work. In Tallahassee, Florida, the Leon County Courthouse holds the county deed books, some of which (1827-1863) were used for information on property transfers and mortgages. Legal papers pertaining to the Call estate (filed September 30, 1862) were of much

value in revealing activities on Call's plantation, the extent of his property at
death, and his debts. Wilkinson Call and Thomas J. Perkins were the executors
of the estate. A typescript copy of the "Parochial Records of St. John's Episcopal Church, Tallahassee, Florida, 1832-1880," prepared by Evelyn Whitfield
Henry and located in the P. K. Yonge Library of Florida History, provided information about births, deaths, and marriages in the Call family.

Official Documents

FEDERAL

Annals of Congress, 18 Congress, 1 Session, Washington, 1856.
Biographical Directory of the American Congress, 1774-1949, Washington, 1950.
House Executive Documents, 22 Congress, 2 Session, No. 44; 24 Congress, 1
     Session, No. 14; 26 Congress, 1 Session, No. 136; 26 Congress, 2 Session,
     No. 111.
Journal of the House of Representatives of the United States, 18 Congress, 1
     and 2 Sessions.
Journal of the Senate of the United States of America, 22 Congress, 1 Session.
Miller, David Hunter (ed.): *Treaties and Other International Acts of the
     United States of America,* 8 vols., Washington, 1931-48.
Peters, Richard (ed.): *Reports of Cases Argued and Adjudged in the Supreme
     Court of the United States,* Vols. VI, VIII, IX, Washington, 1832, 1834-35.
Register of Debates in Congress, 18 Congress, 2 Session, Washington, 1825.
Reports of Committees in the House of Representatives, 18 Congress, 2 Ses-
     sion, No. 87.
Senate Documents, 23 Congress, 2 Session, No. 38; 24 Congress, 1 Session, No.
     346; 24 Congress, 2 Session, No. 224; 26 Congress, 1 Session, Nos. 278, 449.
Senate Papers, 17 Congress, 1 Session, No. 1.
Senate Reports, 42 Congress, 3 Session, No. 379; 46 Congress, 2 Session, No.
     648.
State Papers, 15 Congress, 2 Session, No. 100; 16 Congress, 1 Session, No. 73;
     17 Congress, 1 Session, No. 42; 18 Congress, 2 Session, No. 111.
United States Statutes at Large, Vols. III and IV, Boston, 1846.
Yearbook of the United States Department of Agriculture, 1911, Washington,
     1912.

STATE

Acts and Resolutions of the Legislative Council of the Territory of Florida,
     1839, 1842-1844, Tallahassee.
Acts and Resolutions of the General Assembly of the State of Florida, 1848,
     1851, Tallahassee.
*A Journal of the Proceedings of the House of Representatives of the Territory
     of Florida,* 1840, 1842, 1844, Tallahassee.
*A Journal of the Proceedings of the Legislative Council of the Territory of
     Florida,* 1837-1839, Tallahassee.
A Journal of the Proceedings of the Senate of the Territory of Florida, 1842-
     1843, Tallahassee.
Jenkins, William Sumner (ed.): Records of the States of the United States of
     America. A Microfilm Compilation. Prepared by the Library of Congress
     in Association with the University of North Carolina. Microfilmed by the
     Library of Congress Photoduplication Service, 1949.

Collected Source Materials

Bassett, John Spencer (ed.): *The Correspondence of Andrew Jackson,* 7 vols., Washington, 1926-35.
Carter, Clarence E. (ed.): *The Territorial Papers of The United States,* 22 vols., Washington, 1934-56.
Dodd, Dorothy (ed.): *Florida Becomes a State,* Tallahassee, 1945.
Gordon, William A. (comp.): *A Compilation of Registers of the Army of the United States, from 1815 to 1837,* Washington, 1837.
Hamilton, Stanislaus M. (ed.): *The Writings of James Monroe,* 7 vols., New York, 1898-1903.
Norton, A. B.: *Reminiscences of the Log Cabin and Hard Cider Campaign,* Dallas, 1888.
Seymour, Mary Jane (ed.): *Lineage Book National Society of the Daughters of the American Revolution,* 166 vols., Washington, 1895-1939.

Newspapers and Periodicals

Niles' Register (Baltimore), 1825-1843.
Daily National Intelligencer (Washington), February-March, 1856.
Florida Advocate (Tallahassee), November, 1828-June, 1829.
Florida Herald (St. Augustine), scattered references, 1822-1844.
Florida Intelligencer (Tallahassee), February-December, 1826.
Florida Republican (Jacksonville), scattered references, 1850-1857.
Florida Sentinel (Tallahassee), 1840-1844, 1846-1855, 1862.
Floridian (Pensacola), 1821-1823; (Tallahassee), 1831-1841.
Floridian and Advocate (Tallahassee), 1830-1831.
Floridian and Journal (Tallahassee), 1849-1862.
News (St. Augustine), 1839-1845.
Pensacola Gazette, 1824-1826, scattered references, 1835-1855.
Star of Florida (Tallahassee), 1840-1845.
United States Telegraph—Extra (Washington), 1828.

Pamphlets

Brackenridge, Henry M.: *Judge Brackenridge's Letters,* n.p., n.d. [ca. 1833]
Call, Richard K.: *Address of Past Grand Master R. K. Call, delivered at the Capital of Florida, by request of the Most Worshipful Grand Lodge, on the 24 of June, 1859,* Tallahassee, 1859.
——————: *An Address to the People of Florida from General Richard Keith Call, December 1, 1860,* Tallahassee, 1860.

Autobiographies, Biographies, and Memoirs

Adams, John Quincy: *Memoirs of John Quincy Adams, Comprising Portions of his Diary from 1795 to 1848,* ed. Charles Francis Adams, 12 vols., Philadelphia, 1874-77.
Douglas, Thomas: *Autobiography of Thomas Douglas, Late Judge of the Supreme Court of Florida,* New York, 1856.

Floyd, John: *The Life and Diary of John Floyd*, ed. C. H. Ambler, Richmond, 1918.

Hanna, Alfred Jackson: *A Prince in their Midst*, Norman, Okla., 1946.

James, Marquis: *Andrew Jackson: The Border Captain*, Indianapolis, 1933.

————: *Andrew Jackson: Portrait of a President*, Indianapolis, 1937.

Kennedy, John P.: *Memoirs of the Life of William Wirt*, Philadelphia, 1850.

Long, Ellen Call: *Florida Breezes; or, Florida, New and Old*, Jacksonville, Fla., 1882.

Malone, Dumas, Allen Johnson, and Harris M. Starr (eds.): *Dictionary of American Biography*, 21 vols., New York, 1928-44.

Miller, Stephen F.: *The Bench and Bar of Georgia: Memoirs and Sketches*, 2 vols., Philadelphia, 1858.

Minnigerode, Meade: *Some American Ladies, Seven Informal Biographies*, New York, 1926.

Parton, James: *Life of Andrew Jackson*, 3 vols., New York, 1859-61.

Poore, Ben Perley: *Perley's Reminiscences of Sixty Years in the National Metropolis*, 2 vols., Philadelphia, 1886.

Silver, James W.: *Edmund Pendleton Gaines: Frontier General*, Baton Rouge, 1949.

Van Buren, Martin: *The Autobiography of Martin Van Buren*, ed. John C. Fitzpatrick, Washington, 1920.

Wiltse, Charles M.: *John C. Calhoun*, 3 vols., Indianapolis, 1944-51.

Special Studies

Bates, Ernest Sutherland: *The Story of the Supreme Court*, Indianapolis, 1936.

Carpenter, Jesse T.: *The South as a Conscious Minority*, New York, 1930.

Cash, William T.: *History of the Democratic Party in Florida*, Tallahassee, 1936.

Cole, Arthur C.: *The Whig Party in the South*, Washington, 1913.

Craven, Avery Odelle: *Soil Exhaustion as a Factor in the Agricultural History of Virginia and Maryland, 1606-1860*, Urbana, Ill., 1926.

Jenkins, William S.: *Pro-Slavery Thought in the Old South*, Chapel Hill, 1935.

Knauss, James Owen: *Territorial Florida Journalism*, DeLand, Fla., 1926.

MacCunn, John: *The Political Philosophy of Burke*, London, 1913.

McGrane, Reginald C.: *Foreign Bondholders and American State Debts*, New York, 1935.

Myers, Gustavus: *History of the Supreme Court of the United States*, Chicago, 1925.

Osterweis, Rollin G.: *Romanticism and Nationalism in the Old South*, New Haven, 1949.

Overdyke, W. Darrell: *The Know Nothing Party in the South*, Baton Rouge, 1950.

Pecquet du Bellet, Louise: *Some Prominent Virginia Families*, Lynchburg, Va., 1907.

Pettengill, George W.: *The Story of the Florida Railroads, 1834-1903*, Boston, 1952.

Sprague, John T.: *Origin, Progress, and Conclusion of the Florida War*, New York, 1848.

Sydnor, Charles S.: *The Development of Southern Sectionalism, 1819-1848*, Baton Rouge, 1948.

Thomas, David Y.: *A History of Military Government in Newly Acquired Territory of the United States*, New York, 1904.
Warren, Charles: *The Supreme Court in United States History*, 2 vols., Boston, 1937.

Unpublished Monographs

Dodd, Dorothy: "Railroad Projects in Territorial Florida," master's thesis, Florida State College for Women [Florida State University], 1929.
Doherty, Herbert J., Jr.: "The Florida Whigs," master's thesis, University of Florida, 1949.
Farrell, Louis: "The Descendants of Hugh Jackson and Ellinor Gault," mimeographed compilation in the possession of the author.
Hill, Dorothy E.: "Joseph M. White, Florida's Territorial Delegate, 1825-1837," master's thesis, University of Florida, 1950.
Thompson, Arthur W.: "David Yulee: A Study of Nineteenth Century American Thought and Enterprise," doctoral dissertation, Columbia University, 1954.
Williams, Edwin L.: "Florida in the Union, 1845-1861," doctoral dissertation, University of North Carolina, 1952.
Williamson, Edward C.: "Wilkinson Call: A Pioneer in Progressive Democracy," master's thesis, University of Florida, 1946.

Articles

Abbey, Kathryn T.: "The Story of the Lafayette Lands in Florida," *Florida Historical Quarterly*, X (January, 1932), 115-132.
————: "The Union Bank of Tallahassee," *Florida Historical Quarterly*, XV (April, 1937), 207-231.
Boyd, Mark F.: "Events at Prospect Bluff on the Apalachicola River, 1808-1818," *Florida Historical Quarterly*, XVI (October, 1937), 55-96.
————: "The Seminole War: Its Background and Onset," *Florida Historical Quarterly*, XXX (July, 1951), 3-115.
Brevard, Caroline Mays: "Richard Keith Call," *Florida Historical Quarterly*, I (July, October, 1908), 3-12, 8-20.
Castelnau, Comte Francis de: "Essay on Middle Florida, 1837-38," tr. Arthur R. Seymour, *Florida Historical Quarterly*, XXVI (January, 1948), 199-255.
————: "Notes Concerning Two Itineraries from Charleston to Tallahassee," tr. Arthur R. Seymour, *Florida Historical Quarterly*, XXVI (April, 1948), 300-324.
Davis, Thomas Frederick: "Pioneer Florida," *Florida Historical Quarterly*, XXIV (April, 1945), 287-294.
Dodd, Dorothy: "Florida in 1845," *Florida Historical Quarterly*, XXIV (July, 1945), 3-27.
————: "The Florida Census of 1825," *Florida Historical Quarterly*, XXII (July, 1943), 34-40.
Doherty, Herbert J., Jr.: "Florida and the Crisis of 1850," *Journal of Southern History*, XIX (February, 1953), 32-47.
Hanna, Alfred Jackson: "Diplomatic Missions of the United States to Cuba to Secure the Spanish Archives of Florida," *Hispanic American Essays*, ed. A. Curtis Wilgus, Chapel Hill, 1942.

Haywood, Marshall D.: "John Branch, Secretary of the Navy in the Cabinet of President Jackson, etc.," *The North Carolina Booklet*, XV (October, 1915), 49-103.

"The Home Life of Chief Justice Marshall," *William and Mary Quarterly*, series 2, XII (January, 1932), 67-69.

Hume, Edgar Erskine: "The Virginia Society of the Cincinnati's Gift to Washington College," *Virginia Magazine of History and Biography*, XLIII (January, 1935), 47-58.

Parker, Daisy: "R. K. Call: Whig Leader," *Tallahassee Historical Society Annual*, IV (1939), 12-19.

"Richard Keith Call—Thomas Brown," *Florida Historical Quarterly*, VI (January, 1928), 156-158.

Roberts, Albert H.: "Wilkinson Call, Soldier and Senator," *Florida Historical Quarterly*, XII (January, 1934), 95-113.

Thompson, Arthur W.: "The Railroad Background of the Florida Senatorial Election of 1851," *Florida Historical Quarterly*, XXXI (January, 1953), 181-195.

————: "Political Nativism in Florida," *Journal of Southern History*, XV (February, 1949), 36-65.

"Valuable Letters of Andrew Jackson," *The American Historical Magazine*, IV (April, 1899), 99-104.

Histories and General References

Brevard, Caroline Mays: *A History of Florida from the Treaty of 1763 to Our Own Times*, ed. James Alexander Robertson, 2 vols. DeLand, Fla., 1924.

Dovell, Junius Elmore: *Florida, Historic, Dramatic, Contemporary*, 4 vols., New York, 1952.

Patrick, Rembert W.: *Florida Under Five Flags*, 3rd ed., Gainesville, 1960.

Pickett, Albert James: *History of Alabama and Incidentally of Georgia and Mississippi, from the Earliest Period*, Sheffield, Ala., 1896.

Rerick, Rowland H., *Memoirs of Florida*, ed. Francis P. Fleming, 2 vols., Atlanta, 1902.

Schlesinger, Arthur M., Jr.: *The Age of Jackson*, Boston, 1947.

Index

DATE DUB			
FEB 1 '74			

GAYLORD M-2 — PRINTED IN U.S.A.

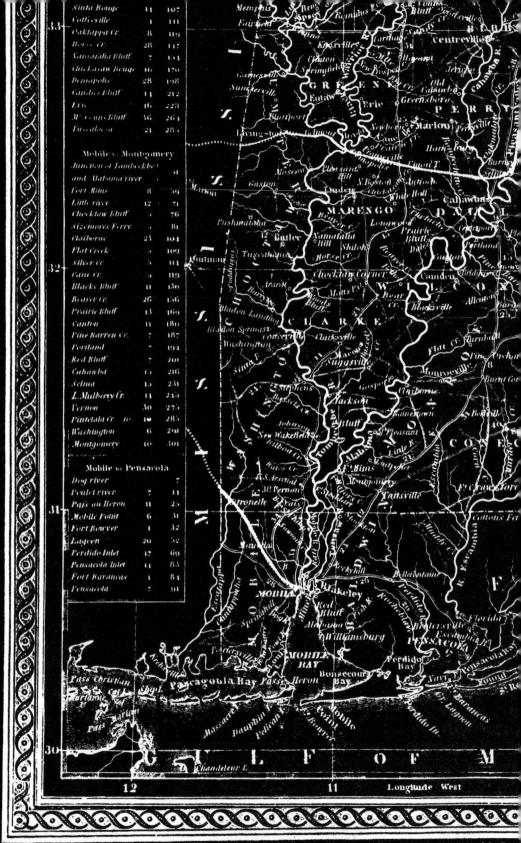